IMPRESSION MANAGEMENT AND INFORMATION TECHNOLOGY

IMPRESSION MANAGEMENT AND INFORMATION TECHNOLOGY

Edited by
Jon W. Beard

QUORUM BOOKS
Westport, Connecticut • London

Library of Congress Cataloging-in-Publication Data

Impression management and information technology / edited by Jon W.
   Beard.
      p.   cm.
   Includes bibliographical references and index.
   ISBN 0–89930–848–1 (alk. paper)
   1. Psychology (Industrial)   2. Identity (Psychology)
   3. Information technology.   I. Beard, Jon W.
   HF5548.8.I475   1996
   158.7—dc20   95–14605

British Library Cataloguing in Publication Data is available.

Library of Congress Catalog Card Number: 95–14605
ISBN: 0–89930–848–1

First published in 1996

Quorum Books, 88 Post Road West, Westport, CT 06881
An imprint of Greenwood Publishing Group, Inc.

Printed in the United States of America

The paper used in this book complies with the
Permanent Paper Standard issued by the National
Information Standards Organization (Z39.48–1984).

10 9 8 7 6 5 4 3 2 1

CONTENTS

FIGURES AND TABLES

ACKNOWLEDGMENTS

No undertaking of this sort is possible without the assistance and understanding of many people. It is nearly impossible to publically acknowledge all of those who have contributed in some form or fashion to this project, so a blanket "Thank You!" is necessary. You know who you are.

A special thank you is needed, however, for those who have contributed to this volume. The topic under consideration is not a mainstream or typical approach to information technology. The involvement and subsequent contribution of those who have participated required taking different perspectives and assuming atypical postures toward the literatures. Without their care, insights, and interest, this project would never have been completed. And, their understanding of and patience with the editor was of immense help.

Finally, special thanks need to go to several people who are especially close to me and my work. First, a special acknowledgment needs to be made to my wife, Caryl, for her patience with and support of this effort. Laura Jarvis was of great assistance in supporting many of the clerical aspects of this project as well as with handling other looming issues while my attention was diverted by this volume.

And two people in particular have provided both professional and personal support. Bob Giacalone, one of the trailblazers in impression management research, provided a significant amount of encouragement, direction, and support in this project, even though he was not directly involved with the effort. He led me to impression management and encouraged me to explore and consider its implications and was always willing to lend an ear when it was needed. Finally, Tim O. Peterson, my "brother," has contributed far more than I could have hoped through his insight, patience, and counsel.

IMPRESSION MANAGEMENT
AND INFORMATION
TECHNOLOGY

IMPRESSION MANAGEMENT AND INFORMATION TECHNOLOGY: NEW PERSPECTIVES ON INDIVIDUAL AND ORGANIZATIONAL COMPUTING

Jon W. Beard

It is commonly acknowledged and understood that information technology (IT) is having a dramatic effect on both our personal and professional lives. IT is also changing the nature of our organizations by providing opportunities to make fundamental changes in the way they do business. Many of the opportunities are recognized and understood. Yet a tremendous number of issues and consequences are only vaguely perceived while other questions are just now being raised.

The technology is changing rapidly, with computing speeds and the number of transistor equivalents available in a given area of a microprocessor chip both doubling approximately every 18 months. Organizations are acquiring more and more technology systems to assist in everything from manufacturing to the management of information to the provision and improvement of customer service. Harnessing and coordinating this computing power is the challenge. New tools and innovative perspectives with which to examine, interpret, and comprehend this rapidly evolving environment are always needed and sought.

This book, and the chapters contained herein, is an attempt at exploring issues related to IT from a relatively new perspective—impression management (IM)—which has not been widely utilized in relation to information technology. The focus, therefore, is on the integration and exploration of concepts derived from the IM literature and applied to issues related to information technology at levels ranging from an individual focus to an organizational perspective.

Information technology will be left largely undefined; each chapter provides its own focus and orientation. However, to contribute the most basic foundation definition as a starting point, we will consider technology to be the set of systems for getting the organization's (and individual's) work done (Perrow,

1967).   For our purposes in this book, the technology we are considering is computer based and/or computer related.   It has both individual effects and larger organizational consequences.   Technology influences person-to-person interaction and organization-to-organization relationships.   It can change how we do our work, where we do our work, and even whether we work at all.   And the IM framework is used to take a new look at and, hopefully, gain increased understanding of the opportunities and consequences of IT.

IMPRESSION MANAGEMENT: AN INTRODUCTION AND REVIEW

According to Rosenfeld and Giacalone (1991), organizational investigations of impression management were few before the 1980s (cf Fletcher, 1979; Wortman & Linsenmeier, 1977).   By the mid-1980s IM had acquired a theoretically distinct identity separate from its origins in the organizational politics literature.

Impression management, also referred to as self-presentation, originates in the sociological work of Erving Goffman (1959).   Goffman suggested that social interaction was much like a "play," with people (and organizations) engaged in "performances" for and with an audience.   There is a constant interaction between the actor and the audience, with a "definition of the situation" evolving between the two and guiding behavior.   According to Schneider (1981), impression management is primarily concerned with the behaviors people exhibit for others to create and maintain the desired perceptions of themselves.   The motives for behavior are driven by the desire to be favorably viewed by others. Whether behavior is consciously manipulated and controlled is the subject of some debate, with some viewing impression management as a malevolent attempt to manipulate the audience (cf Tedeschi, Schlenker, & Bonoma, 1971; Tedeschi, 1981), whereas others view IM as a psychological attempt to construct and maintain one's self-image (Schlenker, 1980).   Still, even with intuitively obvious suggestion that people may have conscious concern over appearances, Goffman's (1959) work had little immediate impact among social scientists. Impression management was often perceived as being an explanation of extreme behaviors, and much of the empirical work in impression management was thought to actually be contaminants of other more important mechanisms (Tedeschi & Rosenfeld, 1981).

Although some tried to limit the reach of phenomena captured by IM theory (cf Baumeister & Tice, 1984; Paulhus, 1982; Tetlock & Manstead, 1985), by the mid-1980s IM had entered the mainstream of social psychological research (cf Tedeschi, 1981, which is largely credited with creating this respectability).   Leary and Kowalski (1990) noted that IM "has attracted increased attention as a fundamental interpersonal process" (p. 35).   Recent extensions of the IM framework have now been incorporated within and targeted toward organizational issues, such as arbitration (Giacalone & Pollard, 1989), business ethics (Konovsky & Jaster, 1989; Payne & Giacalone, 1990), computer-based surveys (Lautenschlager & Flaherty, 1990; Rosenfeld, Giacalone, Knouse, Doherty, Vicino, Kantor, & Greaves, 1991), employment and selection (Fletcher, 1990; Gilmore & Ferris, 1989), marketing (Crane, 1989), and office design (Ornstein, 1989), to name just a few. But, with the exception of the research on computer-based organizational surveys mentioned above, no systematic work has been done using the IM framework to examine issues related to information technology. This collection is an attempt to make the first tentative steps toward spanning that void.

THE BOOK'S ARRANGEMENT

Although there will obviously be some overlap, each of the chapters to follow presents a different approach to impression management and information technology. It has been left to each contributor to define and structure the concepts relevant to their specific approach.

The contents of the book are roughly broken into two sections. The first section, consisting of Chapters 2, 3, 4, and 5, works largely from a theoretical focus with the arguments derived from and built on the literature. They are more suggestive and inductive in nature and, if they succeeded in their goals, probably raise more questions than they answer. They progress from a (perhaps) more traditional IM approach and structure, through the symbolism of IT, to a historical assessment, and, finally, to a pattern for creating and maintaining relationships among various groups who must interact due to technology. The second section of this volume consists of Chapters 6, 7, and 8. Although obviously still derived from and built on previous research issues and results, these chapters take an active approach to the topic of impression management and information technology through the reporting of actual research.

THE CHAPTERS

Increasingly individuals and organizations are adopting electronic communication methods, such as electronic mail, computer bulletin boards, and computer conferencing, because they foster a more efficient and rapid exchange of ideas and information. In Chapter 2, Bill Gardner, Mark Martinko, and Joy Van Eck Peluchette examine both the benefits and the "hidden consequences" of these computer-mediated communication systems (CMCS). The benefits of CMCS include better communication, improved decision making, enhanced documentation, tighter coordination, and the ability to monitor employees. The hidden consequences are largely social in nature, resulting from the absence of the nonverbal behaviors and visual cues to which we are accustomed. Although a substantial amount of work has been done to investigate a number of issues,

Steinfield and Fulk (1987) have noted that minimal work has been done to synthesize or integrate the impact of computer-mediated communication on human behaviors.   Gardner and Peluchette (1991) employed impression management at the micro-level of analysis of the self-presentational behaviors people exhibit when communicating via CMCS. This chapter expands on that investigation by incorporating recent research into the discussion of the effects of CMCS and suggesting additional areas that warrant further research.

In Chapter 3, Susan Winter broadens the discussion by examining the symbolic value of computers. Her approach suggests that the common argument of information technology allocation occurring based on their function as a tool in the workplace may be false. Instead, computers may actually hold a great deal of symbolic value for both those who interact with them and those external to the technology. If this is true, then the symbolic value of the technology could be, and perhaps should be, actively managed to create and reinforce the desired impression.

Following the symbolic orientation of Chapter 3, George Marakas and Dan Robey use a historical context to apply impression management to the concept of the "productivity paradox" in Chapter 4. One would think that the value of large investments in IT should be easy to demonstrate. Most organizations, however, have been unable to demonstrate the economic payoffs from investments in information technology (IT). Yet, despite the lack of a clear connection between IT and economic return, investments in IT continue to represent a significant portion of capital expenditures throughout the world. In this chapter, the authors argue that the symbolic role of IT may help to explain the absence of demonstrable economic reasons for IT investments.   An organization may implicitly justify the acquisition and possession of IT because of its symbolic importance rather than its economic value. IT's symbolic role, therefore, may have an indirect effect on economic performance, especially in cases where an organization is able to sustain its legitimacy and survive within an institutional environment. Impression management is used to explore and explain the patterns of acquisition and deployment of IT in three distinct periods of time: (1) the glass-house era (circa 1960-1980), (2) the desktop era (1980-1990), and (3) the current era of the boundaryless organization.

When defined as the "process by which individuals attempt to control the impression others form of them" (Leary & Kowalski, 1990, p. 34), impression management not only has application to interpersonal relations and interaction, but also to interaction among teams and departments within organizations. Chapter 5, by Jane Carey and Afsaneh Nahavandi, uses impression management as an approach through which to examine the negotiation and implementation of successful service-level agreements between information systems dapartments and their "clients" within an organization. Service-level agreements are defined and their use in a quality-focused environment are emphasized.

Chapters 6, 7, and 8 use impression management as a tool to actually examine issues related to information technology. In addition to the basic issues of integrating concepts from IM with the IT literatures, these chapters each contain examples of research on the practical merits of this integration. The focus and approach in each of these chapters is somewhat different, providing support for the conclusion that IM may be a useful, and as yet largely unused, tool for examining and exploring IT-related concepts and issues.

In Chapter 6, Lyne Bouchard and Lynne Markus study the impression management opportunities and realities of electronic data interchange (EDI). EDI is argued to provide major benefits to the organizations that use it for exchanging business data across organizational boundaries. However, the benefits of EDI are not shared equally among business partners, since the larger partners stand to gain more through a larger volume of transactions. Consequently, large firms find themselves working hard to convince their smaller business partners to adopt EDI. Bouchard and Markus use the innovation diffusion perspective, the critical mass perspective, and the impression management and bargaining literatures to examine the persuasive strategies used and the extent to which they work. These perspectives are applied specifically to the case of EDI adoption in the retailing industry, with particular attention to the efforts of one large retailer and two of its suppliers.

Information production and distribution is growing at a staggering rate. Technology for providing and distributing that information is having profound effects on individuals as they are bombarded by information, or more accurately, by attempts to gain the person's attention so that information may be received by the person (Huber, 1984). Increasingly sophisticated presentation formats are being used, user interfaces are evolving away from command-driven structures toward graphics-oriented icon manipulation, and sound, video, and powerful imaging capabilities are available to almost everyone. Yet, little systematic work has been done to determine whether these system capabilities can be manipulated to influence the impressions formed by others. In Chapter 7, David Paradice investigates the impression management consequences of multimedia through a study of the IM effects of and opportunities created by IT.

In Chapter 8, Paul Rosenfeld and Stephanie Booth-Kewley employ the impression management framework to look at the implications of utilizing computers to administer organizational surveys. Recent research has made some initial explorations of the effects of computers in the administration of organizational surveys, but few studies have investigated the psychometric and statistical comparability of responses of computer- versus paper-administered surveys. Many of the studies that have been done have been inconsistent in their findings and difficult to replicate. This chapter examines past research and presents the Navy's computer survey research program. It also offers an analysis of past inconsistencies by proposing a "Big Brother Syndrome" integration of recent research.

In the concluding chapter of this volume, Chapter 9, K. Vernard

Harrington and Jon Beard investigate the appropriate use of computer-based information technology (CBIT) using an impression management framework. Forces within organizations both promote and resist change. Understanding the dynamics of change within an organization is important, and how CBIT is affected by these dynamic forces may go a long way toward resolving the challenges of automation. Finally, the chapter, and the book, conclude with suggestions for future research and exploration as encouraged by the various approaches from throughout this volume.

CONCLUSION

As will be noted in most of the chapters to follow, the combination of impression management and information technology is a new and evolving field of study. The opportunities are tremendous, the paths numerous, and the possibility of incorrect and inappropriate applications abound. The material to follow is a first attempt at exploring these issues, establishing a coherent set of questions to consider, and stimulating discussion.

2

A SELF-PRESENTATIONAL PERSPECTIVE OF COMPUTER-MEDIATED COMMUNICATIONS

William L. Gardner III
Mark J. Martinko
Joy Van Eck Peluchette

An ever increasing number of today's organizations are adopting computer-mediated communications systems (CMCS) (Gardner & Peluchette, 1991; Hiltz & Johnson, 1990; Hiltz & Turoff, 1985), such as electronic mail (E-Mail), computer bulletin boards (CBB), and computer conferencing (CC). These systems foster communication more efficiently and rapidly than could be achieved through the postal service or by telephone (Culnan & Markus, 1987; Finholt & Sproull, 1990; Kiesler, 1986; Rice, 1984, 1988; Sproull & Kiesler, 1986). Such widespread adoption is due to the benefits of CMCS, including rapid and efficient communication, more and better information for improved decision making, enhanced documentation, improved coordination, and the ability to monitor employees (Culnan & Markus, 1987; Gardner & Peluchette, 1991; Szewczak & Gardner, 1989).

Although CMCS have tremendous potential for enriching organizational communication (Hiltz & Johnson, 1990; Komsky, 1991; Smolensky, Carmody, & Halcomb, 1990; Verity & Lewis, 1987; Zuboff, 1982), there are "hidden consequences" of these technologies. Since nonverbal behavior and visual cues are absent within CMCS, concerns have been expressed about the social ramifications of these systems. These concerns have prompted research focusing on group decision support systems (GDSS) (Connolly, Jessup, & Valacich, 1990; DeSanctis & Gallupe, 1987; Jessup, Connolly, & Galegher, 1990; Nunamaker, Applegate, & Konsynski, 1987) and group processes (e.g., participation, efficiency, consensus, group choice) (Kiesler, Siegel & McGuire, 1984; Siegel, Dubrovsky, Kiesler, & McGuire, 1986). Others have concentrated on the behavioral consequences of specific CMCS such as E-Mail (Finholt & Sproull, 1990; Komsky, 1991; Sproull & Kiesler, 1986; Steinfield,

1986, 1992), and the Electronic Information Exchange System (EIES) (Hiltz & Turoff, 1981; Kerr & Hiltz, 1982; Rice & Case, 1983).

Steinfield and Fulk (1987) note that little has been done to synthesize or integrate the research on the impact of computer-mediated communication (CMC) on human behavior. In particular, insufficient attention has been devoted to the motivational, cognitive, and affective processes of CMCS users (Sproull & Kiesler, 1986; Trevino, Lengel, & Daft, 1987). Recently, Gardner and Peluchette (1991) used impression management (IM) theory to provide a micro-level analysis of the self-presentational behaviors that people exhibit when communicating via computer networks. The purpose of this chapter is to expand that analysis by incorporating recent research into CMCS and identifying areas that merit additional research.

A MODEL OF THE SELF-PRESENTATION PROCESS

The self-presentational model depicted in Figure 2.1 builds on the earlier model advanced by Gardner and Peluchette (1991) and the general model of IM processes proposed by Gardner and Martinko (1988). A key difference between the current model and general models of the IM process is that it focuses on self-presentation. *Impression management* is the process whereby individuals seek to control the impressions that other persons form of them (Leary & Kowalski, 1990; Schlenker & Weigold, 1992). In contrast, *self-presentation* involves "the manipulation of information about the self by the actor" (Schneider, 1981, p. 25). Thus, self-presentation is a narrower construct confined to presentations made directly by an individual relating to their personal image.

There are also important differences between this model and the earlier model presented by Gardner and Peluchette (1991). This model is more articulated since it specifically identifies (1) information richness and features as key aspects of communication media, (2) the specific personality traits that mediate actors' definitions of their situated identities, and (3) the social context cues that influence self-presentations and media choices.

As Figure 2.1 indicates, an opportunity for interaction between individuals serves as the impetus for self-presentation. Once such an opportunity arises, the attributes of the actor, audience, and the environmental setting serve as static social context cues. Dynamic cues are provided by the emergent behaviors of each party. Through a variety of cognitive, motivational, and affective processes, the actor and audience selectively perceive and interpret specific aspects of these social context cues to form their situated identities. Importantly, the communication medium selected by the interaction participants mediates this entire process. The parties can choose among face-to-face, telephone, written, numeric, CMCS, or other media that vary with regards to their "richness" and features.

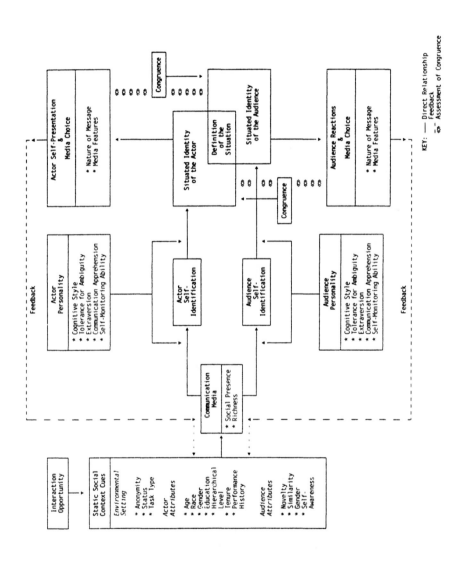

Figure 2.1
A Model of the Self-Presentation Process

The self-presentational model also indicates that the personality attributes of both the actor and the audience (e.g., cognitive style, tolerance for ambiguity, extraversion, communication apprehension, and self-monitoring ability) influence their situated identities. Moreover, the extent to which these parties agree on each others' roles is depicted schematically by the area in which their situated identities intersect. Although considerable overlap between the situated identities normally exists, sizeable discrepancies are also common.

Based on their situated identity, actors choose self-presentational behaviors that are congruent with their interaction objectives and situational demands. Two important aspects of this decision are the selection of the medium and message. The extent to which the actor's behavior and the audience's situational definition are seen as congruent has a substantial impact on the impression the audience forms of the actor. The process of assessing congruence is depicted in the figure by the double arrows, which appear between the actor's behavior and the audience's situated identity. (A parallel process of assessing the congruence of the audience's response relative to the actor's situated identity is also depicted). Congruent actor behavior often leads to positive impressions and responses, whereas perceived incongruence may produce unintended impressions and negative reactions. Such reactions, in turn, provide the actors with feedback that may cause them to alter their situational definition, identify a new target for influence, and/or modify their performance. Given this overview of the self-presentational model, each portion of the model will now be discussed in greater detail.

SELF-PRESENTATION STRATEGIES AND COMPUTER-MEDIATED COMMUNICATIONS

A number of recent studies have shed considerable light on the self-presentations of CMCS users. The three areas that have received the greatest attention revolve around (1) the impact that various social context cues (e.g., anonymity, status) and personality variables exert on behavior during electronic communications; (2) the influence of media choice, the nature of the message, and media features on actor self-presentations; and (3) the influence of audience reactions on actor self-presentations.

Static Social Context Cues

Static social context cues include the demographic attributes of the actor and audience, as well as various factors in the environmental setting.

Environmental Setting. Numerous situational factors provide a backdrop, or "set the stage" for how the actor and audience perceive and communicate with one another. Anonymity, status, and the type of task being performed have been identified as key components of the environmental setting.

With regard to *anonymity,* research on deindividuation (e.g., Festinger, Pepitone, & Newcomb, 1952) lead Gardner and Peluchette (1991) to propose that actors would be less concerned about their image when communicating electronically than with richer forms of media. Since CMCS often provide for anonymity, this medium may promote uninhibited and socially undesirable behavior (Siegel et al., 1986). Still anonymity may prove to be beneficial by encouraging participation and the expression of unpopular ideas (DeSanctis & Gallupe, 1987; Turoff & Hiltz, 1982).

Hiltz, Turoff, and Johnson (1989) compared group decision making during "pen name" and "real name" computer conferences. The results revealed little uninhibited behavior during either type of computer conference. However, recent studies indicate that anonymity can impact on user behavior. Jessup et al. (1990, p. 318) found that members of GDSS groups "felt that they could more safely make critical comments or ask questions about proposed solutions" when they were anonymous. Moreover, when members were less self-aware and concerned about their image, group processes were improved. Similarly, Connolly et al. (1990) concluded that anonymity produced a larger number of original solutions and overall comments. Thus, anonymity may provide important benefits to groups by allowing more freedom of expression.

Status differences can also impact communication process. Actors tend to be more aware of the image they portray during interactions with high- as opposed to low-status audiences (Gardner & Martinko, 1988). However, due to the reduced salience of social context cues, the impact of audience status on actor self-presentations has generally been found to be less pronounced during CMCS communications (Sproull & Kiesler, 1986). Nonetheless, a recent study by Weisband, Schneider, and Connolly (1992) indicates that status effects do influence electronic self-presentations in certain settings. Contrary to expectations, the contributions of low- as opposed to high-status members were evaluated less favorably within the computer-mediated groups. In addition, high-status users participated more frequently and were perceived as contributing more to the final decision. In comparison, low-status members were evaluated more favorably within face-to-face groups. These results suggest that physical presence and the existence of nonverbal cues, such as nodding or smiling, allowed the low-status members to overcome the status difference during face-to-face interactions.

Weisband et al.'s (1992) findings have important implications for CMC, since visual cues are limited by this medium. Indeed, as increasing numbers of persons at all organizational levels use electronic media, opportunities to favorably impress others via visual cues will be reduced. Thus, additional research is necessary to clarify the circumstances under which CMCS extenuate, rather than reduce, status effects. Based on Weisband et al.'s (1992) findings, however, it appears that it is inappropriate to assume that reduced social context cues will cause status to be less pronounced during electronic exchanges.

Although it is recognized that task characteristics impact self-presentational behaviors (Gardner & Martinko, 1988), the importance of *task type* has only recently been examined with respect to CMCS. Smolensky et al. (1990) found that uninhibited speech was greatest for members of preacquainted triads performing a definitive solution task (the NASA Moon Survival Problem) as opposed to groups that were not acquainted or had choice dilemma tasks (i.e., highly interpersonal value judgments). The authors explained their results suggesting that the preacquainted groups had moved through several stages of group development and felt comfortable in expressing their opinions. Smolensky et al. (1990, p. 268) speculated that the clear-cut nature of the task convinced the preacquainted groups "that they were not risking anything by engaging in uninhibited speech," since the task did not require them to reveal personal values. Nonacquainted triads were more inhibited in their speech and seemed more concerned about how they were presenting themselves to others in their groups. However, these groups were more expressive than the preacquainted groups on the choice-dilemma task. Presumably, the nonacquainted members felt more anonymous and hence more willing to express the kinds of value judgments that this relatively inflammatory task required. Thus, it appears that task type plays a key role in determining how individuals choose to present themselves via CMCS.

Actor Attributes. Actor demographics, such as age, race, and gender, exert a strong influence during interpersonal interactions (Gardner & Martinko, 1988), including those which employ CMCS. Although little empirical research exists on the impact of age and race, the effects of gender on computer-mediated negotiations was explored by Matheson (1991). When no information on an opponent's gender was provided to the subjects, there were no differences between men's and women's expectations regarding their opponent's fairness or negotiating strength. However, when females were informed that their opponent was female, they expected her to be more fair, cooperative, and less exploitative than did males. Thus, gender stereotypes appear to impact users' perceptions and expectations regarding the behavior of males and females during computer-mediated negotiations.

Since managerial characteristics, such as education, hierarchical level, tenure, and performance level, also influence communication decisions, Russ et al. (1990) explored these relationships. Prior research indicated that managers who use "lean" media (e.g., written memos, CMCS) for unequivocal messages and "rich" media (e.g., face-to-face) for equivocal messages are more effective (Daft, Lengel, & Trevino, 1987). Based on this finding, Russ et al. (1990) anticipated positive relationships between such variables as hierarchical level, organizational tenure, and educational level—which may reflect differing levels of managerial skills—and the degree to which managers match media richness with message equivocality. Although tenure and education were found to be unrelated to media choices, managers who used richer media for equivocal messages occupied higher positions and were rated as more effective. Thus, it appears that managers who select appropriate media, are more effective and promoted more often than those who use media less appropriately.

Audience Attributes. As indicated by Figure 2.1, the situated identities of both the actor and the audience are shaped by audience characteristics. Since electronic communication provides fewer cues about the audience, the ways in which known versus unknown attributes of the audience impact on communications between the two parties are important. For example, Matheson's (1991) study demonstrated that knowledge of gender influences perceptions during negotiations.

Further insights regarding audience attributes is provided by Matheson and Zanna (1988), who found that the perceived similarity of the audience influenced perceptions of actors in both face-to-face and CMCS groups. The audience was described as one of two bogus "orientation types"—"proximal" versus "distal spatial orientors." All subjects were told that they were "proximal spatial orientors." Matheson and Zanna (1988) found that subjects exhibited greater attitude change when the audience was viewed as similar (i.e., proximal), regardless of the medium employed. However, the manner in which perceptions of the audience influenced attitude change varied across face-to-face and computer-mediated groups. As predicted, computer users exhibited significantly higher levels of self-awareness. Moreover, among highly self-aware subjects, evaluations of the audience appeared to have a two-step impact by initially biasing subjects' evaluations of the audiences' arguments, which in turn lead to attitude change. In contrast, subjects who interacted face-to-face and/or experienced low levels of private self-awareness, were directly influenced by both audience and argument evaluations. The authors concluded that the task sensitized both computer-mediated and face-to-face groups to social cues, although the use of this information was moderated by the subjects' self-awareness and the medium used.

Communication Media

As Figure 2.1 indicates, the static social context cues perceived by both the actor and the audience must first pass through one or more communication media. Thus, it is necessary to consider the characteristics of different media and how these might impact an actor's choice of media for self-presentation purposes. In examining media differences, we will focus on two constructs from the communication and management literatures: social presence and information richness.

Social Presence. The concept of social presence refers to "the degree of salience of the person in the interaction and the consequence salience of the interpersonal relationships" (Short, Williams, & Christie, 1976, p. 65). Although such cues as facial expressions, voice, eye contact, and race are apparent during face-to-face communications, many of these cues are absent when other forms of media are employed. According to Short et al. (1976), social presence is highest for face-to-face communications, followed by television, multispeaker radio, telephone audio, and business letters. More recent research on the social presence of CMCS suggests that, due to the speed of information exchange and its relative flexibility, this medium falls between the telephone and business letters in terms of its social presence (Rice, 1984). Clearly, the differences between the media with regard to social presence have implications for media choice and actor self-presentation.

Information Richness. Closely related to social presence is the concept of information richness which is defined by Daft and Lengel (1984, p. 196) as "the potential information-carrying capacity of data." More specifically, richness is determined by feedback capability, the communication channels used, the source, and language. Because face-to-face communication provides immediate feedback, uses audio and visual channels, is personal in nature, and allows for both natural and body language, it is considered the richest medium. Electronic forms of communication tend to be positioned between telephone and written communication (Fulk, Steinfield, Schmitz, & Power, 1987). Although electronic media use natural language and provide quick feedback, they normally lack audio cues as well as many visual cues.

Both social presence and information richness play a key role in identifying differences between the various media and how these may impact media choice for self-presentation purposes. The effects of these attributes are considered in subsequent sections.

Actor and Audience Personality Traits

As indicated in Figure 2.1, personality traits mediate the processes whereby the actor and audience define the situation and form their situated identities. Potential personality moderators include cognitive style, tolerance for ambiguity, extraversion, communication apprehension, and self-monitoring ability.

Cognitive Style. Trevino et al. (1990) explored the relationship between media choice and cognitive style as measured by the Judging/Perceiving (JP) scale of the Myers-Briggs Type Indicator (MBTI). Js are believed to be more interested in gaining closure and making decisions, as opposed to Ps, who are viewed as more open, curious, and adaptable. Consistent with predictions, Js were found to use leaner media to present themselves in low-equivocality situations than did Ps. These findings suggest that judging and perceiving actors define similar situations differently, which causes them to choose different media to present themselves when contextual constraints are low. Furthermore, these findings suggest that Ps may be reluctant to use the relatively "lean" CMCS medium.

Tolerance for Ambiguity. Trevino et al. (1990) tested the hypothesis that persons who possess high as opposed to low tolerance for ambiguity prefer to use richer media to communicate low-equivocality messages. Although no significant differences were found, the authors suggest that the results may be misleading due to a restriction in the range of scores. Many of the tolerance for ambiguity scores clustered in the middle of the range. Alternatively, it may be that a high tolerance of ambiguity does not necessarily mean that one will actively choose communication media that transmit more ambiguous information. Thus, more research is needed to clarify the extent to which true variance in tolerance for ambiguity accounts for differences in media selection.

Extraversion. Although Russ et al. (1990) hypothesized that extraverted rather than introverted managers (as measured by the MBTI) would select richer media for communicating messages, they did not find a significant relationship between the proposed variables. In contrast, Smolensky et al. (1990) found strong support for their prediction that extraversion (as measured by the Eysenck Personality Inventory) would be positively related to uninhibited speech during CMC. Smolensky et al. (1990, p. 268) explained their results by noting that "extraverted people are, by definition, more outspoken." Thus, these findings suggest that extraversion is an important personality attribute which can impact upon self-presentations via CMCS, although more research is needed to identify the exact circumstances under which this influence is important.

Communication Apprehension. Although this construct was originally limited to oral apprehension (McCroskey, 1977), it has been expanded to include writing apprehension (Daly, 1985). Prior research suggests that some individuals avoid either type of communication, even when it is the most appropriate medium for the message (Daly, 1985; McCroskey, 1977).

In an effort to clarify the effect of individual differences on managerial media choice decisions, Alexander et al. (1991) investigated the impact of communication apprehension on the managers' media sensitivity. Although the authors examined a range of media that varied in richness, including face-to-face, telephone, group meeting, note or mail, individual memo, and group memo, CMC were not included. Nevertheless, the finding that oral, but not written, apprehension was significantly related to overall media sensitivity, suggests that managers who experience oral apprehension will be more likely to use electronic media inappropriately. Consistent with Trevino et al.'s (1990) findings, this relationship was found to be especially pronounced for oral and written apprehension regarding low-equivocality messages.

Self-Monitoring Ability. Gardner and Peluchette (1991) speculated that high as opposed to low self-monitors may be more attuned to the limited number of social context cues provided by CMCS, and hence more likely and capable of using this medium to strategically present themselves to others. When Alexander et al. (1991) specifically examined the relationship between self-monitoring behavior and media sensitivity, they failed to identify a significant correlation between these variables. Still, it seems likely that self-monitoring ability is related in other ways to users' effectiveness in presenting themselves via CMCS, since high as opposed to low self-monitors have consistently been shown to be more successful at managing impressions using other media (Snyder, 1987). Thus, research is necessary to validate and describe the nature of the relationships between self-monitoring and the IM strategies of CMCS users.

Actor Self-Presentation and Media Choice

Although media differ with regards to their social presence and information richness, there are other factors that interact with these attributes to influence media choice for self-presentation purposes. These include the nature of the message as well as media features. We consider these below.

Nature of Message. Daft and Lengel's (1984, 1986) model of managerial information processing proposes a positive relationship between situational and message complexity/ambiguity and media richness. This perspective asserts that actors use rich media (e.g., face-to-face meetings) to process equivocal messages (e.g., strategic planning, employee motivation), and lean media (e.g., electronic mail) for unambiguous messages (e.g., routine information exchange). Subsequent research supports these predictions. Trevino, Lengel, Bodensteiner, Gerloff, and Muir (1990) confirmed that message equivocality influences media choice such that managers are more likely to select rich media for equivocal messages. Similar findings were obtained by Alexander, Penley, and Jernigan (1991). However, their results were not entirely consistent with Daft and Lengel's (1984, 1986) model, since the face-to-face medium was overutilized for high-equivocality messages (59 percent of media choices), whereas the telephone was overutilized for low-equivocality messages (30 percent). The other media (group meeting, note, personal memo, group memo) were underutilized. Alexander et al. (1991) speculate that the information richness model may be more prescriptive than descriptive, and suggest that the influence of personality and situational variables (e.g., convenience) on media choice decisions should be considered in future studies.

Other researchers (Fulk, Schmitz, & Steinfield, 1990; Markus, 1990; Steinfield, 1992) also assert that the contingency theory foundations of the information richness model are conceptually inadequate. Steinfield (1992) interprets the empirical evidence as suggesting that time and distance constraints, social norms, symbolic meanings attributed to the medium, and media experiences impact media choices. He also notes that "lean" electronic media are often used for interpersonally involving and nonroutine communications. Empirical evidence suggests that CMCS are often used for social purposes (e.g., cross-locational games; Steinfield, 1986), broadcast uses (e.g., Finholt & Sproull, 1990), and for conflicts or heated discussions (Kiesler et al., 1984).

To address these shortcomings, Fulk et al. (1990) suggest a social influence model that asserts that media perceptions are socially constructed, such that social cues frame individuals' perceptions of media and communications tasks to guide their choices. This perspective is consistent with the self-presentational model, which asserts that actors' situational definitions/situated identities guide their media choice decisions and their self-presentations. Thus the self-presentational model takes into account the subjective nature of media choice decisions.

Media Features. A critical consideration of media choice is that each medium possesses unique features that can be used for self-presentational purposes. This is apparent in a recent study by King, Dent, and Miles (1991), which examined the persuasive effect of dynamic and static computer graphics, as compared to written text. They found that subjects in both treatment groups were more easily persuaded than those exposed to written text only. They concluded that graphics can be very effective in changing attitudes and behaviors. Future research is required to further delineate the unique self-presentational features that different forms of electronic media possess.

Audience Reactions and Media Choice

As the double arrows in Figure 2.1 indicate, audiences assess the degree of congruence between their definition of the situation and the actor's behavior. When the actor's behavior is perceived to be congruent and appropriate for the situation, audiences tend to respond favorably toward the actor; conversely, perceived incongruencies typically elicit less desirable responses.

Some insights into how audience feedback shapes actor self-presentations via CMCS are provided by Connolly et al. (1990). This study explored the influence that anonymity (anonymous versus identified) and evaluation (supportive versus critical) exert on the performance and satisfaction of GDSS groups. As hypothesized, anonymous groups outperformed identified groups by generating more original solutions and comments on an "Electronic Brainstorming" task. Contrary to expectations, however, both anonymous and identified groups exhibited further gains in idea generation when they were exposed to critical versus supportive audiences. In interpreting these findings, the authors suggest that the observed effects are mediated by member affect toward the audience, with affect being more positive for the supportive audience. Connolly et al. (1990, p. 399) go on to speculate that V4,32 increased liking for others leads both to increased attention to their comments (increasing blocking, and reducing idea production), and to increased desire not to look foolish in front of them (increasing evaluation apprehension and social inhibition). As well as accounting for the main results, this explanation is bolstered by the finding of increased critical comments in the anonymous and critical groups, which is certainly consistent with the various satisfaction measures that suggest that these groups were experienced as less attractive to their members."

Importantly, this explanation is completely consistent with the self-presentational model in that it suggests that CMCS users will be most concerned about their image when they are identified and interacting with an audience that they wish to favorably impress. Unfortunately, such concerns can also lead to the same kinds of inhibitory group processes (e.g., self-censorship) that limit the performance of face-to-face groups. Thus it is clear that audience attributes and audience reactions play a critical role in shaping both the self-presentations and the performance of CMCS users.

FUTURE DIRECTIONS

This chapter has reviewed recent research and expanded a model that has important implications for self-presentations within the context of CMCS. Although a substantial amount of research was identified, much of it has focused primarily on media choice. Although media choice is important, future research should address a wider range of issues. Three broad areas where research attention is needed are situational factors, personality variables, and self-presentational behaviors.

Situational Factors. A host of situational factors are likely to influence the situated identities of CMCS users and their subsequent presentations. These include the type of CMCS (e.g., E-Mail, GDSS, computer conferencing), accessibility, nature of the task (e.g., routine information exchange, strategic planning), and spatial separation of users (e.g., local-area network, wide-area network), as well as other attributes of the larger organizational context (e.g., culture, norms, structure, physical layout, etc.). Of particular interest is the extent to which the CMCS includes safeguards to protect the privacy of users, since people will be more likely to censor their communications if they believe that unintended targets may gain access to their messages. Research is also needed to determine the degree to which electronic exchanges elicit IM motives that have been identified in other contexts, such as desires to be perceived as attractive, competent, trustworthy, intimidating, morally worthy, and/or helpless (Jones & Pittman, 1982; Tedeschi & Norman, 1985). Although many have argued that such motives will be less pronounced during computer-mediated exchanges due to the lack of social context cues (Kiesler, 1986; Kiesler et al., 1984; Siegel et al., 1986), others have shown that CMCS can and do provide sufficient cues to elicit such motives (e.g., Connolly et al., 1990; Finholt & Sproull, 1989). Thus, additional research is necessary to identify situational attributes that elicit particular self-presentational motives.

Personality Variables. During our literature review, a number of personality variables were discussed that probably influence the media choices and self-presentational behaviors of CMCS users. As Figure 2.1 indicates, these included extraversion, communication apprehension, cognitive style, tolerance for ambiguity, and self-monitoring ability. Although empirical evidence of the mediating role of the first three, but not the latter two, variables is available, all of these variables may account for differences in users' interpretations and responses to social context cues. Additional personality variables that have been shown to influence self-presentations in other contexts include needs for social approval (Crowne & Marlowe, 1964), social anxiety (Weary & Arkin, 1981), self-esteem (Baumeister, Tice, & Hutton, 1989), public self-consciousness (Fenigstein, Scheier & Buss, 1975), and Machiavellianism (Christie & Gies, 1970). Hence, research that seeks to ascertain the manner whereby these and other personality traits interact with situational variables to influence the IM motives and self-presentational behaviors of CMCS users is warranted.

Self-Presentational Behavior. IM researchers have catalogued a wide variety of strategic behaviors that actors choose from as part of their efforts to create and retain desired impressions (Cialdini, 1989; Gardner, 1992; Gardner & Martinko, 1988; Jones & Pittman, 1982; Leary & Kowalski, 1990; Schlenker, 1980; Schlenker & Weigold, 1992; Tedeschi & Norman, 1985). These strategies range from assertive behaviors that are intended to secure a desired identity (e.g., ingratiation, self-promotion, exemplification, acclaiming, entitlements, enhancements) to defensive or face-saving tactics that are designed to protect or repair the actor's image (e.g., defenses of innocence, excuses, apologies, justifications). Indirect methods of IM, such as "BIRGing" (basking in reflected glory), "Burying" (disclaiming a positive link to an undesirable other), and "Boosting" (minimizing the unfavorable features of a positively linked other) are also available (Cialdini, 1989). To date, systematic research on the extent to which actors use these and other strategies when interacting via electronic media is unavailable. Indeed, the insights into CMCS users' self-presentational behaviors that have been obtained, have primarily been generated by studies that were not specifically focusing on IM behaviors. As such, research that seeks to directly ascertain the extent and circumstances under which actors use IM strategies is required. Essentially, such research would be designed to further explicate the "Actor Self-Presentation and Media Choice" component of the proposed model, and the situational and personality factors that influence it. Although it may be that novel approaches to using familiar tactics will be uncovered, it is also possible that strategies that are not commonly used in conjunction with other media (e.g., graphical images), are more prevalent during electronic exchanges.

CONCLUSIONS

From the preceding review, it is clear that a substantial amount of research informs our knowledge of the self-presentational behaviors of CMCS users. It is equally apparent, however, that relatively little research has been conducted that focuses specifically on the IM behaviors which organizational members display during electronic exchanges (Steinfield & Fulk, 1987). Until such research is forthcoming, the potential contributions that IM theory and research can provide with regards to our understanding of CMC will go unrealized. Particularly valuable would be designs which examine the interactions between the situational, personality, and behavioral variables identified by the model. Smolensky et al.'s (1990) study could serve as a prototype for such research, since it examined the interactive effects that situational (task type, group structure) and personality variables (extraversion) exert on the behavior (uninhibited speech) of CMCS users. Investigations along these lines that focus directly on self-presentations could provide valuable knowledge regarding the image-related tactics that actors employ during CMC. The model suggested in this chapter represents an initial attempt to provide a conceptual framework for such research. Ultimately, it is hoped that research into the proposed relationships will provide insights that will enable organizations to capitalize on the benefits of CMCS, while minimizing the undesirable social consequences that too often accompany this technology.

3

THE SYMBOLIC VALUE OF COMPUTERS: EXPANDING ANALYSES OF ORGANIZATIONAL COMPUTING

Susan J. Winter

From at least as long ago as the Hawthorne studies of illumination levels, there has been considerable interest in the design of work areas. Davis (1984) identified several influential aspects of offices. These include the physical structure (e.g., walls, furniture), physical stimuli or cues such as the time on a clock or a ringing telephone, and symbolic artifacts. This chapter focuses on computer technology as symbolic artifacts displayed in office settings.

During the last decade, microcomputers have become increasingly common in organizations. Almost forty percent of capital spending in the United States is being used to acquire information technology to improve productivity. Much of this spending is going toward automating white-collar office work (Davis, 1991). However, hopes of productivity gains among white-collar workers are not being realized and many managers are disenchanted with their computer systems' ability to improve worker productivity (Bowen, 1986; Kletke, Trumbly, & Nelson, 1991). Perhaps one of the reasons computers have not alleviated the productivity problem in white-collar work is that they have not been distributed to workers solely on the basis of their appropriateness to the tasks performed (efficiency potential) but according to their symbolic value.

The predominant metaphor used by professionals in the management of information systems (MIS) to describe the relationship between information systems and their users (people) is that of a neutral tool (Gutek, 1989; Hirschheim, 1986; Hirschheim & Newman, 1991). Technology is seen as a tool in the hands of the workers to be used when and where appropriate to make their work more efficient, to raise the quality of life in general, and to provide competitive advantage for the organization. The tool itself is seen as neutral and can be used in many ways. One of the missions of MIS professionals is to describe tasks or problems in detail and identify or develop computerized "tools" to aid in performing those tasks or solving those problems (Brancheau & Wetherbe, 1987).

However, it is possible that computers have not been allocated based on their function as a tool. Rather, distribution may actually have been based on the value attached to them by powerful stakeholders and guided by concerns for impression management. Research in the area of organizational culture has suggested that physical artifacts (the built environment) such as computers can hold symbolic value for those who interact with them (Schein, 1985; Sundstrom, 1986). This chapter explores the implications of computers acting as value-laden symbols rather than just neutral tools to improve efficiency.

Awareness of their symbolic value allows computer technology to be actively managed to create a desired impression. If it symbolizes a worker's status in an organization, it can be integrated into the organizations' compensation packages and strategic plans for managing employee performance. For example, a valued recruit could be given a powerful computer primarily as a symbol of her value to the organization, though the capabilities of this equipment would not be required. Using computers in this fashion would improve the ability to attract, retain, and motivate high-quality employees. If computers are negatively valued or inconsistent with the desired impression, this information could help organizations manage computer acquisition and allocation and to interpret stakeholder's reactions to them. For example, companies that want to portray a caring, human atmosphere to clients, such as those that provide social services, may choose to locate computers in an area that is not usually visible to clients. However, they may want to convey an impression of efficiency and rationality to other stakeholders, such as regulators or donors. Managers should then locate computers in areas that are visible to regulators and donors, but not to clients.

This chapter will call attention to the symbolic nature of computers. It will also help clarify and describe the use and display of computers as symbols in organizational life. The questions to be answered are How can computers function as symbols for individuals, groups, and organizations? and What do computers symbolize? Future research should focus on describing when and how computers are used as symbols. The next section provides a discussion of organizational symbols focusing on the definition of symbols, how they relate to organizational culture, and on their functions in organizational life. Contingency variables that may affect the symbolic value of computer technology and appropriate levels of analysis are discussed. Evidence supporting the symbolic value attached to computers is presented from three diverse areas: organizational sociology, the research on individual-level impacts of use, and the literature on information technology development. Implications for impression management for multiple audiences are discussed and suggestions for future research are presented.

BACKGROUND

Symbols

As symbols, computer technology can be displayed or used to manage impressions about an individual, a group, a firm, or a society. Computers can convey both positive and negative information. They can affect impressions of an individual's competence, modernity, intelligence, rationality, and status in the organization (Feldman & March, 1981; March, 1987; Safayeni, Purdy & Higgins, 1989; Winter, 1993). They can also symbolize to stakeholders a department, plant, or firm's modernity, legitimacy, and competitiveness (Anderson, Hassen, Johnson, & Klassen, 1979; Bikson, Gutek, & Mankin, 1987; Danziger, Dutton, Kling, & Kraemer, 1982; March & Sproull, 1990). Of course, it is also possible that computer technology symbolizes negative characteristics or portrays an image that is antithetical to that which is desired. For example, use of a keyboard may indicate that an individual is a low-status clerical worker or the presence of computer technology may symbolize sterile rationality in a setting where emotional support should be emphasized (e.g., an Alcoholic's Anonymous meeting).

Recently, attention has been focused on the topic of organizational symbols and their role in corporate climate (James & Jones, 1974) and culture (Martin, Feldman, Hatch, & Sitkin, 1983; Schein, 1985). Most theorists suggest that a symbol is any object or event that conveys or transmits meanings, images, feelings, and values to those who encounter it (Dandridge, Mitroff, & Joyce, 1980; Morgan, Frost, & Pondy, 1983). Symbols have received much attention because they are believed to be used in forming impressions, in rapid communication of information to those inside and outside of an organization, in motivating employees, and in maintaining social systems (Dandridge, 1983; Dandridge et al., 1980; Morgan et al., 1983; Sundstrom, 1986). Though little research attention has focused directly on computers as symbols, previous work has shown that they do transmit meanings and so can be considered symbols.

Most researchers in the organizational culture field agree that culture is composed of shared values, patterns of beliefs, common understandings, and assumptions. However, their models differ in nature, though most propose that visible artifacts are surface manifestations of a culture's underlying values. Schein (1985) suggests that culture is composed of three levels: artifacts (the built environment) that are visible, values (the sense of what "ought" to be), and basic assumptions that are invisible and preconscious. Symbols would be visible artifacts that embody the underlying values of the group. Norms, values, beliefs, and cognitions established by previous interaction with the object all play a role in the interpretation of symbols. Dandridge et al. (1980) suggest that symbols can be verbal (e.g., stories, slogans, jokes), actions (e.g., parties, rites of passage, meals), or material (e.g., status symbols, logos, pins). Clearly, computers would be classified as material symbols (though stories told about them could be verbal symbols and rituals surrounding computer use could be action symbols).

It is not yet clear whether computers transmit the same images, feelings, and values in all situations and to all people. It is possible that the meaning of computers varies consistently with characteristics of the computers themselves, the situations in which they are found, and the people encountering them. The following section reviews evidence of contingency factors affecting the social meaning of computers and tried to identify consistent patterns of meaning.

Contingency Factors

Organizational symbols' connotations depend upon their social meaning within the context of specific work situations, as distinct from the social meaning connoted when found in other contexts (Safayeni et al., 1989). The concept of social meaning refers to the way in which others interpret and understand a situation within a certain context or frame. It is similar to the concepts of attitude and organizational climate and culture, but differs in that it is sensitive to specific situations rather than stable across many situations. Though social meanings may vary from situation to situation, there may be some consistent patterns in the connotations attached to computers. Since the meaning of a symbol is determined partly by cognitions established through interacting with the symbol, those that are most similar to each other in their physical characteristics, purposes, and uses would likely have more similar connotations. Though computers do differ from each other, those developed for each type of user are likely to share many characteristics and elicit some of the same responses from their users.

Type of System

The literature in sociology, MIS, ergonomics, and public health focusing on the individual-level impacts of computers on their users and includes both positive and negative effects. This is not too surprising since computers may differ markedly from each other in their physical characteristics, implementation, purpose, history, and social meaning (Kling & Scachi, 1982). Computers designed to support executives do differ markedly from those designed to support clerical workers (Rockart & DeLong, 1988).

The effects of computer use on the quality of work life have been found to differ based on participants' occupations. Often, researchers have found positive effects (i.e., decreased tedium, increased speed of work, more fun) for managerial, executive, and professional workers and have found negative effects (i.e., decreased control, increased stress) for clerical workers (Alcalay & Pasick, 1983; Grandjean, 1987). Therefore, the value attached to computers by

avoid displaying computers because they are considered antithetical to creativity. Symbols can similarly be used and displayed by entire organizations or by societies. The group and organizational levels of analysis have been investigated primarily by organizational theory and sociology. The societal level of analysis has been discussed by anthropologists. The focus of this chapter does not include the societal level (which is omitted from Figure 3.1), though it is acknowledged that societal norms should influence the social meaning of computers.

Figure 3.1 also shows that each of the functions of symbols can be investigated at each of the levels of analysis, yielding nine cells. The next section will review the possible symbolic uses of computers and the research literature for each of these nine cells. First we will consider the informational function of symbols when used by individuals.

INDIVIDUAL LEVEL OF ANALYSIS

Informational Function

Much of the research on office design and the role of symbols has been done by social psychologists and architects. Organizational symbols are seen to rapidly convey many types of information about an employee. For example, the occupants of semienclosed work spaces in one large open office attached drawings of small doors across the entries of their workstations. These served no practical value, but were "closed" to let others know that the occupant wanted to be left alone (The trouble with open offices, 1978). This is an example of a symbol used to communicate the workers' current desires for privacy.

Impression Management

The informational value of symbols at the individual level of analysis has also been the focus of a considerable body of research on impression management. Impression management (IM) is predicated on the theatrical analogy of people as actors working to create and maintain desired perceptions of themselves (Schneider, 1981). IM provides one framework for understanding the use of computers for their symbolic value and also alerts us to both the positive and negative information conveyed by computers. The majority of IM research has focused on behavior (Giacalone & Rosenfeld, 1989), but the crucial role of elements in the behavioral setting has also been recognized (Ornstein, 1989; Gardner & Martinko, 1988).

Though most of the IM literature has focused on behaviors performed to create and maintain desired impressions, the theories underlying this work assign a critical role to the setting in which these behaviors take place. Three theoretical perspectives on social interactions have been suggested as supporting the premises of IM (Ornstein, 1989); the role of the physical environment in the dramaturgical perspective, the symbolic interactionist approach, and the situated identities approach is described below.

In Goffman's (1959) dramaturgical perspective, people are viewed as "actors" engaging in "performances" before "audiences" in various "settings." Within a social setting a team of performers may cooperate to present an audience with one agreed on definition of the situation. Often the setting is divided into a "backstage" area where a routine is prepared and an "onstage" area where the performance is presented; the audience is generally not allowed "backstage." An individual acts a part based on how he or she wants to be seen by the audience. In support of this goal, people may focus on creating physical settings that are consistent with the image they are trying to convey. From this perspective, computers should be prominently displayed in the onstage area when their symbolic information is consistent with the image an individual wants to convey and hidden when they are inconsistent with that image.

In contrast, the symbolic interactionist approach (Blumer, 1969) suggests that people act in ways that are consistent with the expectations of their audiences. People are seen as caught up in a longitudinal process of interaction in which they have to fit their developing actions to one another. Interaction includes indicating to others what they are to do and interpreting similar information from others. The role taken on by an actor may change to fit the different expectations and desires of various audiences. The meanings attached to objects are seen to guide an individual's orientation and actions. The physical setting is important as a visual cue that helps create and support the role being played. From this perspective, computers can be displayed to guide others' actions or when others expect them to be displayed.

Finally, the situated identities approach (Alexander & Knight, 1971) suggests that people use the social context in which they find themselves as the basis for determining appropriate roles and behaviors. One major factor in defining the social context is the physical setting (Schlenker, 1985). From this perspective, people will assess their social context to determine whether or not they should display computers and situations where computers are prominent should affect actors' behaviors and roles.

Though the details of the role played by the setting vary among the three perspectives, it is clear that the environment is an important factor in impression management and that computers, as part of the social setting, can convey important symbolic information. Though there has been little systematic empirical research focusing on the social meaning of computers (and none informed by the IM perspective) the few studies have shown surprising agreement in their results considering their wide variety of research methods. Safayeni et al. (1989) found that managers and professionals associated having a computer in one's office with being more status conscious, career oriented, dynamic, logical, open-minded, younger, and less conservative. Similarly, the use of computers has been found to signal competence and rationality (Feldman & March, 1981; March, 1987). Computers have also been noted to appeal to people as entertaining or status-improving technology (Beatty & Gordon, 1988; Katz, 1987; King, 1983; Malone, 1980; Ord, 1989).

The next section provides a review of the literature on one common type of symbol use to convey information at the individual level of analysis, status symbols.

Status Symbols

One commonly researched class of symbols is that associated with status, or the relative standing of an individual in the organization's hierarchy of authority and influence. For the individual, the symbols of status represent concrete and visible evidence of rank in the organization and the power that accompanies it. Status markers (characteristics of work spaces that signify the occupant's status) can perform several functions. They can efficiently communicate the hierarchy of influence in the organization, serve as incentives for performance, or serve as props for use in carrying out the duties associated with specific jobs (Konar & Sundstrom, 1985; Sundstrom, 1986).

Several features of work spaces in offices have apparently become more or less traditional signs of status. These include location near a window, accessibility by others (a private office), amount of floorspace, furnishings, and degree of personalization permitted (Konar & Sundstrom, 1985; Konar, Sundstrom, Brady, Mandel, & Rice, 1982; Steele 1973). There is little systematic empirical research on this subject, but anecdotes abound and aspects of the work space apparently symbolize status in the hierarchy in many offices (Sundstrom, 1986). For example, many organizations (including CBS in New York City and the Civil Service) have developed formal policies detailing the appropriate size and furnishings of offices for each level in their hierarchy (Wotton, 1976). On entering an office, any individual familiar with the organization's policy can easily assess the occupant's level in the hierarchy.

Within an organization, symbols of status will be allocated differentially to workers based on their rank in the hierarchy. When information about individuals' standings in the organization is scarce, any aspect of the workplace that is closely tied to rank (even if it is also necessary for performing the job) can be given significance and operate as a symbol of status (Steele, 1973). The allocation of status symbols simultaneously reflects the value of the individual to the organization, the props required to perform the job, as well as indicants of success. Top executives may receive the largest incomes, the largest private offices, and the nicest furnishings because they are the most valued employees, or because of the perception that they need these props, but this does not diminish the significance of the symbols in transmitting information about the employee to others.

Much of the individual-level research on organizational symbols has been done in the field of social psychology and has focused on conveying information about an employee to other individuals inside or outside of the organization. Previous research has shown that computer technology is distributed according to status particularly for professional workers and so can act as a status symbol (Winter, 1993). Computers have also been mentioned as one of the items respondents would want in their work spaces to indicate their new status if they were promoted (Sundstrom, 1986). Safayeni et al. (1989) also found that managers and professionals associated having a computer in one's office with having higher status.

Energy Controlling Function

Symbols can also perform an energy controlling function (Dandridge et al., 1980) at the individual level of analysis. Energy controlling symbols can inspire or attract a worker, or can repel her. They can also provide catharsis and decrease the amount of tension an individual perceives. A status marker can also act as an incentive to the extent that it is itself valued or it indicates the relative standing or allocation of promotions valued by the employee. A status marker can also indicate negative status and act as a disincentive or be repellent to employees.

If computers symbolize a worker's status in an organization, they can be integrated into the organizations' compensation packages and strategic plans for managing employee performance. For example, a valued recruit could be offered a powerful computer primarily as a symbol of her value to the organization and to increase her feeling of attraction to the company in hopes of getting her to take a position there instead of with the competition. This offer may be made even though the capabilities of this equipment would not be required to perform the job. The symbolic use of computers for controlling an employee's energy has not been systematically investigated but may be widespread.

System Maintenance

Symbols can also perform a system maintenance function (Dandridge et al., 1980). This refers to the use of symbols to justify or reinforce the patterning or stability of the system. Symbols can be used to provide coherence, order, stability and integration. Lavish work spaces for high-ranking members of an organization are often justified as props required for performing their jobs. The executive may need a large, well-furnished office because he or she needs to hold meetings with many important people who would expect a lavish office. However, at the same time low-ranking employees may have difficulty in obtaining the necessary props for their own jobs (Sundstrom, 1986). The allocation of identical computer equipment to all members of a particular group of workers may provide a symbol of that group's coherence and of each individual's membership in the group. The use of computers for system maintenance has not been studied at the individual level of analysis.

In summary, research on the symbolic functions fulfilled by computers at the individual level of analysis is sparse with only the informational function addressed in previous work. However, generally positive perceptions have been found of computer users. Most of this work has been done with managers and professionals and little of it has been theoretically driven or informed by previous work on impression management or status symbols. The next section reviews the symbolic functions fulfilled by computers at the organizational level and will be followed by a discussion of the group or mezzo level of analysis.

ORGANIZATIONAL LEVEL OF ANALYSIS

Most of the literature on the use of computer technology as a symbol at the organizational level of analysis has been done by researchers in the fields of sociology and organizational theory. The literature on organizational sociology includes work on the impact of computerization on power and status, the assessment of characteristics of those who have computers, and the institutionalization of computers in organizations.

Computers have been found to perform a descriptive function transmitting information about an organization. Several researchers have stated that they symbolize modernity and competitiveness among organizations (Anderson, Hassen, Johnson, & Klassen, 1979; Bikson, Gutek, & Mankin, 1987; Danziger, Dutton, Kling, & Kraemer, 1982; March & Sproull, 1990). Computer technology can also be a symbol of power and control at the industry, class, or societal level. The use of computer technology by management has been seen as a form of control over workers (Clement, 1988; Danziger, Dutton, Kling, & Kraemer, 1982; Edwards, 1979; Zuboff, 1988).

Considerable interest has also been generated in using energy controlling symbols throughout an organization in order to inspire and attract workers (Dandridge et al., 1980). However, little empirical research has been done in this area and a theoretical model relating organizational symbols to motivation remains to be developed. No systematic research has focused on the energy controlling function of computers as symbols at the organizational level.

However, some sociologists have investigated the use of commonly accepted forms and symbols for system maintenance and particularly to attain legitimacy under conditions of uncertainty. When it is not clear what process ought to be followed to obtain the desired results, institutional theory predicts that firms will mimic the forms and display the symbols of those that have good reputations and are, therefore, socially legitimate. For instance, if it is not clear how one ought to teach students at the university level, but it is widely agreed that Carnegie Mellon University does a good job and requires each student to obtain a personal computer, therefore, other universities will require the same. Powerful stakeholders (e.g., parents, benefactors, top high school students) will then feel that all universities that require personal computers of their students must be doing a good job.

Though the institutionalization of computer use has not been widely investigated, the institutionalization of computer use in classroom instruction and in organizational settings has been described (Davis, 1983; Dickson, 1981). Some researchers have also found that professional employees expect and demand access to computers at work (Kling & Iacono, 1989), providing indirect evidence of the institutionalization of computing in the work place.

In summary, little systematic research has been done on the symbolic functions fulfilled by computers at the organizational level of analysis. However, both the informational function and the system maintenance function have been addressed in previous work. Organizations using computers have generally been perceived positively and computer use appears to be institutionalized in educational and work settings.

GROUP OR MEZZO LEVEL OF ANALYSIS

The symbolic role of computers has not been systematically investigated at the level of the group or department. Though no research has focused on the descriptive role of computers in transmitting information about a group, the interpretation of computer technology by its users has been found to differ by organizational culture and between firms (Brown, 1994) and the value attached to computers by their users has also been found to depend partly on the organizational function of the group to which they belong (Winter, 1993). The literature on organizational sociology includes work on the impact of computerization on the power and status of groups of workers within an organization. Researchers have also shown that control over computer resources is related to the power and status of groups within an organization (Kling & Iacono, 1984; Kraemer & Dutton, 1979: Markus, 1981).

We can also trace the process by which computers as symbols could be used for its informational value at the group or mezzo level of analysis. Information can be conveyed about a department or workgroup to powerful stakeholder groups or to individuals with whom it makes contact. At this mezzo level we may see a combination of the individual-level influence process and the macro-level mimicry and institutionalization process. For example, a top engineering student interviewing for an entry-level position will be making site visits to engineering departments in various firms. The computer technology displayed may symbolize for the candidate the modernity, wealth, competitiveness, and desirability of the department. Comparisons between the offices in the engineering department and other areas will provide information about the status or legitimacy of engineering within the firm and (at the organizational level) the modernity, wealth, competitiveness, and desirability of the firm as a whole. Also comparisons made regarding the computer technology available to engineers within the same department can indicate the relative status of various branches of engineering (e.g., electrical versus mechanical) or of individual engineers within the same field.

Energy-controlling symbols could also be used at the group level in order to inspire and attract workers (Dandridge et al., 1980), but little empirical research has been done is this area and, again, a theoretical model relating group symbols to motivation has not been determined. No systematic research has focused on the energy-controlling function of computers as symbols at the group level. Similarly, though it is possible to investigate the use of computers as system maintenance symbols at the group level of analysis, this area has also remained unexplored.

SUMMARY

In summary, it is possible to study the symbolic function of computers as providing information, controlling energy, and maintaining systems at the individual, group, or organizational level. However, previous literature has focused on the informational function at the individual level and the informational and systems maintenance levels at the organizational level. The symbolic effects of using computers at work do not seem to be neutral and may covary with the nature of the work performed by the individual, the nature of the work group, or the organizational culture. Indirect or symbolic effects may be closely related to direct effects because interaction with the object and the resulting cognitions play a role in the creation of its social meaning. Though the social meaning of computers has yet to be fully investigated empirically, computers do seem to be value-laden objects. As symbolic artifacts, computer technology can be used to manage impressions of an individual's competence, modernity, or status. It can also be used to convey impressions of a firm's competitiveness, modernity, status, or legitimacy to powerful stakeholders. The symbolic value of computer technology can also convey information about a group. Additionally, computers may fulfill both energy controlling and system maintenance functions at the individual, group, and organizational levels.

IMPLICATIONS

Previous research indicates that any object or event that conveys meanings, images, feelings, and values to those who encounter it can act as a symbol (Dandridge et al., 1980; Morgan et al., 1983) and may have a role to play in providing information, managing impressions, controlling motivation or energy, and in maintaining social systems. If it is allocated differentially to workers, groups, or organizations based on their rank in the hierarchy, it can be a symbol of status (Steele, 1973). As a symbol, computers can also be subject to the forces of institutionalization which may guide their diffusion throughout organizations. There is evidence that computer technology is acting as a symbol at several levels of analysis conveying various meanings. It may act as a symbol of status, competence, modernity, rationality, and intelligence among individuals. It can also indicate the same for work groups, departments, or firms and can be used to enhance social legitimacy. The meaning conveyed may vary and can be either consistent or inconsistent with the desired impressions.

Though some organizations may negate the status effects of computer resources by allocating identical equipment to each worker, in many situations the allocation of computers may engender the same degree of conflict as the allocation of office space. Managers who recognize the nonrational, power-related implications of computer resource allocation decisions should be better able to understand "irrational" responses to computers and, therefore, should be able to manage more effectively.

For example, a manager supervising an engineer may consider his or her strong requests for a modem with direct-dialing capability frivolous and irrational since it would only be used a few times each day. However, management may want to purchase the modem (investing a relatively small amount of money) in order to retain and motivate a valued employee (especially if engineers at other companies are receiving these modems). Either decision (purchasing or not purchasing) may also provide a signal to the employee regarding his or her value to the organization.

The amount and distribution of computer resources can also provide a signal about the organization to prospective employees, clients, competitors, and regulators. Many firms choose office furnishings to portray a particular image to their clients (e.g., waiting areas in law offices, banks, and hospitals look very different from each other). If a manager recognizes the symbolic value of computer resources, he or she can take the same care in choosing and displaying computers in order to enhance the firm's preferred image.

As computer equipment becomes less expensive, it represents a relatively small fraction of managerial and professional compensation packages and may play a pivotal role in signaling both the modernity of the organization and the value of an employee to the company. Organizations recognizing the symbolic value of computer resources can choose to integrate them into their compensation systems and use them to attract, retain, and motivate the best employees. Some organizations (such as universities) have already moved in this direction because of market pressures (e.g., competition for scarce professors of business and engineering); many more may be able to do so profitably. Additionally, computers may be used to maintain social systems through providing legitimacy and coherence. Those who want to enhance their legitimacy may want to mimic the computing arrangements of highly regarded members of society.

FUTURE RESEARCH

Research Questions

Several interesting research questions not previously investigated are suggested by this review of the literature. Among them are the following possibilities:

1. What are the social meanings conveyed by computer technology?
2. Are there communalities in the social meanings conveyed by computers among types of workers, groups, departments, and firms? If so, what are the forces affecting this communality (e.g. educational experiences, surrounding culture)?
3. What is the process by which computers' social meanings are developed over time?
4. When do the symbolic aspect of computers perform an energy controlling function providing inspiration and motivation at the individual, group, and organizational levels?
5. Under what conditions do computers function as symbols providing the system maintenance functions of legitimation and integration?

Research Methods

Exposing the social meaning of any artifact (such as computers) is not a simple task since the insiders of a culture are not necessarily aware of their own artifacts and their social meaning (Schein, 1985). When questioned, respondents may even deny the symbolic value of an artifact and attribute the differences in its distribution to its utility in the performance of various jobs (Lipman, Cooper, Harris, & Tranter, 1978). Even social meanings and values that are consciously articulated may indicate only what people will say rather than what they actually think or do (Argyris & Schon, 1978). Therefore, one cannot ask about the value attached to computers directly. However, an outsider can observe the distribution of an artifact, in light of its instrumental nature, and infer from that distribution the underlying value of the artifact to the group (Schein, 1985; Sundstrom, 1986).

Because respondents are generally unable to describe (or are unaware of) many of the symbols they encounter (Argyris & Schon, 1978), the study of organizational symbols has remained primarily an idiographic, qualitative endeavor drawing heavily from anthropological research methods and anecdotal evidence. Though this methodology has yielded considerable insight into the nature of symbols, the information it can provide is limited. A fuller understanding of the nature and use of symbols could be developed if additional methods of research were used. However, few studies have taken a normative approach by attempting to identify consistent patterns, classify common symbols, or test causal theories or models by collecting, comparing, and testing quantitative data from respondents in multiple organizations (though see Ornstein, 1986; Safayeni et al., 1989; Winter, 1993 for notable exceptions).

Though it is possible to use questionnaires to study symbols, it may be extremely difficult to collect accurate information more directly relevant to the symbolic value of computers from average workers responding to written questionnaires. Symbols embody the values of the group (the sense of what "ought" to be), but members do not usually (and may be unable to) examine the underlying assumptions that explain why things "ought" to be this way rather than another; these underlying assumptions are generally invisible and preconscious (Schein, 1985). Additionally, respondents may be heavily influenced by social desirability bias. This may make them extremely unwilling to espouse an "irrational" power-based or impression management-based allocation of computer equipment. It may also lead respondents to be reluctant to discuss the importance of status and its symbols in societies that are not supposed to have rigid social classes and that have been founded on the assumption that all its members were created equal. Thus, direct questions about organizational symbols, even if embedded in a carefully crafted questionnaire and skilfully worded, may yield inaccurate or questionable information.

A quantitative, indirect research method that focuses on relating the distribution of computer technology among workers, departments, or firms that differ in perceptions of their status, competence, rationality, and the like, may further efforts to identify and classify organizational symbols whose meanings remain fairly consistent across organizations, groups, or jobs. A policy capturing study using scenarios describing employees, the nature of the work they do, and the type of firm can be used to abstract the decision rules used by allocators. Comparing results with different wordings of the decision would indicate the amount of slippage between allocators' ideal policy and organizational reality. Another possibility that should be explored further is the use of photographic stimuli representing offices with different types computer resources and asking respondents what they symbolize about the incumbents of those offices and about the organizations in which they work. A third possibility would be to ask respondents to describe or draw the work space they would want or expect to use for various types of jobs. Any of these methods could allow the true size of the symbolic effect of computer resources to be more closely estimated by providing some experimental control and while still allowing respondents considerable freedom in providing information they feel is relevant.

CONCLUSION

The major purpose of this chapter has been to call attention to an important but neglected phenomenon, the symbolic nature of computers. The "neutral tool" metaphor used by professionals in MIS does not adequately describe the relationship between information systems and their users. As cultural artifacts, computer resources are transmitting information and seem to have significant symbolic value in motivating and in maintaining social systems. Managers should not ignore this aspect of computers in managing impressions, motivating workers, and gaining legitimacy at the individual, group, and organizational levels. For researchers, there is a wealth of qualitative and quantitative data waiting to be collected that pertains to the symbolic functions of computers in organizational life. Organizational symbolism provides a complementary and important view of computerization that will allow a much fuller understanding of this phenomenon.

4

MANAGING IMPRESSIONS WITH INFORMATION TECHNOLOGY: FROM THE GLASS HOUSE TO THE BOUNDARYLESS ORGANIZATION

George M. Marakas
Daniel Robey

The inability to demonstrate the economic payoffs from investments in information technology (IT) has become known as the "productivity paradox." One would think that the value of large investments in IT should be easy to demonstrate. Yet despite the lack of a clear connection between IT and economic return, investments in IT continue to represent a significant portion of capital expenditures throughout the world. In this chapter, we argue that the symbolic role of IT may help to explain the absence of demonstrable economic reasons for IT investments. An organization may implicitly justify the acquisition and possession of IT because of its symbolic importance rather than its economic value. IT's symbolic role may have an indirect effect on economic performance, especially in cases where an organization is able to sustain its legitimacy and survive within an institutional environment. Thus, we consider a symbolic analysis of investments in IT to complement more circumscribed economic analyses.

The purpose of this chapter is to apply a recently developed theory from the study of organizational behavior—impression management—to the productivity paradox. We argue that information technology has symbolic consequences and that it is acquired in part as a means for an organization's members to manage impressions they make on peers, customers, competitors, and others. We trace the origins of impression management theory, articulating its basic constructs and propositions, and show how it may be applied in organizational settings. We apply the logic of impression management to explain the patterns of acquisition and deployment of IT in three distinct periods of time: (1) the glass-house era (circa 1960-1980), (2) the desktop era (1980-1990), and (3) the current era of the boundaryless organization. We conclude by discussing the relationship between economic and symbolic explanations of IT investment arguing that, by creating positive impressions, members of an organization may produce economic returns on its investments in IT that are not directly included in standard economic analyses.

INTRODUCTION

The word "potential" appears frequently in the literature on information technology (IT).   Leavitt and Whisler (1958), who also coined the term information technology, spoke of the potential of IT to reshape individual tasks, eliminate certain levels of organizational hierarchy, alter organizational structures, reshape boundaries, recentralize, shorten feedback loops, and improve the quality of decisions. Thirty years later, Applegate, Cash, and Mills (1988) revisited these predictions and concluded that, while Leavitt and Whisler were "downright visionary," much of the potential attributed to IT had yet to be realized.   As the twenty-first century approaches, potential remains a major selling point for IT and its ancillary services.   IT has the potential to provide an organization with strategic opportunity (Jarvenpaa & Ives, 1990; Johnston & Carrico, 1988; Vitale, Ives, & Beath, 1986; Banker & Kauffman, 1988), competitive advantage (Copeland & McKenney, 1988; Ludlum, 1989; Porter & Millar, 1985), improved customer service (Ives & Mason, 1990), and increased productivity and efficiency (Banker, Kauffman, & Morey, 1989; Weill, 1992; Zimmerman, 1988).

Although both academics and practitioners have provided accounts in which IT has realized this potential (e.g., Bender, 1986; Brynjolfson & Hitt, 1993; Harris & Katz, 1988), other authors have reported neutral or negative effects of IT on performance (e.g., Cron & Sobol, 1983; Banker, Kauffman, & Morey, 1989).   On balance, there is no consistent evidence that investments in IT generate positive financial returns (Kauffman & Weill, 1989; Olson, 1965; Roach, 1988).   Indeed, most of the evidence has been inconclusive.   For example, Loveman (1988) showed no evidence of any positive relationship between IT investment and business performance, after controlling for the time lag between the development and acquisition of IT and its effect on the acquiring organization.   A more recent study (Dos Santos, Peffers, & Mauer, 1993) indicated that the average net present value to the firm of an investment in IT was zero.

The inability to demonstrate the economic payoffs from investments in IT has become known as the "productivity paradox" (Due, 1993; Powell, 1992; Drucker, 1991; Haynes, 1990).   It is paradoxical that investments with an average net present value of zero would account for 32.5 percent of all U.S. capital equipment expenses in 1986, exclusive of expenditures for software and systems development (Roach, 1987).   One would think that the value of such large investments should be easier to demonstrate.   Yet despite the lack of a clear connection between IT and economic return, investments in IT in the service sector increased threefold between 1970 and 1988, becoming almost 20 percent of capital stock (Weill, 1992). Even more pronounced increases have occurred in the manufacturing sector, where IT investment grew from 1.6 percent to 10.6 percent of capital stock between 1970 and 1988 (Roach, 1989).

The purpose of this chapter is to apply a recently developed theory from the study of organizational behavior, that is, impression management, to the productivity paradox. Impression management regards people's conscious and unconscious behavior as attempts to create and maintain desired perceptions of themselves by others. We argue that IT has symbolic consequences and that it is acquired in part as a means for an organization's members to manage impressions they make on peers, customers, competitors, and others. Feldman and March (1981) argued that the production and use of information in organizations may symbolize competence, rationality, and other social virtues. March and Sproull (1990) extended this argument to include the technologies for processing information, stating that IT's value depends partly on its contribution to institutional reputation and legitimacy. They suggested that some of IT's benefits may be derived merely by adopting and possessing IT, independent of any instrumental economic return from its use. In this light, IT becomes a cultural artifact, capable of reflecting an organization's values and assumptions, particularly those of efficiency and progress (Robey & Azevedo, in press; Robey & Rodriguez-Diaz, 1990).

The symbolic role of IT may produce value that is difficult to measure, but is nonetheless real. IT's symbolic role may have an indirect effect on economic performance, especially in cases where an organization is able to sustain its legitimacy and survive within an institutional environment. Thus, we consider a symbolic analysis of investments in IT to complement more circumscribed economic analyses.

We begin by tracing the origins of impression management theory, articulating its basic constructs and propositions, and showing how it may be applied in organizational settings. We then apply the logic of impression management to explain the patterns of acquisition and deployment of IT in three distinct periods of time: (1) the glass-house era (circa 1960-1980), (2) the desktop era (1980-1990), and (3) the current era of the boundaryless organization. We conclude the paper by discussing the relationship between economic and symbolic explanations of IT investment. We argue that, by creating positive impressions, members of an organization may produce economic returns on its investments in IT that are not directly included in standard economic analyses.

IMPRESSION MANAGEMENT

Sociologist Erving Goffman (1959) is most often credited with the modern-day popularization of impression management. The theory is concerned with the behaviors that people direct toward others in order to create and maintain desired perceptions of themselves (Schneider, 1981). Impression management behavior was originally regarded as an experimental artifact, referred to as "evaluation apprehension" (Rosenberg, 1965), that threatened the validity of laboratory research. Through the work of scholars such as Schlenker (1980) and Tedeschi (1981), however, the theory has attained acceptance by the community of researchers in social psychology. Currently, impression management is a mainstream theory in the field of organizational behavior (Rosenfeld & Giacalone, 1991).

Despite the common belief that impression management involves insincere, deceptive, and manipulative behavior, impression management actions can be considered as sincere components of social behavior. According to Tetlock and Manstead (1985), "there is no compelling psychological reason why impression management must be either duplicitous or under conscious control. Impression management may be the product of highly overlearned habits or scripts, the original functions of which people have long forgotten" (p. 60). Research in impression management includes such organizational behaviors as employment and selection interviews (Fletcher, 1990; Gilmore & Ferris, 1989), ethical conduct (Konovsky & Jaster, 1989; Payne & Giacalone, 1990), arbitration (Giacolone & Pollard, 1989), and responses to computer-based organizational surveys (Lautenschlager & Flaherty, 1990).

Impression management is an extension of Goffman's (1959) dramaturgical metaphor to the organizational context. The theory regards the members of an organization as "actors" engaging in "performances" before "audiences" (other organizational members, customers, competitors, and stakeholders) in various "settings" (environments and markets). The actor and audience interact to develop a "definition of the situation" (Goffman, 1959), which provides the environmental cues to stimulate action (Gardner & Martinko, 1988). For Goffman, the environment provides a stage and set that includes decor, layout, scenery, and props for managing impressions. Organizations provide familiar stages and sets for the performances of individuals, who are attempting to create and sustain perceptions of competence, innovativeness, productivity, and so on.

Impression management behaviors are not necessarily limited to conscious actions (Tedeschi & Reiss, 1981). Schneider (1981) has found that an actor can exhibit impression management behavior that is either conscious or unconscious and either intentional or unintentional. As such, actors can be engaged in impression management behavior without conscious awareness of either their actions or of the specific impressions being conveyed. Impression management theory is not limited to studying specific motor or spoken behaviors, and has been applied to more complex combinations of behavior, such as the acquisition of material artifacts and their deployment and configuration within one's work space (Hatch, 1990).

As a form of self-presentation, acquiring and displaying material artifacts provide two types of image cues—aesthetic and professional. Aesthetic image cues signal the quality of the environment for employees, and professional image cues convey the nature of the organization's business. Both aesthetic and professional image cues produce consequences for organizations. For example, Klein and Ritti (1980) found that the aesthetic design of office facilities and the physical plant conveyed impressions that affected the recruitment of professional staff. Also, Becker (1982) studied the professional image cues conveyed by the office environment. Unlike creative and administrative offices, client-centered offices provided cues aimed primarily at confirming the organization's professional status and attending to the client's need for comfort, security, and confidence in the business relationship. Becker referred to the client-centered office as "99 percent image."

Like other material artifacts, IT potentially provides both aesthetic and professional image cues. Choices to acquire specific IT products and to locate and display them in specific areas within an organization all convey cues that generate impressions. Positive impressions may lead to consequences that have economic benefits, but are difficult to measure. For example, if IT's aesthetic and professional cues create the impression of an organization that is conducive to professional development and growth, it may be easier for an organization to attract and retain a qualified workforce and clientele. Of course, negative impressions may also be gained from the acquisition and display of IT, and these may reduce the economic benefit from IT. In these ways, the impressions conveyed symbolically by IT potentially affect its economic consequences.

In this chapter, we adopt an anecdotal, historical perspective to examine these issues. Specifically, we draw portraits of typical impression management behaviors involving IT in three distinct eras: the glass-house era that existed between 1960 and 1980, the desktop era that existed between 1980 and 1990, and the current era of the boundaryless organization. In each of these periods, IT conveys different impressions, both favorable and unfavorable. For each era, we describe the typical practice of configuring and displaying IT and speculate on the impressions conveyed.

HISTORICAL PATTERNS OF IT ADOPTION AND USE

1960-1980: From the Glass House to the Embattled Fortress

In the early years of corporate computing, the computer's primary role was to attain efficiencies in corporate accounting by reducing clerical costs. The computer was not yet considered critical for running the day-to-day business, and the information systems (IS) function was primarily a support service. However, between 1960 and 1980, IS departments in many organizations grew to become formidable entities within a heavily controlled and secure environment

(Tapscott & Caston, 1993). A common metaphor for the corporate data center was the glass house, in reference to the glass walls that typically surrounded mainframe computers of the day. Originally, walls were needed to separate the climate-controlled rooms that housed the computers from adjacent areas, many of which were not air conditioned. The use of transparent glass walls provided the additional symbolic benefit of displaying the computing resource. Even in fully climate-controlled buildings, glass houses persisted and the prominent display of computers enabled important cues to be sent to other members of the organization and to visitors.

Viewed from the perspective of impression management, the conspicuous deployment of IT during the glass-house era may have served to increase the power and status of IS professionals in the organization. The era's mainframe computers were rather similar in appearance—large blue or gray boxes with lighted panels and spinning tapes, raised on elevated floors that covered vast networks of wiring (Scholz, 1990). The glass house was often located centrally so that members and visitors saw it frequently during their travels through the building. The conspicuous display of IT conveyed the impressions of power, mystery, intelligence, and knowledge. These impressions also extended to the personnel who could be seen operating the computer behind the glass walls.

In many IS facilities, IT was treated as though it possessed biological properties that required specific environmental and atmospheric treatments. The image of bio-sterility was conveyed by the operators' practice of wearing white laboratory coats and, in some installations, headcoverings and footwear similar to those worn by surgeons. As an example, one data center, located at the headquarters of a midwestern U.S. pharmaceutical company, installed a two-door air-lock at the entrance to the main floor of the computer area. Although this practice was commonly used to isolate the climate-controlled data center from the "common area," the bio-sterility image was advanced to new extremes by the presence of a vibrating grid in the floor of the air lock. When a person stepped on the grid, it vibrated in order to shed particles of dust from the entrant's clothing. The device presumably protected the computer from the same airborne particles that threatened the company's pharmaceutical products. Although the resultant cleaner air could not have hurt the computer's operation, it is doubtful that a vibrating floor was necessary to achieve the degree of cleanliness required. An alternative explanation is that the design of the data center conveyed the impression that computers deserved equal or greater protection from environmental contaminants and equal stature in the organization to the pharmaceuticals that were being manufactured. Interestingly, the packaging area for the pharmaceuticals manufactured by this same firm was not subjected to similarly rigid environmental protections.

The central location of the typical data center in the glass-house era allowed for both visitors and workers to be regularly exposed to the presence of information processing in an organization. Users were typically denied direct access to the mainframe interacting by means of card-punch machines and terminals located adjacent to the glass house. This permitted the performance in the glass house to be viewed by the "audience" who had come to obtain services. By placing the stage in clear view, and by physically separating it from the audience's seats, the actors in the data center were able to control the performance and manage the impressions it gave. The images received by the audience had little to do with the actual functions of the technology.

Goffman (1959) suggested that different regions, bounded by perceptual barriers, reflect different impression management behaviors. The front stage is where the performance is given. The back stage area is generally hidden from the audience and is accessible only to the cast and a select few with back-stage passes. Back stage, the actors can step out of character and perform activities that might detract from the impressions given on the front stage. The back stage conceals the secrets of the illusions created during performance. In the typical data center of the glass-house era, much was hidden from view, despite the overt display of equipment and activity. Without a detailed knowledge of computer operations, most organizational members were unable to decipher the mysteries of the computer. As a result, IS personnel preserved their back-stage secrets and built their organizational power.

In time, the impressions of exclusivity and mystery became negative images for IS personnel. IS departments began to lose ground toward the end of the 1970s, and the glass house became the "embattled fortress" (Izzo, 1987). Instead of viewing IS departments as centers of knowledge and power, members of the organization began to see them as drains on corporate resources. The attitudes of IS personnel were often viewed as arrogant, and their bureaucratic approaches to the development of systems added to this image problem. IT became the target of criticism from an increasingly dissatisfied and widening user population who required a more immediate response to their computing resource needs than the burgeoning IS bureaucracy was able to provide. Simultaneously, the advent of microcomputers removed the rationale that initially had made the glass houses necessary. Together, client dissatisfaction and microcomputers ushered in the desktop era and a new set of impression management behaviors.

1980-1990: The Desktop Era

With the emergence of the microcomputer, the capabilities of organizational members to manage impressions took a dramatic turn. The material attributes of the IT gained a new importance and the functionality of the desktop computer allowed for impressions to be made through its use as well as its appearance.

The most obvious change in IT between the glass-house and desktop eras was the smaller size of computers, which earned them the "desktop" label. The personal, desktop computer rapidly became a symbol of status and power for the individual and symbolized users' independence from the IS department. Individual users of IT became the managers of impressions in the desktop era. Having the latest CPU, a high-resolution color monitor, a high-speed communications modem, and the most recent version of software became measures of status and presumed ability to perform one's job. Dunlop and Kling (1991) suggest that the ability of organizational members to obtain high-performance IT is a sign of power because of the costs involved. Felson (1981) notes that impressions formed regarding the status of an individual can serve to determine that person's ability to attain other rewards and additional power. An ability to manage impressions with IT, therefore, can widen the gap between individuals with power and those without it. With every desktop now a potential stage for impression management, those who regularly upgraded their personal computing resources demonstrated not only their knowledge but also their control over financial resources.

The impression of technical prowess was further enhanced by sophisticated users who assumed a central position in an informal hierarchy within departments. Expert users, or local computer gurus, gained status through their ability to decipher cryptic error messages, create shortcut procedures in commonly used software, avoid the copy-protection schemes employed during the period, install new boards and cables in others' machines, or make simple repairs to computers. Such experts formed the vanguard of user-developed applications, or end-user computing, and they were seen as adding value to their organizations by making users more productive. In addition, many of the office gurus were welcomed by the user community as an alternative to the seemingly lethargic service provided by the organization's data-processing department.

As IT advanced and as personnel at all levels mastered its use, desktop publishing emerged as a primary example of impression management. Many of the software products developed for microcomputers provided the user with a variety of formatting and presentation options. Spreadsheets evolved beyond their original conceptions of electronic worksheets to support elaborate layout and typesetting of text and data. Wordprocessing and desktop publishing packages allowed individual users to become self-contained media departments with the ability to create professional documents with little effort. Foster and Flynn (1984), for example, reported a typical case wherein secretaries became "publishers" of departmental documents when IT was introduced, in sharp contrast to their earlier work of typing single-page hard copy, analyzing routine data, and typing updates to manuals.

Desktop publishing gives the impression of a vastly more efficient and productive office workforce. Desktop technologies allow individuals to furnish their documents with superficial signs of professional work, but may not allow for a material alteration of the contents. Style may be more important than substance to the consumer of such reports.

As the 1980s drew to a close, the ubiquitous desktop technology diminished the ability of the individual to manage impressions with desktop IT. The appearance of portable, laptop, and notebook computers—each progressively smaller and more powerful—signaled the dawn of a new era of IT. No longer could a manager or professional depend on conveying a favorable impression by simply displaying the latest personal computer on his or her desk. The knowledge and skills of the typical office worker were growing such that simply displaying the IT without demonstrating an observable level of prowess with it began to become bad impression management. An even more positive impression could be conveyed if the person were away from the desk, accompanied by a small, integrated grouping of IT products. A transition from the managing of impressions through the display of desktop IT to the creation of a myriad of impressions via the functional nature of the IT had begun. The new portable technologies were to play a central role in managing impressions in the approaching era of the boundaryless organization.

The 1990s and the Boundaryless Organization

The boundaryless organization (Maccoby, 1991) is based on the principle that temporal and geographic boundaries are irrelevant to organizational form. In lieu of a centralized physical facility in which people interact face-to-face, boundaryless organizations place their personnel virtually anywhere, linking them both synchronously and asynchronously via telecommunications. Transactions among remote members can be mediated by "invisible" IT. Boundaryless organizations also use IT to support such relationships with their suppliers, customers, and business partners, making a wide variety of interorganizational designs feasible (Tapscott & Caston, 1993).

Although the physical attributes of IT played a prominent role in impression management during both the glass-house and desktop eras, they play almost no role in the era of the boundaryless organization. Although there may be some favorable impressions gained by possession of a mobile phone or notebook computer, these technologies are normally used in isolation from people whose impressions might matter. Users of IT in the boundaryless organization create impressions through their use of IT, rather than its conspicuous display. It is during the electronic mediation of interaction that impressions are formed.

Many organizations have employed IT to reduce the importance of geographical location to their many stakeholders. By reaching their audience through investments in IT, successful relationships can be formed quickly and with greater impact than ever previously imagined. The ability of the IT to replace the need for direct contact has become the focus of attention. As in the other eras, it is difficult to evaluate the precise economic benefits of using IT in this way.

The impression of immediacy and efficiency can now be conveyed to a customer or business associate literally anywhere in the world. An automated teller machine located either across town or across the ocean can create the impression of the existence of a global, boundaryless bank to its customers. A theatrical set designer in Europe can provide immediate response through fax and high-speed image transmission technologies to a Hollywood director's request for required changes in staging as a result of a last minute change in the story line. Such response creates the impression of flexibility and personal attention so vital to the fast-paced, competitive theatre and motion picture production environments of today. Likewise, geographically remote business executives can manage impressions using videoconferencing technology to simulate the face-to-face meetings. The physical attributes of IT are not on display in these examples. Rather, their functional capabilities are responsible for creating the positive impression of a remote, but connected executive.

The impressions created by the use of IT in boundaryless organizations may also be negative. Institutionalized business practices, such as face-to-face meetings and the generation of a paper trail of transactions, are difficult to replace, and many people are still uncomfortable with computer-mediated communication. Employees may miss the nonverbal cues, face-to-face encounters, and other social opportunities afforded by regular staff meetings. Likewise, the positive impressions of universal access to timely and accurate data may be offset by negative impressions of the "faceless organization," which commits "computer errors." Customers whose main contact with an organization comes from an 800 number may become completely bewildered over where the organization is, who owns it, and how it functions. In addition, many customers find it difficult to define precisely what relationship, if any, actually exists between themselves and the organization.

Boundaryless organizations may partially offset these negative impressions by linking new technologies with more familiar ones. For example, facsimile technology satisfies the need for physical confirmation of an electronic transaction. In organizations where the need for paper documents is pervasive, IT can also remove the need for rooms full of paper files by storing documents on compact laser discs. The laser technology solves the problem of storing paper while providing high-quality reproduction capabilities. In addition, favorable impressions may also be gained by providing access to electronic databases through the familiar touch-tone telephone. In these ways, the image of the boundaryless organization can be sustained by combinations of familiar and advanced information technologies.

CONCLUSION

March and Sproull (1990) suggest that some of the benefits of information technologies are derived simply from possessing, adopting, or claiming access to them. In this chapter, we have argued that information technology may add considerable value to organizations by virtue of its symbolic importance, that is, its role in producing and sustaining favorable impressions of organizations. We have not argued against the traditional economic analyses that are used to evaluate investment decisions. Rather, we suggest that the positive impressions of competence and efficiency that are conveyed by information technology should be included in such evaluations. Considering such intangible benefits may help to remove the paradox of demonstrating IT's productivity by identifying benefits that are not typically captured in traditional economic analyses. The value generated by such favorable impressions may increase the total return on investments in IT.

We have supported this argument by showing how the acquisition and display of IT conforms to the expectations derived from the theory of impression management. In addition, we have shown how impression management behaviors have changed as applications of computer technology have evolved since the 1960s. Although we have not prescribed particular methods for valuing the impressions created through information technology, it should, nevertheless, be possible in principle to assign economic value to intangibles.

Academic research can take an active role in the investigation of methods to quantify the presently intangible nature of positive impressions created through IT. Winter (1993) has already shown possession of IT to be a surrogate for compensation at certain levels of the organization. Research using pictorial manipulation could provide further insight into the value perceived to be associated with the presence or absence of information technology in a situation or relationship. Admittedly, it is presently difficult to weigh the relative contribution of a document's style and substance or to place economic value on the enhanced quality of life as a result of information technology. Nevertheless, it is reasonable to assume that such contributions can be measured in quantifiable terms and that the true value of the impressions can be factored into the economic justification of the IT. If researchers can increase the level of consciousness held by managers regarding the impressions of modernity and competitiveness (Danziger, Dutton, Kling, & Kraemer, 1982), as well as the signals of competence and rationality (Feldman & March, 1981; March, 1987) that are potentially conveyed through IT, the practitioner community may move a step closer toward resolving the productivity paradox and gaining a broader appreciation for the benefits of information technology.

Wexler (1986) has suggested that success in a service economy is determined by the ability to perform with one eye on the task at hand and the other on the audience. Information technology certainly enables task performance, and investments in IT have historically been justified on the grounds of efficiency. Perhaps it is time to consider the impressions that IT makes upon the audience more carefully. In the current era of the boundaryless organization, customers increasingly depend on IT to acquire products and services. But IT also produces impressions of competence, knowledge, security, intelligence, soundness, responsibility, and so on. The evaluation of investments in IT should consider these impressions along with more traditional economic criteria. We believe that economic returns may be substantially affected by the impressions conveyed by information technology. By becoming more conscious of their own impression management behavior, managers may realize greater benefits from their investments.

NOTE

An earlier version of this chapter was presented at the 1994 conference of ACM's Special Interest Group on Computer Personnel Research. The authors wish to acknowledge the useful comments of Elizabeth Roberts, Paul Hart, and James Musarra.

5

USING IMPRESSION MANAGEMENT TO ESTABLISH SUCCESSFUL SERVICE-LEVEL AGREEMENTS

Jane M. Carey
Afsaneh Nahavandi

The introduction of impression management and self-presentation into organizational research is a relatively new phenomenon. However, in spite of the recency of the application of the concepts, impression management has proved to be a highly powerful and useful tool to explain and predict a variety of events from gender and cultural differences (e.g., Bond, 1991; Larwood, 1991) to performance management (Eden, 1988, 1990). When defined as the "process by which individuals attempt to control the impression others form of them" (Leary & Kowalski, 1990, p. 34), impression management has application not only to interpersonal relations and interaction but also to interaction among teams and departments within organizations. This chapter discusses the use of impression management in the negotiation and implementation of successful service-level agreements between information systems departments and their "clients" within an organization. Service-level agreements are defined and their use in a quality-focused environment is emphasized.

INFORMATION SYSTEMS DEPARTMENTS AND NEGATIVE IMAGE

Information systems (IS) departments in a majority of organizations have relatively negative impressions (Singleton, McLean, & Altman, 1988). There are many reasons for this condition, including historical power struggles between users and IS departments, historical power abuse of IS departments when their expertise was unavailable from other sources, perceived lack of responsiveness, lack of attention to usability issues, lack of adequate outward positive communication, lack of understanding of service role that IS should play, and inability of IS departments to manage client expectations.

In the early days of IS (known as electronic data processing at that time), computers and their support were new to organizations and the world in general. There was little understanding of how computers worked and what they could do for organizations. Managers and other end-users of computer information had little contact with the programmers and technicians who controlled computers. Their main points of contact with computers were printouts, which provided them with summary data that may or may not have been useful in performing their jobs. When new systems were developed, no one thought to ask the end-users what they needed. Instead, programmers set about automating existing manual systems.

As time went on and the basic accounting systems were functional, end-users began to make requests from IS for computerized functions and reports. The balance of power was on the side of IS and, since they had a backlog of requests, they often told end users that their requests could not be filled quickly or at all. There was no systematic method for determining which requests were critical and which were not. Intentional and unintentional abuse of this power occurred and end-users began to be frustrated because their informational needs were not being met.

Also, the systems that were being developed were not very user-friendly or even usable. One reason for this was that they were primarily mainframe applications and the user interfaces were limited. When end-users finally got the systems they requested after waiting too long, the target system was probably unfriendly and did not meet informational needs. Information requirements change so rapidly that between the time of design and implementation of a system, new requirements are likely to surface and not be met.

In addition, the skills that lead to good analysis and programming are not likely to coexist with good communication skills. The use of technical jargon and acronyms do not help end-users understand or sympathize with the work of the programmer/analyst. As a whole, groups of technicians (who are often led by managers who were former technicians), do not understand how to communicate. They do not appreciate the notion that success is dependent, in part, on the ability of the group to communicate in order to convey what they do and the value of that work to the organization.

It is only recently that IS departments have begun to understand the role they play as service units and consultants. Information systems are not an end in themselves, they are only as valuable as their ability to provide useful information and functionality to the end-users. They must be aligned with the mission and goals of the organization. The learning of this lesson was rather painful. As microcomputers became pervasive, entrepreneurial vendors offered competitive products with attractive price tags, and end-users became more sophisticated, IS began to lose its client base. The loss of an internal client base means loss of power and potential loss of existence. Now most modern IS departments have come to realize that they are service providers not dictators of the IS resource, but they have been slow to embrace the management tools and philosophy that most service providers have adopted to make themselves viable.

In making the transition from IS resource guardian to IS service provider, a common mistake is lack of management of customer expectations. For example, as a resource guardian, customers expect IS departments to offer little or no support of their needs. Yet, as IS departments announce and sell themselves as service providers, clients or customers suddenly increase their expectations of service beyond the performance capability of IS departments. There is a compelling need to set and meet realistic client expectations in order to improve user satisfaction and impression management.

It is very important to understand that the IS department of any organization serves as an internal consultant to a number of "client" departments, groups, and individuals within an organization. It is therefore essential for these consultants to maintain a relationship with their clients that would allow for effective, efficient, and fair exchanges where the needs of all involved parties are satisfied and the basis for continuous long-term exchanges is established. As previously mentioned, the role and power of IS departments has undergone a great deal of change. A few years ago an IS department could dictate its terms to largely uninformed individuals within their organization; however, it now has to approach the people its serves as customers and clients. This change puts an IS department in a very different negotiating position. In the past, the IS department satisfied many strategic contingencies such as dependency, substitutability, and coping with uncertainty (Salancik & Pfeffer, 1977). Satisfying these contingencies provided the IS department with power. Today, more and more, other departments can find IS expertise elsewhere. Therefore, the power balance between the IS department and its clients is become more equal. Although IS departments have the expertise that others need, such an expertise can be obtained elsewhere (e.g., by calling manufacturers and suppliers directly). The power that comes from expertise is therefore balanced by loss of power due to the reduction in dependability (Emerson, 1962) and substitutability (Hickson, Hinnings, Schneck, & Pennings, 1971).

SERVICE-LEVEL AGREEMENTS

One technique for combating the aforementioned problems and improving the organizational impression of IS is to establish service-level agreements (SLA). SLAs are negotiated contracts between IS departments and clients that spell out specific details of service and the conditions under which service will be provided. SLAs provide a means of measurement of service and service satisfaction, which in turn allow IS departments to assess service performance and to improve that performance over time.

The typical SLA includes the following components (Frenzel, 1992):

1. effective date of agreement;
2. duration of agreement;
3. specific type of service;
4. measures of service:
   - availability,
   - amount,
   - performance, and
   - reliability;
5. resources needed or costs charged;
6. reporting mechanism; and
7. signatures.

IS should take the initiative in setting up SLAs. However, the process is iterative and negotiated. In the first trials, service levels may be set too low or high; both of which can create problems. Since the goal is to set realistic expectations and increase the positive impression of IS in the organization, it is better to err on the low side. Over time, the levels can be adjusted to realistic amounts.

What types of service can be articulated in an SLA? The answer is dependent on the nature of the organization and will vary from firm to firm. Most common services have to do with problem, change, recovery, capacity, and performance management.

Problem Management

Problem management is responding to individual and system-wide obstacles. In the problem management-oriented SLA, the method for reporting problems, an acceptable response time for initial contact, a maximum time frame for problem correction, and other details are all negotiated. In large organizations, it may be advisable to set up a severity classification scheme (user negotiated) in order to attend to the most severe problems first. In the past, the squeaky wheels and big wheels got quicker responses regardless of the nature and severity of their problems. This can lead to overall loss of productivity if severe problems are allowed to languish while support staff are running around fixing the minor problems of noisier clients. It also encourages an impression of inequity and lack of fairness, which can be highly damaging to long-term client/service relationships. The summary reports that are generated as part of the SLA process, give the user a clear understanding of the workload of the IS department and work to enhance the positive image of the IS department.

Change Management

Change management is primarily concerned with responding to requests for enhancements to existing systems or development of new applications. It is very important that users have a mechanism for requesting changes. A steering committee should meet on a routine basis to assess the change requests and determine the order in which they will be implemented. A side benefit of the SLA technique is that it provides a basis for personnel staffing requirements. The steering committee should be composed of end-users, management, and IS support staff. The formation of this committee allows face-to-face communication, which has the potential of alleviating communication gaps.

Recovery Management

Recovery-based SLAs focus on recovery from service interruptions, regardless of cause. If an information system goes down, end-users must have a clear understanding of the procedures and time frame for recovery. Timely communication of the nature of the interruption and the time frame for correction allow the end-users to plan their time accordingly rather than waste time and become frustrated.

Capacity Management

Capacity-based SLAs, are important in organizations where mainframe computer resources are limited. In today's organizations, there is a trend toward downsizing or migrating applications off the mainframes onto distributed networks with a client-server architecture. This trend has lessened the contention for mainframe capacity. Consequently, capacity-based SLAs are not very common.

Performance Management

The last type of SLA is performance based, which defines acceptable performance levels and lays out mediation processes for lack of conformance. Performance can be as simple as response time (in seconds or subseconds) or as complex as operational scheduling. Most dimensions of performance are quantifiable. That makes performance easy to measure and to report. Ease of measurement does not mean ease of improvement. Improving performance in a significant manner usually means high dollar investment.

SLAs have high potential for improving IS impression management. They can also serve as an internal mechanism for personnel performance appraisal and compensation adjustments. High credibility and an increased understanding of the IS workload is another important benefit of SLAs; however, the most important benefit is to set and meet realistic client expectations. Realistic expectations are the key to satisfied IS clients.

NEGOTIATING THE SLA

As mentioned, the change in power of the IS department creates a new environment and bargaining position for IS in relation to other departments. In the past, as the party with most of the power, an IS department could take a "tough" negotiating position (Wall, 1991). The negotiating strategy it used could have been unilateral (Savage, Blair, & Sorenson, 1988) whereby negotiating could simply be avoided. With more equal power among the IS and other departments, an impression needs to be created whereby the negotiation "assists one's interaction with an opponent" (Wall, 1991, p. 134). A more appropriate negotiating position is one that would focus on soft impressions that are nonalienating. A softer, nonalienating style is particularly appropriate with opponents who have equal power in situations where the outcome of the negotiation is visible to other constituents (Wall, 1991). Therefore, the approach that an IS department needs to take is one that would cultivate an image of cooperation, openness, honesty, and competence.

KEYS TO A POSITIVE IS DEPARTMENT IMAGE

Competence

As consultants to other departments and groups within an organization one of the most important impressions that an IS department needs to cultivate and maintain is competence. The need for such an impression is particularly important in light of the recent changes in the power and substitutability of IS departments. Even if the clients do not have many alternatives, they have to trust that the IS department is capable of solving their problems (Eden, 1991). An image of competence is first and foremost built on actual past and continued performance. However, the clients need to be made aware of such performance and evidence of it has to be provided and advertised. By having knowledge and proof of past performance, the clients come to believe in their consultant's competence. The image of competence is also cultivated through the projection of self-confidence. The consultant has to have a high expectations of his/her own capability. Such beliefs have been suggested to serve as self-fulfilling and therefore lead to high actual performance (Eden, 1991). The projection of an image of self-confidence needs to be tempered by realistic expectations and clear messages about potential limitations. Much the same way as realistic job previews provide employees with an accurate and reasonable expectation of their jobs, the IS department needs to provide a realistic image of its capabilities. The presentation and clarification of limitations increases the image of competence.

Aside from being its own impression of competence, the IS department plays a key role creating a positive image of the client (Eden, 1991). The consultant has to believe that the client is reasonably competent and interested in solving its problems. If the client is perceived by the IS department as helpless, a negative prophecy is likely to be created. The consultant either consciously or unconsciously and through direct statements or nonverbal leakage (Babad, Bernieri, & Rosenthal, 1989) conveys the message that the client will not be effective. As in other self-fulfilling situations, the message is quickly picked up by the client who then becomes helpless and incompetent, therefore leading to failure for both parties.

Consequences of Competence

Developing and preserving the image of competence allows an IS department to fulfill its role in helping other departments perform. Without such an image, other departments are hesitant to seek IS help, less likely to implement IS recommendations fully and precisely, and more prone to seek outside assistance. In the first two situations, organizational performance may be affected as problems do not get addressed and delays and errors affect the quality and efficiency of the work. In the latter situation, the cost of seeking outside assistance may be higher than using internal sources and may also lead to lack of coordination and uneven implementation and application as the outside consultants' recommendations may differ from established procedures followed by others within the organization.

An image of competence is not only likely to lead to more "business" for an IS department, it is also likely to energize those who are using its services. Eden's (1990, 1991) work on the role of consultants in inspiring and energizing their clients suggests that by maintaining and confidence and competence, a consultant has the opportunity to serve as a quasi-charismatic leader for its client. Such a "messiah" (Eden, 1990) motivates clients to believe in themselves and perform beyond their own expectations. The key to such inspiration is, first and foremost, the consultant's proven past competence and performance and high expectations for future performance.

Fairness

Fairness is the basis for any satisfactory social exchange and interaction (Cohen, 1986). It is also key to the success of service-level agreements. In order for both the client and the consultant to be satisfied with their interaction and for them to feel positive about future exchanges, they both have to evaluate their interaction as balanced and equitable. Impression management is key to the process since fairness is more often than not in the eyes of the beholder

(Greenberg, 1990). The arduous task for the IS department becomes not only to be fair and equitable in its exchanges with its clients, but also to maintain the impression and image of fairness. Several issues need to be considered in cultivating such an image of fairness (Greenberg, Bies, & Eskew, 1991).

First, in negotiating and implementing a SLA, the IS department has to give its internal clients' point of view and ideas adequate consideration. Although the consultant is the expert, the needs and preferences of the client have to be respected and included in the recommendations and solutions. Without sufficient input from the client, the consultant is likely to be perceived as unfair and unreasonable. Second, the SLA has to be neutral and consistent across the various internal clients. Preferential treatment, real or perceived, for one group in the form of quicker response, broader and higher quality services, and the like will quickly erode the image of professionalism and impartiality necessary for long-term interaction (Sheppard & Lewicki, 1987) One of the easiest ways to maintain consistency and neutrality is reliance on well-established and agreed-upon procedures. However, the image of consistency and neutrality has be carefully balanced with one of flexibility (Greenberg et al., 1991). Being overly rule bound and following procedures too closely without allowing room for exceptions can easily give an impression of unfairness and unresponsiveness (Tyler & Bies, 1990).

Dignity

Another key to building an image of fairness is treating the clients with respect and dignity (Greenberg et al., 1991). This involves timely feedback in the form of response time answer to queries and questions as well as adequate explanation for actions and decisions. A timely response has been found to be the basis for fairness evaluation in many settings. Receiving a timely response not only promotes a sense of respect and fairness, but also allows the client to continue his or her work or plan for delays adequately, factors which are key to quality performance. In addition, even though the clients have to rely on the expertise of the IS consultant and may not have knowledge to challenge their decision, it is key that they understand why the consultant has selected a certain procedure and the ramification of such a decision for their own operation. Having an explanation for the decisions enhances the sense of fairness in the exchange (Bies & Shapiro, 1988). Overall, a timely response and an adequate explanation for the actions that are taken provide the client with an image of respect and dignity, which in turn are key to a sense of fair and equitable treatment.

Consequences of Fairness

In addition to what may be the obvious benefits of an image of fairness, having such an image also provides an individual or a group with other benefits. Greenberg et al., (1991) pointed out that an image of fairness is likely to create a positive halo affect, which would enhance the holder's power and acceptance within an organization. Being perceived as fair by others also may provide a group with increased idiosyncracy credit (Hollander, 1958), which can then be used to create change or simply provide room for mistakes. For example, an IS department with a reputation for fair treatment of its clients may also be assumed to be highly competent and efficient. Furthermore, that same department may not be judged very harshly if it fails to respond in a timely fashion once in a while. The positive halo created by the image fairness will protect to some extent from the negative evaluation. In addition to creating a positive halo, research has found a reputation of fairness to be highly beneficial to organizations in terms of recruiting (Schwoerer & Rosen, 1989) and even profitability (Greenberg et al., 1991). Such results can be applied to the image of a department within an organization suggesting that the image of fairness is likely to lead to more resources and higher effectiveness.

With the potential benefits of a fair image come a special responsibility and burden of maintaining it (Greenberg, 1990). Maintaining such an image may limit a person or a department's options for actions. Even minor deviations from this image may be evaluated very negatively. For example, the IS department may have a very legitimate reason to disregard an inappropriate request from one of its client departments. However, refusing the request may affect its image and its future interaction with others so negatively, that it may have difficulty doing so. Without the image of fairness, treating a client in what may appear to be an arbitrary fashion is much easier, since it may simply be perceived as "business as usual." Overall, though, aside from the burden of continuously cultivating the image of fairness, having such an image is more positive than negative and is key to the success of negotiating and implementing exchanges with the various internal clients. Without such an image, interaction are bound to be wrought with suspicion and attempts at one-upmanship which affect the quality of the outcome for all involved.

SLA TACTICS

In cultivating and controlling its image and the impressions others have of it, an IS department has a number of direct and indirect tactics it can use. The direct tactics generally involve presenting oneself in a better light by highlighting roles, actions, and accomplishments. The indirect techniques tend to rely on associations with positive or negative others, rather than on any action taken by the group or individual.

Direct Tactics

Impression management is all about self-presentation and the roles that we play in our personal and professional life (Schlenker, 1980). Therefore, one of the primary techniques of direct impression management is the definition of roles a person or department wants to play. The past role often taken on by IS departments is considerably different that its current role in most organizations. By clearly defining and stating its service and support-oriented role to its internal customers, an IS department can set the stage for its interaction with them. The selection and public announcement of that role becomes the first step in managing impressions. In addition, such action is both legitimate and ethical as it helps the IS department find its place in the overall mission of the organization.

Another direct tactic of impression management, ingratiation, is generally considered to be more on the unethical side, as it often implies deceit and trying to play up to an audience by providing them what they want (Schlenker, 1980). Ingratiation is designed to "influence a particular other person concerning the attractiveness of ones's personal qualities" (Jones & Wortman, 1973, p. 2). The behaviors can range from flattery, opinion conformity, and doing favors to attractive self-presentations (Jones & Wortman, 1973). The last type, self-presentation is one of the most legitimate and accessible types of impression management. It is essential for an IS department that is trying to establish long-term positive working relationship with other units through the negotiation of SLAs to present itself in a positive way. This self-presentation need not be deceiving; it can be accurate by still emphasizing the positive aspects. In other words, the IS department needs to put on a public relations campaign by, among other things, proving old stereotypes wrong, by admitting its errors and weaknesses, and by being responsive and advertising its speed. As long as the IS department is striving to match this self-presentation with actual actions, the ingratiation can be positive. Such self-presentation can even work as self-fulfilling prophecy and encourage actions that are consistent with it.

Among the direct impression management techniques, is the careful management of verbal and nonverbal communication. The verbal communication has been discussed in the self-presentation section above; the nonverbal communication can also be a powerful tool in managing impressions. Members of an IS department have projected a look of competence (Mehrabian, 1971), energy (Korda, 1977), and cooperativeness. The use of office design and the setup of the work space can also be used to support the image that an IS department is cultivating. Although the research about the use of office design in impression management is relatively new (for a review see Ornstein, 1989), the existing results indicate that the manipulation of space often sends a powerful message. In the case of an IS department seeking to project an image that is customer- and service-oriented, the key to the use of space may be the almost total giving up of space. In this instance, a service-oriented IS department would always visit others in their space rather than invite them into its own.

The use of the various direct impression management tactics can be highly effective and legitimate if the goal is accurately represent a person or group. The line to unethical behaviors is crossed the moment the self-presentation becomes inconsistent with actual facts and behaviors. With this in mind, the use of impression management tactics can help an IS department achieve its goals and help the mission of its organization.

Indirect Tactics

In addition to the direct impression management techniques described above, an IS department can rely on a number of indirect tactics to maintain its positive image. These indirect tactics have been defined as "techniques undertaken to enhance or project one's image by managing information about the people and things with which one is simply associated" (Cialdini, 1989, p. 46). Direct impression management techniques build on performance and action; whereas, indirect techniques are characterized by the fact that the person or group using them are not responsible for success.

One of the techniques of indirect impression management that can be used in the negotiation and implementation of SLAs is "boasting." During boasting, one attempts to link oneself with a successful other (Cialdini, 1989; Richardson & Cialdini, 1987). Boasting allows an IS department to be perceived as competent, responsive, and generally a positive element by either having a good working relationship with a well-respected person or department or having endorsements from such individual or group. On the positive side, boasting can be the use of idea champions in order to encourage acceptance of new idea (Galbraith, 1982). For example, an IS department that is trying to get the idea of a system upgrade accepted by several departments and is facing resistance may seek association and endorsement from a respected manager. The association enhances the positive image of the IS department and allows it implement the change more easily. On the negative side, boasting, like other indirect techniques of impression management is somewhat unproductive and likely to cross the line to unethical impression management since the positive impression is not based on any action or accomplishment of the user.

Two other indirect techniques of impression management, "burying" and "blaring" (Cialdini, 1989) distance and disassociate the person or group from unfavorable others. For instance, an IS department can try to dissociate itself from an unsuccessful project it had originally proposed or from one of its group members when he or she either makes a mistake or develops a negative image for a variety of reasons. Although both of these disassociation techniques may have the immediate outcome of boosting the positive image of a department or person, in the long run, they may discourage risk-taking and innovation and hamper the possibility of reaping the benefits of learning from one's mistakes.

Several other indirect techniques focus the "observers' perception of others to whom one is clearly connected" (Cialdini, 1989, p. 52). These other-focused techniques, whether enhancing or belittling others, tend to have many potential negative consequences for the organization. The result of such approaches is to shift attention away from the "actors." For example, a department may attempt to place all the blame for its own failure on the incompetence and lack of motivation of those it services. As result, although the department's positive image is not tarnished, it may fail to address genuine internal problems that are likely to continue affecting performance.

SLAs AND IMPRESSION MANAGEMENT THEORY

Accountability and SLAs

Schlenker and Weigold (1989) posit that accountability makes social control possible. Without accountability, no one would be interested in the impression that is being made on the rest of the organization and therefore impression management would not exist. Accountability is also linked to performance. Quality performance occurs because of accountability, which is then linked with reward, avoidance of punishment, or adherence to norms.

SLAs are a form of articulation of IS accountability. The SLA articulates the responsibilities for which IS is accountable and the mechanism for measurement of performance achievement. SLAs are a proactive mechanism. Rather than let management or clients dictate accountability and performance, IS takes the initiative and negotiates an agreement that is acceptable to both sides and is in the best interest of the organization as a whole.

According to Schlenker and Weigold (1989), the link between accountability and performance results in the following desirable outcomes: makes salient organizational goals, standards, and rules (in SLAs, service levels are set within organizational standards); makes expectations salient (SLAs allow expectations to be clearly articulated, negotiated, and settled on); increases intensity of information gathering to accomplish task that unit is accountable for (measurement and reporting is a part of SLAs); makes salient the notion of projecting a positive identity or image (SLAs are a direct mechanism for enhancing impressions); and causes people to determine defensibility of actions (important when SLAs are up for renegotiation).

SLAs and Management Style

Good managers are self-monitoring and therefore engage in active impression management (Riordan, 1989). They understand that there are desirable self-images and undesirable self-images and that projecting a desirable self-image is critical to success. The desirable images for IS departments and any other unit in an organization include among others: cooperative, possessing open channels of communication, and possessing real concern and empathy for others.

SLAs project and support all three of these dimensions, but particularly the first and second. When SLAs are initiated by IS departments, users perceive the IS department to be cooperative and open. Whether or not they are seen as possessing real concern and empathy for others is more a function of the front-line employees who deliver the service than a function of the mere existence of a SLA. Therefore, once SLAs are negotiated, it is important that the service providers themselves exhibit real concern and empathy for the problems of the clients while teaching them to be self-sufficient.

SLAs and Goal Setting

Huber, Latham, and Locke (1989) propose the management of impressions through goal setting. They articulate the process from both the supervisor and subordinate orientation. The supervisor follows these steps to project a positive image:

1. sets specific goals,
2. serves as a role model,
3. provides appropriate participation in goal setting,
4. dispenses initial task information,
5. increases self-efficacy,
6. sets proximal goals (subgoals),
7. provides feedback, and
8. provides rewards.

SLAs follow these steps very closely with moderate departures:

1. SLAs are used to set service levels or goals.
2. SLAs are set using a participative and iterative process.
3. SLAs use initial data or task information set service levels.
4. SLAs should increase self-efficacy for both the end-user's and the service provider.
5. SLAs are used to set proximal goals (subgoals).
6. Reporting mechanisms in SLAs are used to provide feedback.
7. SLAs should be used to provide rewards. The performance appraisal and reward system for service providers should be closely tied to the SLA process.

Establishing these links between SLAs and impression management theory strengthens the argument for use of SLAs by IS departments. It is clear that SLAs have positive benefits that result in impression and expectation management.

CONCLUSION

The changes in the role of IS departments in most organizations is forcing them to adopt a mission that revolves around service and customer orientation. Such a mission involves a change in the identity and role that IS employees play. They have to not only view themselves as support personnel to other departments, but they also have to actively cultivate and maintain such an image. It is in this area that the research and practice of impression management can be used to help guide their actions. Particularly, SLAs are one of the processes through which a positive working relationship and therefore a positive image can be established. By specifying the nature, process, and timeline for service, SLAs set up accurate expectations that contribute to the positive image of the IS department. In negotiating the SLAs, an IS department needs to particularly focus on its image of competence and fairness as these two elements are key to a successful and long-term relationship with internal clients. Through the use of SLAs and action impression management, IS departments become accountable and responsive to their clients.

Much of the research used in this chapter has not been tested or applied in the information technology setting. The opportunities for future research are therefore very rich. It is also interesting to note that the service management literature (e.g., Bowen, Chase, & Cummings, 1990), barring a few examples (e.g., El Sawy & Walls, 1986), has not been fully integrated with the role of IS departments and their relationships with their internal clients. Such integration also provides considerable avenues for future research.

6

MANAGING ONE'S BUSINESS PARTNERS: THE SELLING OF EDI

Lyne Bouchard
M. Lynne Markus

The technological innovation known as electronic data interchange (EDI) is argued to provide major benefits to the organizations that use it for exchanging business data across organizational boundaries. Suppliers and retailers can use EDI to transmit purchase orders, advance shipping notices, invoices, and even payments, thus reducing costs, streamlining operations, and increasing the timeliness of business activity. The benefits of EDI are not shared equally among business partners, however, since the larger partners stand to gain more through a larger volume of transactions. Consequently, these firms find themselves working hard to convince their smaller business partners to adopt EDI. What persuasive strategies do they use and to what extent do these strategies work?

In this chapter, we address these and other questions derived from three theoretical perspectives on the adoption and diffusion of collective technological innovations: the innovation diffusion perspective, the critical mass perspective, and the impression management and bargaining literatures. We apply these perspectives to the case of EDI adoption in the retailing industry, with particular attention to the efforts of one large retailer and two of its suppliers. We find that the critical mass and impression management literatures explain nonadoption better than the innovation diffusion perspective, but that the impression management and bargaining literatures add considerably to our understanding of why and how some suppliers actually adopt.

INTRODUCTION

Imagine a situation in which you can get tremendous benefits from a technological innovation, but only if your business partners adopt the innovation, too. Clearly, you will try to persuade your partners to adopt it. Unfortunately, the benefits your partners will receive from adopting the innovation are not nearly so great as yours—they may not even offset the costs of the sizable up-front investment. And your business partners know both what you stand to gain and what this will cost them. How will you attempt to persuade them? And how will they react?

This is the situation facing large retailers with respect to electronic data interchange (EDI). EDI involves replacing paper and telephonic business communications (purchase orders, invoices, payments, etc.) between customers and suppliers with computer-to-computer transmissions using telecommunications standards. When transaction volumes are large, EDI can substantially cut the costs of paper handling, while increasing transaction speed, streamlining internal operations, and improving responsiveness to changing market conditions. The benefits to be had from adopting EDI have been claimed to reach millions of dollars per year (Belitsos, 1988; *EDP Analyzer*, 1989; Keefe, 1980).

Unfortunately, retailers can only achieve the benefits of EDI if their suppliers also adopt it, which requires that the suppliers must also make sizable up-front investments in computer hardware, software, telecommunications, and changed business practices. Indeed, in order for retailers to achieve these benefits, suppliers need not only to send and receive EDI transactions, they must also integrate EDI into their internal business processes and information systems, an activity that requires considerable effort and expense. If the rewards to the suppliers were comparable to the benefits achieved by retailers, these required investments would probably pose few barriers to the adoption of EDI. But the benefits of EDI depend on the volume and proportion of transactions that can be exchanged through EDI. Thus, large retailers stand to gain much more than their smaller suppliers. And both parties tend to benefit most when they can use EDI for the majority of their business transactions. This means that large retailers want all their suppliers to use EDI, but that their smaller suppliers may not want to adopt EDI at all and certainly not with a retailer that accounts for only a small fraction of their total sales.

These conditions provide a fruitful field in which to observe impression management and bargaining at work. The retailer needs the supplier to provide the products that consumers want to buy; suppliers need the shelf space in the retailer's stores to sell their products. Although retailers and suppliers need to cooperate, they are not willing to do so at any price; to do so would jeopardize the partners' chances of maintaining a profitable business. Thus, retailers and their suppliers face a range of choices and strategies with respect to EDI. Retailers can try to force suppliers' adoption with the threat of severing the relationships or they can try a more considerate approach of being helpful and sharing the costs. Suppliers can give in, refuse outright, or bargain for time and as much help as possible. Furthermore, the strategies of one partner have consequences for the subsequent choices open to the other, as in the case of a couple engaged in a ballroom dance.

In this chapter, we examine the impression management tactics of retailers and suppliers around the adoption of EDI. After a brief introduction to EDI, we look at three theoretical lenses for understanding the adoption of EDI: the diffusion of innovation literature, critical mass theory, and the literatures on impression management and bargaining. Through historical reconstruction, we focus on efforts to diffuse EDI throughout the retail industry at the end of the 1980s. Then we present data from a case study of one large retailer, Sears, Roebuck and Co., and two of its suppliers. Although no single theoretical background explains all of the phenomenon under study, researchers interested in the diffusion of innovations and interorganizational behavior stand to gain tremendously from taking into account and further developing the impression management literature. To this end, we propose several propositions for future research based on this study.

BACKGROUND

Electronic data interchange involves the transfer of business documents between business partners, using computers and standard transaction formats. Examples of documents exchanged through EDI are purchase orders, advance shipping notices, invoices, and payments. The elimination of paper documents and verbal orders has the immediate benefit of reducing the costs and increasing the speed of business communication. But, because EDI documents are handled by computers, EDI can also be used to streamline internal operations by eliminating unnecessary activities and to improve responsiveness to changing market demands. Because these benefits of adopting EDI have been claimed to reach millions of dollars per year (Belitsos, 1988; *EDP Analyzer*, 1989; Keefe, 1980), Sokol (1989) predicted that, by 1992, 70 percent of all U.S. companies would be making significant use of EDI.

EDI benefits increase with the volume of transactions, due to economies of scale (Benjamin et al., 1990; *EDP Analyzer*, 1987; Sokol, 1989). Benefits are greatest when all transactions, at least of a certain type (e.g., purchase orders), are transmitted through EDI. When some transactions are processed through EDI and others are handled manually, EDI benefits are reduced by the costs of maintaining additional, less efficient processing systems. As a result of these factors, three conditions obtain. First, large retailers stand to gain more from EDI than small retailers because of the larger volumes of transactions they process. Second, larger retailers stand to gain most from EDI when all their suppliers, regardless of size, also use EDI. Unfortunately, third, small suppliers may not be willing to participate in EDI given their much lower benefits.

Consequently, large North American retailers have tried several persuasive strategies to induce their business partners to adopt EDI, with very mixed results. In July 1987, "EDI, spread the word!" reported 1,465 EDI users from all business sectors; this number rose to 12,200 by September 1990, and to 31,000 by October 1992 (EDI, spread the word, 1992-1993). Within five years, the global rate of EDI adoption had increased by 2100 percent. But this apparent success pales in comparison to the number of business that could use EDI, estimated at over 5 million in the U.S. alone. At the beginning of the 1990s, Thomas Colberg, a partner in Price Waterhouse's EDI Consulting Group, voiced the feeling of many experts: "EDI should be growing faster than it is. Frankly, it's embarrassing to be an expert on EDI and to forecast explosive growth year after year after year" (Anthes, 1990). In the sections that follow, we discuss three theoretical perspectives—innovation diffusion, critical mass, and impression management and bargaining literatures—that might help shed light on the slow diffusion of EDI between retailers and their suppliers.

Innovation Diffusion Literature

The first research perspective is summarized in Rogers' classic work, *Diffusion of Innovations* (1983). There, Rogers writes: "An obvious principle of human communication is that the transfer of ideas occurs most frequently between two individuals who are alike, similar, or homophilous" (p. 18). Homophily is defined as the degree to which pairs of individuals are similar with respect to certain attributes, such as beliefs, values, education, social status, and the like (Rogers and Bhowmik, 1970-1971). Although the innovation diffusion perspective was developed primarily to explain adoption by individuals, it has also been applied at the organizational level, notably by Becker (1970), Burt (1982), Galeskiewickz and Burt (1991), and Walker (1971). In this stream of research, "similar" organizations are those that occupy the same economic network position and are comparable in terms of organizational-level characteristics, such as size, technical competence, organizational values, and geographic markets (Burt, 1982; Rogers, 1983). So, for example, the jeans manufacturers Levi Strauss and Lee would be considered peers, but they would be viewed as dissimilar to companies that manufacture upscale children's clothing for local markets, and they would also be viewed as dissimilar to the retailers that carry their products.

Homophilous communicators share common beliefs, meanings, and subcultural language, and are similar in personal and social characteristics (Berger & Calabrese, 1975; Rogers & Bhowmik, 1970-1971). Therefore, people and organizations are likely to perceive the credibility of a communicator to be greater when the communicator is more similar; ultimately, communication from similar people and organizations is likely to be more effective and influential (Rogers, 1983; Rogers & Bhowmik, 1970-1971).[1] Through discussions with similar adopters, potential adopters acquire the beliefs and evaluations of these adopters, obtaining a normative understanding of the innovation, resolving the uncertainty associated with its adoption "in their own minds, if not in fact" (Burt, 1987, p. 1290), and benefiting from the "trial by others" (Rogers, 1983, p. 172). Having formed positive attitudes through answers to questions such as "what will the innovation do for someone like me?" potential adopters are likely to adopt the innovation. Thus, Rogers (1983) writes: "The dependence of the communicated experience of near-peers suggests that the heart of the diffusion process is the modeling and imitation by potential adopters of their network partners who have adopted previously" (p. 18).

Individuals tend to disbelieve information originating from interested parties, which Rogers (1983) called "change agents." Change agents can create awareness of the existence of the innovation and explain the innovation to potential adopters, thereby achieving "competence credibility." But, because of their selfish or even manipulative motives, they lack "safety credibility" and are not perceived as credible for evaluative information about the innovation. They are, therefore, bound to fail in their attempt to induce attitude changes and innovation adoption. However, there are two exceptions to this rule (Rogers, 1983). The first concerns heterophilous sources (including change agents) who are empathic to receivers, that is, able to project themselves into others' situations and thereby gain safety credibility. The second exception has to do with the fact that frequent communicators tend to become homophilous.

According to the innovation diffusion literature, then, we would expect that large retailers would be unsuccessful in their attempts to influence suppliers about EDI, because they are likely to be perceived as dissimilar and interested in the outcome, especially since they often have much more to gain from suppliers' adoption of EDI than do the suppliers themselves. The major exception to this expectation would be retailers who are perceived as credible and trustworthy by their suppliers. By contrast, the critical mass and impression management literatures, reviewed below, suggest that similarity and safety may not be the most important factors in generating the desired impressions.

Critical Mass Theory Literature

Critical mass theorists are concerned with collective innovations, those that require collaboration among potential adopters, if any adopter is to benefit (Hardin, 1982). The adopters of a collective innovation can either be persons or organizations (Fireman & Gamson, 1979). Work related to collective innovations is known in economics under the labels of the "prisoner's dilemma" (Samuelson, 1954) and "demand externalities" (Allen, 1988; Artle & Averous, 1973; Rohlfs, 1974), and in sociology under the labels of "critical mass theory" (Oliver et al., 1985), the "logic of collective action" (Olson, 1965), and "threshold models" of collective behavior (Granovetter, 1978). Critical mass theory has been applied to riot and union demonstrations, participation in community activities, the behavior of cartels and investment groups, and the adoption of communication media (Markus, 1987, 1990; Gurbaxani, 1990). Critical mass theory argues that actors' decisions to adopt a collective innovation are based on their perceptions of what others do. Their decision is influenced by how many others have already participated, how much the others have contributed, and/or who has participated (Allen, 1988; Artle & Averous, 1973; Granovetter, 1978; Markus, 1987, 1990; Oliver et al., 1985; Olson, 1965; Rohlfs, 1974).

Critical mass theorists argue that it would be nonrational for actors to participate in a collective innovation in the absence of a sufficient number of participants. Thus adoption of collective innovations is often unlikely, even when potential adopters are convinced of the positive benefits obtainable with widespread participation. "The concept of threshold, then, is purely behavioral, connoting nothing about what the actor thinks is the 'right' thing to do" (Granovetter, 1978, p. 1435; emphasis added). In the case of communication media, Markus (1990) writes that "in settings where an interactive medium has not yet achieved universal access, individuals are likely to weigh the extent of a medium's diffusion (known or believed) more highly than appropriateness in deciding whether or not to use the medium" (p. 211). Attitudes toward a collective innovation are thus formed by watching the group (Allen, 1988). Perceptions shift as more individuals decide to participate (or stop participating), since the benefits for each participant increase (or decrease). If the innovation attracts a critical mass, the innovation achieves legitimacy, triggering the actions of members who have held back thus far.

Markus (1990) further notes that universal participation in a communication medium can be increased by providing the resources needed to access the medium or by lowering the skill and effort requirements to use it. Oliver (1980) called these resources "positive incentives" and argued that they are effective for motivating small numbers of cooperators. When nearly everyone must participate for group members to achieve high payoffs, and where any one's participation adds little to the payoff unless enough others cooperate, negative incentives are more effective and less costly for their users. In this last case, however, the risk may be high that hostilities will arise to disrupt the cooperation that incentives were supposed to lead to in the first place.

Under critical mass theory, large retailers would be expected to be very influential in inducing their own suppliers to adopt EDI. Because of their interdependence, concerns about similarity or selfish motives would not be so important, because suppliers would take these for granted. To help spur adoption, large retailers would be expected to use positive incentives, such as lowering the technological requirements for their partners, or negative incentives, such as dropping partners who refuse to use EDI. But critical mass theory would also generally expect the number and identity of other adopters to weigh heavily in suppliers' decisions.

Table 6.1 summarizes the discussion thus far. As shown, innovation

Table 6.2
Summary of the Three Theoretical Backgrounds

	Innovation Diffusion	Critical Mass Theory	Impression Management and Bargaining
General rule	The transfer of ideas occurs between individuals or organizations who are alike, similar, or homophilous.	The transfer of ideas occurs between individuals or organizations who are members of the relevant collectivity.	The transfer of ideas may occur through the management of impressions and the use of bargaining tactics.
Rationale	Similarity brings safety credibility. Credible communications induce positive attitudes toward the innovation.	When a critical mass of adopters has been reached, the benefits of adopting become positive for those who have not adopted yet.	Through negotiations, adopting the innovation becomes acceptable for both parties.
Organizations expected to be influential	Similar organizations.	Organizations in the relevant collectivity, similar or not.	Organizations who show firmness but cooperative motives.
How, if at all, can large retailers influence their suppliers' adoption of EDI?	Generally, large retailers will be unsuccessful because of their vested interest resulting in poor credibility in the eyes of their suppliers.	Large retailers may be able to influence their suppliers' adoption of EDI, because the technology affects their relationship directly. Each large retailer's efforts may remain ineffective, however, if their actions are not reciprocated and if a critical mass is not achieved.	Large retailers can use bargaining strategies to appear firm but cooperative, thereby increasing suppliers' willingness to cooperate.

diffusion and critical mass theory literatures lead to different conclusions about whether large retailers can successfully influence their suppliers' EDI adoption decisions.   Both perspectives have limitations, however.   Because it was developed mostly to explain individual behavior, innovation diffusion research does not take into account the possibility of dissimilar business partners engaging in influential relationships not based on feelings of empathy.   For example, retailers surveyed by Andersen Consulting (1992) for the National Retail Federation indicated that they favor "strategic vendor partnerships" with their suppliers, even though they do not trust vendors.   Critical mass theory clearly emphasizes interdependencies among business partners.   However, it does not address the question of why dissimilar partners might be perceived as trustworthy in situations where they have vested interests.   The relevant explanations can, however, be found in the works of impression management theorists interested in bargaining behavior.

Impression Management and Bargaining Literatures

As noted in the introduction, large retailers can decide to impose the adoption of EDI on their suppliers as a condition of continuing to do business with them.   However, the real benefits of EDI, for both parties, occur when suppliers integrate EDI with their internal business processes and information systems.   This the retailers cannot mandate.   However, they can attempt to change how suppliers view EDI as an innovation as the retailers themselves are change agents, thus promoting suppliers to adopt EDI and full business integration.   In so doing, retailers engage in impression management behaviors, as understood by Schlenker (1980), to concern the ways that people attempt to create and maintain desired impressions on others.

Of course, large retailers want much more than suppliers' favorable impressions of themselves and EDI: retailers want suppliers to use EDI now! Because of time constraints and differential benefits, retailers and suppliers have to engage in bargaining, defined by Pruitt and Smith (1981) as "an effort by two parties to make a joint decision about a matter on which their preferences are initially opposed because of differing goals or aspirations" (p. 247).   Although impression management does not necessarily involve bargaining, and although bargaining is not the only method of resolving conflicting situations, Zartman (1977) noted that it is a commonly used method.   In a situation where a behavior cannot be unilaterally imposed, bargaining can lead to an acceptable solution for both parties, which is important in the context of the ongoing relationships among business partners.

In their chapter, Pruitt and Smith (1981) discuss two types of images that bargainers often seek to project: the image of firmness and the image of trustworthiness.   They define firmness as the reluctance to make concessions. Use of this strategy can lead to one of three benefits: a reduction in the use of pressure tactics by the other party, an increase in the other's willingness to make concessions, or an interest by the other party to search for a mutually acceptable solution. The danger exists, however, that the strategist will appear intransigent, causing the other party to withdraw. Pruitt and Smith (1981) also identify factors and strategies that contribute to perceptions of firmness: (1) the firm party seems more powerful than the other and is highly accountable to tough constituents who watch the negotiation closely; (2) there exists an alternative that dominates all others for both parties; (3) the firm party defends his demands vigorously, using threats or persuasion tactics, for example, by starting with large demands and conceding slowly, matching the other party's concessions or lack thereof, and communicating his position clearly.

For these strategies to succeed in producing the desired results, however, the bargainer must be perceived as trustworthy. For Pruitt and Smith (1981), trustworthiness is not related to credibility (as in Rogers, 1983), but "can be viewed as a belief that the adversary is cooperatively motivated, that is, has abandoned a strictly distributive approach[2] and is seeking a mutually acceptable agreement" (p. 256).[3] The authors also identify from past research the conditions that make search for a mutually acceptable solution attractive: reward structures in which each party controls the other's largest outcomes, the anticipation of future contacts with the other party, friendship, and perceived similarity in attitudes and in race. Finally, Pruitt and Smith (1981) note evidence in support of a general strategy proposed by Osgood (1962, 1966) to increase the trust and level of cooperation of another party in conflicting situations. Briefly, it consists of a unilateral series of cooperative initiatives, where (1) actions to be taken by each party are unambiguously announced ahead of time, (2) reciprocity is expected, and (3) rewards and retaliation are used as needed.

Although the impression management with bargaining perspective has mainly been applied to communications between individuals, some research has addressed the management of impressions by organizations and their members—by organizations toward job applicants, for example (see Gardner and Martinko, 1988, for a review and conceptual framework). However, the study of influential communications between organizations can benefit from explicit consideration of the nature of the interorganizational relationship. Pruitt and Smith's chapter provides further explanations about what may go on in the "heads" of potential innovation adopters, especially where the innovation is collective. Criteria such as how powerful a party is, how clear positions are, and the existence of continuing relationships serve to moderate the other party's negative reactions, thereby increasing willingness to cooperate. A delicate negotiation process emerges between organizational representatives attempting to reconcile their initially dissimilar and conflicting objectives.

Table 6.2 summarizes the comparison between the impression management and the innovation diffusion and critical mass literatures. In short, because EDI

Table 6.1
Summary of Innovation Diffusion and Critical Mass Theory Literatures

	Innovation Diffusion	Critical Mass Theory
General Rule	The transfer of ideas occurs between individuals or organizations who are alike, similar, or homophilous.	The transfer of ideas occurs between individulas or organizations who are members of the relevant collectivity.
Rationale	Similarity brings safety and credibility. Credible communications induce positive attitudes toward the innovation.	When a critical mass of adopters has been reached, the benefits of adopting become positive for those who have not yet adopted.
Organizations expected to be influential	Similar organizations.	organizations in the relevant collectivity, similar or not.
How, if at all, can large retailers influence their suppliers' adoption of EDI?	Generally, large retailers will be unsuccessful because of their vested interested resulting in poor credibility in the eyes of their suppliers.	Large retailers may be able to influence their suppliers' adoption of EDI, because the technology affects their relationship. Each large retailer's effots may remain ineffective, however, if their actions are not reciprocated and if a critical mass is not achieved.

is a collective innovation that several parties must adopt if any are to benefit, the conclusion of the innovation diffusion literature (that dissimilar parties will fail in their persuasive attempts) may not apply. Rather, as critical mass theory suggests, large retailers may be able to influence their own suppliers to adopt EDI, because of their mutual interdependence. But although critical mass theorists emphasize the negative effects on adoption due to problems in achieving a critical mass, the literature on impression management and bargaining shed doubt on the importance of this factor. By acting fairly and cooperatively, large retailers may be able to induce their business partners to negotiate for a mutually satisfying agreement on a one-by-one basis, regardless of how many others have already adopted and who they are.

RESEARCH METHODOLOGY

To examine influential communication among business partners in the context of adopting collective innovations, we chose the case study method. This method results in richer descriptions and, more importantly, provides better explanations of the phenomena studied (Miles and Huberman, 1984; Yin, 1989). As Yin (1989) noted, "the case study allows an investigation to retain the holistic and meaningful characteristics of real-life events" (p. 14), such as organizational and managerial processes. The unit of analysis in this study is the interorganizational relationship between retailers and their suppliers.

Electronic data interchange (EDI) was selected as the focus of investigation for two main reasons. First, EDI represents an interesting opportunity to examine influential communication at the interorganizational level of analysis, which has previously received little research attention. EDI has mainly been promoted by the larger members of business partnerships, in a context where organizations have traditionally sought to maintain autonomy despite their acknowledged economic interdependence. The second reason for studying EDI is that the arguments of EDI promoters have apparently not been as convincing as one might have expected. Whereas industry observers predicted an explosion in EDI adoption, actual adoption rates have been much lower.

The analysis here focuses exclusively on the retail industry and suppliers to it. The retail industry has been one of the most active promoters of EDI[4], but inaction among suppliers led many retailers to change their promotion strategies midstream from persuasion to mandate. Therefore, it is possible to compare the relative effectiveness of different strategies. We focus in particular on the strategies used by one large retailer—Sears, Roebuck and Co. Sears is a particularly good case study because the company achieved disappointing, but typical, results with an EDI promotion campaign that was widely regarded to have been especially innovative and considerate of suppliers (see especially Pastore, 1992).

Data were gathered using two techniques. First, historical reconstruction was used to analyze the retail industry's experience with, and promotion of, EDI. Four publicly available sources were particularly helpful: (1) industry analyses by Standard & Poor's, (2) articles in the computer industry magazines and newspapers (especially *Computerworld*), (3) business magazines (such as *FORTUNE* and *Business Week*), and (4) publicity distributed by Sears Communication Company.

The second data-gathering technique consisted of telephone and face-to-face interviews with two suppliers to the retail industry. The interviews were focused, but open-ended; respondents were free to answer the questions however they believed appropriate. Both suppliers had received letters from one or more customers mandating adoption of EDI. The first organization, MClothing (a pseudonym), refused to adopt EDI even if this meant losing business partners. This manufacturer of children's clothing had received a mandate from Sears to begin using EDI by a certain date. Nevertheless, in June 1992, MClothing decided against EDI implementation. The second case is a small family-run organization that was in the process of implementing EDI with Sears when the research was conducted in the summer of 1992. MJewelry (a pseudonym), which designs, manufactures, and sells jewelry, had been asked by Sears and other large retailers to adopt EDI in early 1991.

All interviews were recorded, and interviewees received a transcript for verification. Transcripts were analyzed using techniques discussed in Miles and Huberman (1984). A complete transcription of the interview with the president of MClothing and a summary of the MJewelry data appear in Bouchard (1992).

RESULTS

The possibility of using computers to transmit information between companies has existed almost since computers were invented. Indeed, a few large retailers, such as Wal-Mart, Sears, Kmart, and JC Penney, have been transmitting purchase orders to important suppliers since the 1960s. However, it was only at the end of the 1980s that retailers began actively promoting EDI with the objective of 100 percent adoption by their business partners. To explain why the change occurred and what promotion strategies were used, we begin our analysis with a review of the retail industry environment throughout the 1980s. We follow this with a history of EDI in retailing. We then present the case of Sears, Roebuck and Co., highlighting the efforts it made to get its business partners to use EDI. Finally, we discuss how two of Sears' suppliers reacted to these efforts.

Retail Industry Analysis

It used to be that, to increase its sales, a retailer only had to increase its number of stores. Contrast this with a recent prediction by Carl Steidtmann, chief economist at the retail consulting firm Management Horizons: by the end of the 1990s, half of the retailers currently operating in the United States will be out of business. This pessimistic prediction illustrates the extent of the changes occurring in retailing, which of necessity affect retail suppliers. The changes are due to three major factors: consumer profile and behavior, the appearance of specialty stores, and the financial difficulties of department stores.

In 1979, over 52 percent of consumers' disposable income went for retail purchases. In 1990, this percentage dropped to about 45 percent. Shoppers not only had less money to spend—due to lower real incomes, heavy debts, and low savings—but they also showed increased dissatisfaction with shopping. A 1990 survey of 1,255 adults in *Business Week* indicated that 63 percent of them found shopping mostly or entirely drudgery. On the other hand, expenditures on services have increased rapidly with the aging of the population and the rising number of more affluent, college-educated consumers. The mass markets of the 1960s have been replaced by micromarkets of highly selective and price-sensitive shoppers. Thus, more consumers buy in specialty stores, the second major source of changes in the retail industry.

The retail winners of the 1980s, such as Nordstrom, Wal-Mart, the Limited, and the Gap, were virtually unknown the decade before. Category-dominant superstores, such as Toys 'R Us, Circuit City, and Home Depot, also did well. For example, in 1980, these companies shared about 1 percent of the nation's general merchandise, apparel, and furniture markets; in 1989, their market share had risen to almost 10 percent. Using consumer research and market studies, they differentiated themselves in the eyes of consumers, in terms of assortment, price, value, and service. They operate with high sales per square foot, healthy profit margins, high inventory turnover, and fewer management layers, and they use information technology to help lower their costs.

But their success has occurred at the expense of department stores. After inflation, department stores' sales per square foot in 1989 were about even with their 1985 level of $151. By contrast, the average sales per square foot in specialty stores, adjusted for inflation, was $219, up 23 percent from 1985.

Although specialty stores stayed close to their markets and to the general economic trends, many department stores and mass merchandisers continued their strategy of expansion. Between 1986 and 1989, the number of malls increased 22 percent. At the same time, merger and acquisition activity was exceptional: by 1990, of the eight companies that constituted the Standard and Poor's department store index at the beginning of 1986, four had been acquired or taken private, and a fifth underwent a major restructuring that split the firm into two separately traded companies. Retailers faced substantial debts as a result of this restructuring. When the Canadian company, Campeau Corp., went into bankruptcy in November 1989, department stores panicked and finally acted. Marginally profitable and unprofitable stores were closed, and personnel were let go. Buying offices were centralized, and the remaining buyers began to use fewer vendors, usually the larger and more reliable manufacturers. Brand-name merchandise suppliers were favored, whereas many mom-and-pop vendors went broke. This benefited large manufacturers, such as Liz Claiborne, because customers wanted brand-name products and shopped at the stores that carried them.

In general, though, retailers gained influence over manufacturers, because the retailers that remained after consolidations were fewer and more powerful. Today, retailers demand more volume discounts, cooperative advertising, and ticketing and pricing of merchandise by manufacturers before shipment. This leaves those suppliers who are able to deliver frequently and in smaller quantities and who can adapt more rapidly to changing consumer tastes better positioned to survive and prosper. However, it is widely believed that achieving this flexibility and integration will require suppliers to implement distribution systems known in the industry as "Quick Response Systems" involving the use of EDI and a number of other innovative business practices. For instance, Kurt Salmon and Associates, a retail industry consulting firm, has estimated that the apparel pipeline, about 66 weeks from material stage to store delivery, can be reduced to 21 weeks through improved (electronic) communication between suppliers and retailers. It has also calculated that as much as $25 billion in sales and profits are lost through leaks in this pipeline, mostly at the retail level, in the form of stockouts (too little of the right merchandise) and markdowns (too much of the wrong merchandise). According to the National Merchants Association, department stores markdowns as a percentage of sales rose to 16.2 percent in 1988, up from 13.8 percent in 1983.

Retailing became a win-lose business in one decade. As traditional retailers started to wake up to the changes, they shook up the whole industry with a message to their suppliers: EDI or DIE.

EDI and Its Promotion in the Retail Industry

By the end of the 1980s, much of retailers' capital spending went for new information technology. Retailers first began installing computers in their stores to collect point-of-sale data in the 1970s. Scanning technology, which automates ticketing and checkout, started in the 1980s. Installation of scanners at Kmart stores was completed in 1990 at a cost of over $1 billion. In the same period, Sears was rolling out new versions of its major systems for distribution, billing, product ordering, store layout, and other important business activities. To improve communications between stores and headquarters, retailers such as Kmart, Wal-Mart, Sears, and Toys 'R Us have begun to use satellites. In 1990, Sears' information systems budget was evaluated at about $300 million, while Wal-Mart's executives said they had spent approximately $500 million in information technology over the last five years.

As noted, large retailers such as Sears, Kmart, Wal-Mart, and JC Penney have used computers to communicate with their suppliers for several decades, as did some large suppliers, like Levi Strauss, with their customers. These communications occurred through what is called "proprietary systems": for each retailer that a supplier communicated with, different protocols and communication formats had to be used. In many cases, these communications also required suppliers to have dedicated telephone lines. Because of the difficulties involved, only large organizations used computers to transmit business documents.

Today, EDI refers to transmissions using standard transaction formats and protocols. The overall standard is continually being improved under the supervision of the American National Standard Institute (ANSI) X.12 committee. Industry standards, which started evolving before ANSI intervened in the late 1970s, continue to exist, but are becoming aligned with X.12. In the retail industry, the most popular standard is VICS EDI (Voluntary Interindustry Communication Standard EDI); VICS's members are retailers, manufacturers, and textile producers, and most of the large retailers helped develop these standards. The first VICS EDI standards were released in 1987, and retailers with proprietary systems started migrating toward this standard. X.12 standards were also quickly adopted by network providers, removing the need for organizations to call each of their business partners directly; instead, they only had to set up connections with one or a few networks, which would then transmit the information to the appropriate business partners. Finally, off-the-shelf EDI software became commercially available, especially for the microcomputer platform. From a technology standpoint, everything needed for EDI fell into place at the end of the 1980s.

Large retailers embarked on a promotional campaign to inform their business partners about EDI. They held educational seminars, talked more directly on the phone or face-to-face, and attended or gave talks at industry and EDI conferences. By mid-1990, Wal-Mart, the largest EDI user, had about 1,800 of its 5,000 suppliers on EDI; Kmart claimed to have 1,000 EDI partners; JC Penney had 300 EDI partners; and Sears had about 400 online and 150 more said to be "in testing." EDI partners were usually major suppliers, representing a large fraction of the retailers' purchases or transactions.

Despite this progress, retailers clearly deemed the number of EDI-ready partners to be insufficient. If retailers were really to leverage their investment in information technology, to streamline their operations, and to decrease their inventory carrying costs, they had to have all their business partners on EDI. Therefore, they took a tougher stance. During the summer of 1989, Dillard's Department Stores informed its 800-plus key suppliers that they had until February 1, 1990, to be up and running on EDI, or at least to submit a schedule for doing so sometime in 1990. When all of Dillard's suppliers missed their first EDI implementation deadline, they were charged $25 per paper-based transaction; those who missed the final deadline of the end of 1991 lost the retailer's business. Wal-Mart and Kmart's suppliers were given deadlines of summer 1990. JC Penney planned to have 1,000 of its 4,500 to 5,000 active suppliers on EDI by the end of 1990. Sears wrote its partners in July 1990 that they were expected to be online by July 1992. EDI usage also became mandatory for the partners of Toys 'R Us, who were told they would be charged $25 for every piece of paper the toy retailer had to process.

Today, in 1994, EDI conferences are still populated with retailers and their business partners, the former wondering why it is taking an eternity for their suppliers to implement EDI. Retail consultants have advised against simply forcing suppliers to adopt EDI, since the benefits of EDI do not come from simple implementation but rather from the more complex and difficult process of integrating EDI into internal business operations. Furthermore, a coercive EDI implementation strategy puts retailers in a difficult position with respect to their suppliers, for close integration of business through EDI demands a high level of trust between business partners, due to the extensiveness of the information exchange about each other's operations.

As noted, Dillard simply dropped from its lists suppliers who were unwilling to adopt EDI. But Kmart judged this option too radical and decided to allow exceptions: "It makes no sense to discontinue a product line just because the manufacturer isn't ready to do EDI," said David Carlson, Kmart's senior vice president of corporate information systems (Pastore, 1992). Unfortunately, EDI implementation programs that involved relatively greater consideration for the problems of suppliers were also unsuccessful in achieving 100 percent adoption, as the case of Sears shows.

EDI at Sears, Roebuck and Co.

Chicago-based Sears, Roebuck and Co. was founded in 1895. At first a mail order catalog company, and a store owner since 1925, Sears remained at the top of retail industry charts until quite recently. Its challenger is Wal-Mart, a chain from Bentonville, Arkansas, that almost no one had heard of a few years ago. As Table 6.3 indicates, Sears faces extremely tough challenges. Its five-year growth rate at the end of 1989 was a negative 25 percent, and its pretax profits represented only 1.1 percent of sales. By comparison, Wal-Mart's profits represented 6.4 percent of sales, while those of the Gap and Toys 'R Us represented 10 percent and 10.7 percent respectively. Sears' difficulties seem so significant that some industry analysts doubt its ability to survive. Carol Farmer, a retailing consultant, was quoted as saying: "The big question to ask about Sears is not if but when, and what sort of tidal wave will it create as it goes under" (Saporito, 1989).

However, predictions of Sears' death may be premature. Today, the company is striving to eliminate bureaucracy and improve its responsiveness to market changes. 1990 marked the end of a six-year plan to revamp Sears' retail information systems. One of these, the Sears Apparel Merchandising System (SAMS), allows apparel departments to plan, buy, and replenish goods through online terminals. SAMS replaced a 20-year old system and went live at the beginning of 1990, after a six-month progressive implementation. This system plays an important role in Sears' EDI strategy.

Sears began using computers to send and receive business documents with its major trading partners in 1967. Its pre-EDI system, SENDEN, used Sears' own communication formats and its private communication network. Most of Sears' suppliers now communicate using the VICS EDI standard, which the Sears EDI team continues to help develop. In 1990, Sears employed over 500 persons in its information systems department; of these, about a dozen worked exclusively on the EDI project at the Sears Merchandise Group. Their expertise was complemented by the Sears Communication Company (a subsidiary of Sears), which oversees Sears' telecommunications network and which has offered network services to the commercial marketplace since 1986.

Sears began promoting EDI among its business partners at the end of 1989. With the help of Andersen Consulting, basic EDI translation software with training and documentation (estimated in value at $3,300 per partner) was

Table 6.3
Financial Indicators for Selected Retailers

Retailer	Retail Sales (Millions)	Pretax Profits	Interest Expenses	5-Year Growth Rate
Dillard	$2558	$173	$81	24.0%
The Gap	$1252	$126	$3	25.0%
The Limited	$4071	$396	$63	24.0%
Nordstrom	$2328	$198	$45	22.0%
Sears	$30,256	$333	$1093	(25.29%)
Toys 'R Us	$4000	$429	$26	19.2%
Wal-Mart	$20,649	$1325	$136	30.0%

Source: Saporito, B. (1989, December 18), "Retailing's Winners & Losers," *FORTUNE*, p. 76.

developed and provided free to interested partners. Sears also offered discounts on the purchase of the IBM Personal System/1 computers, the minimum configuration needed to run the software. A two-day seminar on EDI was first offered in October 1989; Sears assumed half of the fees for each partner attending. And although Sears gave away its own EDI software and offered the services of Sears Communication Network for a fee, it never required its partners to use these proprietary services. Indeed, Sears even went so far as to provide a list of approved alternative EDI software and network providers from which suppliers could choose, considerably reducing the technology search costs of suppliers willing to adopt EDI but unwilling to use Sears' proprietary EDI approach. The company estimated its costs of helping partners convert to EDI at $5 million, and calculated that it would take it three years to recoup this investment. In comparison to the approaches followed by other large retailers, Sears' EDI promotion strategy received praise from both suppliers and the business press (Pastore, 1992).

As noted, Sears had about 400 suppliers (out of approximately 5,000) using EDI in July 1990, and 150 in the testing phase. On July 5, 1990, the chairman and chief executive of the Sears Merchandise Group wrote a letter to all of its suppliers not yet using EDI with Sears. This letter contained one main message: "EDI will become a requirement for doing business with Sears." Sears divided its suppliers into groups and laid down a schedule to bring each of these groups onto EDI, beginning in January 1991. Each group was given 90 days to comply, with all suppliers to use EDI by July 1992.

By fall 1991, Sears had convinced fewer than half of its suppliers to implement EDI. Only 10 percent of Sears' EDI business partners had chosen to use its free software.[5] It was not even the case that all of Sears' suppliers had attended one of its seminars on EDI. Between October 1989 and December 1991, when Sears held its last seminar, close to 30 sessions had been offered across the country. Lance Dailey, then director of EDI implementation for the Sears Merchandise Group, was quoted as saying: "If I look back to '89, I would have expected to be farther along than where I am," and "All the good intentions we've had don't seem to move them [Sears' suppliers]" (Pastore, 1992). To understand why, we next take a detailed look at two of Sears' suppliers.

Supplier MClothing

MClothing is a small manufacturer of children's fashion clothing that decided not to implement EDI. Its president learned about EDI when he received literature from several big customers, with a request that he adopt the technology. According to MClothing's president, the decision to reject EDI was based on one major reason: Its number one account, representing $5 million of business, had not requested EDI adoption and indeed showed no interest in using the technology. EDI specialists had estimated that it would cost between $12,000 and $15,000 to implement EDI at MClothing. To justify such an expense, MClothing would have needed a large volume of steady business with the customer requesting the use of EDI. But the fashion industry is highly volatile, and customer orders fluctuated. Further, MClothing faced ongoing economic difficulties. Said MClothing's president:

> I don't blame them for wanting [EDI], but actually I've got to have some return on my end also. These people that request it from me, where one season I do with them half a million dollars worth of business and the next season I don't see them: why should I go out and spend $12-15,000 to put their system in, when they have no loyalty to me?

MClothing's internal activities were computerized. Like many other suppliers, the company had also been requested by customers to preticket goods, to ship in certain configurations to customer warehouses, and to hold and manage inventories for retailers. These requests were costly to accommodate. EDI was the latest demand in the series, "and it just has to reach a point where you just can't go any further." In addition, MClothing's president did not see any benefit from the use of EDI for the final customer buying fashion clothes at the store, or for enabling MClothing to obtain new customers. For MClothing, then, "it's just not worth it."

Supplier MJewelry

MJewelry became aware of EDI during the first quarter of 1991, when Sears, one of its major customers, asked the company whether it could do EDI. It took about six months for MJewelry's controller to justify the expense and decide to adopt EDI. Three reasons prompted the decision. The first one was the pressure of large retailers: "I looked at it and said, well, if you're going to continue to do business with Sears and other major accounts, it will pay for itself. It's fine, I can live with that, it's an additional asset, we'll depreciate it over time." The cost to implement EDI at MJewelry was estimated at around $15,000, an expense which the controller described as "awfully high with respect to software. It's not that we're not used to it. It's something that we're not used to putting out for something that does not have immediate response, as far as advantages to us. It's just expensive at first, a great start-up cost."

The second reason behind MJewelry's decision to adopt EDI was one of strategy. For the controller, "if you want to play with the big guys, you have to be one of the big guys. You just can't compete anymore on price, quality and service. You've got to compete really at a business level. I think what it's going to do for us is it's going to open doors where we can compete." The controller describes the jewelry market as being very competitive. Several jewelry designers have been forced to close due to the economic crisis, but this was not the case for MJewelry: "The main reason why we are in business is that [MJewelry] sells. That's the bottom line."

The third reason for adopting EDI was to improve the quality of data by eliminating rekeying, and to provide more information on MJewelry's operations through summary reports. However, this was not a big priority for MJewelry, given the company's small number of transactions: "I don't get 400 orders each week from Sears; I don't get 400 orders from anybody each week. If I did, EDI would have been on after the first couple of months, because it would have paid for itself."

Once MJewelry decided to adopt EDI, however, it took over a year and a half before the company started using it. The first consulting company hired to develop a tailored EDI system for MJewelry failed. A second team of consultants hired to integrate an off-the-shelf EDI software with the company's applications worked only part time. But Sears remained patient through most of the process. Here is how MJewelry's controller describes their relationship:

> They understand that there's great costs involved in it; they understand that it's going to take a little while to be able to convert to our system. They understand that and they're willing to work with that. We have a deadline, somewhere near the end of September [1992] for Sears. They've been after us for a year and a half. We're still doing business with them!

> We will be charged by Sears [if MJewelry does not meet the deadline], but then again we would probably not be doing business with them if they were not reasonable enough. That's our choice. We've made decisions in the past not to do business with major accounts because of unfair chargebacks and things such as that. You've got to be able to make money on it. If you can't make money on it, it doesn't make sense to do it. Sears purposely hasn't pushed us to be on EDI by a certain deadline, up until recently, because our jewelry sells good and they're happy with it.

Since the beginning of his involvement in EDI, MJewelry's controller was also asked by four other of its major customers to use the technology, but no specific deadlines were set. He was only asked to inform them when he would be ready.

In order to reach its adoption decision, MJewelry's controller used several sources of information, including programmers, local newspapers, and brochures. However, two sources were critical. The first was Sears, through its seminars and personal contacts over the phone with Sears' personnel. About the seminar, the controller noted that "it just opened my eyes. I said, well, if you want to compete, you've got to have this." Several questions during the interview with MJewelry's controller centered on the credibility of the information given by Sears. For example, it was stated in the seminar that it takes a major company $45 on average to process an order, but the controller found this hard to believe:

> I did not believe this $45: if it's costing somebody $45, how can they be in business? I don't understand. Ten, fifteen dollars. I can understand that it's got to go through a million channels in the corporate ladder. But I said to myself, 'accept the stuff that you can really understand and believe,' and the stuff I could understand and believe was where it came from, why you should do EDI.

More generally, the controller noted:

> It could have been a biased opinion, but my feeling on that was that it was not biased. They were being sincere with respect to if you want to do business with us, you've got to do this anyway, but let me help you out. I was very happy with the type of answers I was able to have answered by Sears and different people at Sears, not only on a technical level, but also on a business level. They taught you how to do it, and they told you who was out there. So that was not biased. Obviously Sears Communications Company wants us to sign on with them, but who wouldn't? And they were not pushing it on us or anything like that. They were very fair and told us about the other companies, told you who to call over there to get the price list and things like that, they told you what to look at when you were going after buying EDI systems, make sure that you had access to your source code, and make sure that they'd been around for a while, and that they've got technical people that always get the UCC updates. They were very good with making you understand it.

A second source was also influential in the decision to adopt EDI at MJewelry. The vice president of the company is the friend of someone working for another jewelry manufacturer; the two companies offer different lines of products and are not in competition. We will call this friend "Arthur," and his company, "Arthur's Co."

> Arthur was very gracious to let me come in and look at their system. Arthur is a whizbang; I don't understand how he does it. They have so much equipment there. Arthur's Co. is big because they can compete. They have that electronic information on a second's notice. He showed me their system and how it works. I saw data coming in, I saw what they were doing with the data, it was great! After that I made the decision.

In short, although MClothing rejected EDI, MJewelry decided to implement the technology even though the investment could not be justified on financial grounds. Although Sears used the same tactics to get these firms to adopt EDI, the reaction of the suppliers was mediated by their different relationships with Sears.

DISCUSSION

Over the years, retailers have used several strategies to promote EDI. At first, they exchanged pre-EDI transactions with their largest suppliers, as both parties had the volume and expertise required. But the changing economics of the retail industry encouraged them to promote EDI adoption with all of their suppliers, including the smallest. Initially, they did this by distributing information, holding seminars, and attending conferences. They proceeded under the assumption that the existence of EDI standards—which they had helped develop—and the availability of PC-based software would tear down suppliers' resistance. But when the crisis came to retailing in 1989 and suppliers had not yet adopted the technology, retailers decided to mandate adoption of EDI. In this section, we look at how these strategies were received by suppliers and at the extent to which each of the three theoretical perspectives described at the outset accounts for the strategies and reactions to them.

In the innovation diffusion perspective, large retailers are expected to be unsuccessful in inducing positive attitudes toward the innovation on the part of suppliers, because retailers lack safety credibility due to their dissimilarities and vested interests. The large retailers were indeed unsuccessful, but the data in our study contradict the explanation provided by the innovation diffusion perspective. First, the decision of whether or not to adopt EDI at MClothing and MJewelry was not based on characteristics of the innovation per se, nor did it focus on the dissimilarity and vested interests of retailers. The characteristics of EDI, and consequently, suppliers' attitudes toward it, were quite secondary in the adoption decision to the quality of the relationship between the business partners. MClothing's president talked about steady business and loyalty, while MJewelry's controller attended to the way in which the company was treated by its major partners in the course of doing business, including the implementation of EDI. Second, the perceived dissimilarities and vested interests of the large retailers did not prevent suppliers from actively seeking information about the innovation from retailers. Among the information they sought from business partners was information about what EDI would do for the relationship between them.

This observed behavior is consistent with the predictions of critical mass theorists, who emphasize the interdependencies among business partners. In fact, the more interdependent the parties are, the more likely that a collective innovation will be adopted, according to the critical mass perspective. Like most North American suppliers to the retail industry, neither MClothing nor MJewelry had a large enough volume of transactions to justify the cost of EDI on purely independent economic terms. The investment had to be amortized over a number of years, and suppliers were only willing to adopt the technology if they could count on a long-term relationship with their EDI-using customers. This is precisely why MClothing declined to implement EDI. The instability of its relationship with Sears made adopting EDI unfavorable: Sears was seen as asking too much for the strength of the relationship, and MClothing was not willing to spend so much to preserve it. Contrast this with the attitude of the controller at MJewelry, who saw EDI as a demonstration of the seriousness of his company "to play with the big guys" and hoped that his use of EDI would secure his future relationship with Sears and other major customers.

The desire to become one of "the big guys" cannot, however, be interpreted as an expression of perceived similarity between MJewelry and Sears. The controller's description of a similar supplier is revealing in this regard: "Arthur's Co. is big because they can compete [with other suppliers for the business of big retailers]." Furthermore, MJewelry's controller doubted the veracity of some information about EDI provided by Sears and recognized Sears' vested interest in MJewelry's adoption of the technology. Thus, this supplier was influenced by its customer despite the latter's dissimilarity and vested interests.

As Oliver et al. (1985) and Markus (1990) have noted, differences in interests and resources may be essential to "start the ball rolling" in the diffusion of collective innovations. Critical mass theory, then, helps explain why dissimilar information communicators can be influential. However, it leaves largely unexplained the issue of why differences in interests do not drive the whole process—why don't all suppliers adopt EDI when pressured to do so by their business partners? To return to the metaphor we used in the introduction, dissimilar interests set the stage for a dance party: someone has hired a hall and a band and issued invitations. But this alone is insufficient to get dancers paired up and moving around the floor. To explain whether or not and how people actually dance, another perspective is needed.

The impression management literature can contribute substantially to our understanding of the process by which business partners actually adopt collective innovations, like EDI, when one of the partners has made the first move. First, large retailers have to manage the impressions they make on their suppliers as they try to induce them to undertake an action that is not necessarily in their short-term economic interest. It is always possible for retailers to issue an ultimatum: EDI or DIE. But this, of course, is not always in the retailers' best interests, and so it may not be perceived by suppliers as a credible threat. As Kmart's senior vice president of corporate information systems observed: "It makes no sense to discontinue a product line just because the manufacturer isn't ready to do EDI." Although retailers may be willing to drop non-EDI-adopting suppliers of less profitable products, they would be foolish to drop all their good suppliers just because the latter hesitate to make an expensive and possibly uneconomic change in their business practices. Retailers, therefore, have to rely heavily on noncoercive strategies, such as creating and maintaining favorable impressions on their suppliers. They need to convey with credibility the message that, if both parties adopt EDI, both will be better off, especially when compared to other retail partnerships that do not use EDI. This message sends the signal that retailers are looking out for suppliers' long-term interests, as well as their own short-term needs. Consistent with this perspective, we observed that retailers expended enormous energy and resources conducting promotional campaigns and educational seminars about the partnership benefits of using EDI.

Although suppliers got the message that using EDI would eventually become a business necessity, they did not adopt it fast enough to satisfy the retailers. Therefore, retailers started to bargain for an increased rate of EDI adoption. They projected an image of firmness by sending letters mandating EDI adoption within specific deadlines and used the threat of penalties for subsequent nonelectronic transactions. The impression of firmness was reinforced by the simultaneous actions of several large retailers during the same time period. Although there is no evidence of collusion in retailers' behavior, their collective tough stance forced suppliers to make a deliberate choice at a particular moment in time.

In order not to jeopardize their relationships with suppliers through this tough stance, some retailers also tried to enhance the image of consideration and trustworthiness that they had nurtured in their earlier promotional campaigns and educational seminars. The extensiveness of Sears' efforts in this regard accounts in large measure for high esteem in which its EDI strategy was held. Sears generally gave suppliers more time to prepare for, and implement, EDI than did Dillard and Kmart. By providing free software and free training, and by not imposing the use of a particular software or network provider, Sears projected an image of understanding suppliers' situation and being willing to share the costs. Sears was therefore perceived as more trustworthy and fairer than other retailers. For MJewelry's controller, "They understand that there's great costs involved in it; they understand it's going to take a while to be able to convert to our system. They understand that and they're willing to work with that."

In response to Sears' considerate approach, MJewelry went to some pains to impress Sears with its own good faith and cooperative intentions when it incurred major delays in implementing EDI. Additionally, MJewelry created favorable impressions on its four other major customers by pointing to its work with Sears when they too asked MJewelry to use EDI. In consequence of Mjewelry's cooperative intentions as evidenced by its efforts with Sears, these other customers did not pursue coercive tactics with MJewelry, but contented themselves with MJewelry's estimates of a reasonable time frame for implementing EDI.

We see, then, that it is the critical mass and impression management perspectives, rather than the innovation diffusion perspective that explain the small rate of adoption of EDI in the retail industry. For some supplier-retailer relationships, EDI will never be used, because suppliers do not judge the relationship sufficiently important to warrant the expense and disruption of EDI adoption. However, in this case study, it is the impression management perspective, rather than the critical mass perspective that better explains why some suppliers actually do adopt this collective innovation. Suppliers appear to be quite unswayed by the evidence that others are doing EDI, as critical mass theory suggests. Rather, they make the difficult decision in the context of a fair and trusting relationship with a valued, though dissimilar and interested, business partner. In this situation, the question for the retailers is how to appear fair, trustworthy, and considerate, while maintaining a hard line. And, for suppliers, the question becomes, not whether to adopt EDI, but when, which means bargaining for time and attempting to appear cooperative even when there is no immediate progress.

These apparent contradictions make sense when the whole prior relationship among the bargainers is taken into account. At least in the case of the diffusion of EDI, therefore, trustworthiness is not a feature of a specific situation, as argued by Pruitt and Smith (1981), but of the entire past and future relationship among the business partners. Once interdependence has been acknowledged, the general strategy of cooperation in conflicting situations as proposed by Osgood (1962, 1966) explains the adoption of EDI, which the two other perspectives reviewed here failed to do. The adoption of EDI involved (1) unambiguous advance announcements by retailers of their expectations of suppliers and their own resource commitments, (2) the expectation on the part of retailers that the suppliers would respond with a clear decision, (3) the use of rewards and retaliation to motivate quick response.

FURTHER RESEARCH

Further research is needed to understand the adoption of innovative business practices, especially those involving collective innovations. The research reported here suggests that the following propositions—not all fully supported by our research, but suggested by it—will provide a fruitful basis for further research.

P1: When the potential users of a collective technological innovation are already engaged in a continuing relationship, the importance of this relationship, as seen by each participant, strongly affects the adoption decision.

P2: The perceived importance of the relationship depends on the perceived overall quality and fairness of the relationship, and the behavior of a relationship partner with respect to the adoption of collective technological innovations plays an important role in shaping these perceptions.

P3: To improve the perception of relationship quality and fairness, large organizations can manage the impressions of their smaller business partners by:

a: clearly communicating their adoption expectations to their business partners, in addition to making their position toward the innovation known, and by

b: offering active support for their business partners' efforts to implement the innovation.

P4: The use of an adversarial approach, such as mandating the adoption of a collective technological innovation without providing support, will affect negatively the long-term relationships between business partners.

The current study does not provide real evidence for the last proposition. It seems that some retailers may have given their suppliers more leeway than they really wanted to, and so few retailer-suppliers relationships were strained to the breaking point.[6] However, the opportunity to compare the long-term effects of adversarial versus cooperative exists in the latest saga of EDI diffusion. Retailers are now demanding that suppliers manage retailers' inventory in a concept called "vendor-managed inventory" (Betts, 1994). Retailers are currently approaching this innovative business practice with the same strategy they used with EDI: retailers are sending suppliers letters mandating that suppliers use retailers' point-of-sale or warehouse data as a basis for making decisions about when to replenish the retailers' inventories. Interestingly, this innovation may shift some power in the relationship back to the suppliers, and the experience of EDI leads us to expect considerable efforts on the part of suppliers to use this power to negotiate more favorable implementation and other business terms.

CONCLUSION

In this chapter, we have focused on issues of impression management in the adoption of collective innovations, and in particular, of electronic data interchange. We have observed that, for such innovations, cooperation among actual and potential adopters is required. Our main conclusion is that studying the dynamic, ongoing relationships among the members of the collectivity is essential if we are to understand how such innovations diffuse. In particular, we found some evidence inconsistent with traditionally assumed mechanisms of diffusion among homophilous communicators and of critical mass as an essential consideration in the adoption of collective innovations.

The work reported here has relevance for researchers interested, not only in EDI, but in other collective technologies and innovative business practices, including electronic mail, just-in-time and quick response programs, total quality management, and business process reengineering efforts, in a wide range of industries. We see fruitful possibilities in the use of the impression management and bargaining literatures to elucidate the strategies by which participants of unequal power interact dynamically through the lengthy process of innovation adoption and use. The characteristics of technologies and partners may set the stage, but the magic is in the dance.

NOTES

This research was supported by grants from Universite Laval (Quebec City), the Social Sciences and Humanities Research Council of Canada, and the Information Systems Research Program at UCLA.

1.   The importance of similarity in managing impressions has also been noted by researchers such as Schlenker (1980), Gardner and Martinko (1988), and Tedeschi and his associates (see, for example, Tedeschi & Reiss, 1981).
2.   A distributive approach is a strategy where one seeks a personally advantageous distribution of the resources under discussion.
3.   For Pruitt and Smith, trust is a feature of a specific situation and does not refer to a continuing perception that the other party is likely to be cooperative.
4.   See, for example, coverage in *Computerworld* during 1989 through 1992.
5.   This probably had to do with the fact that Sears' software could only be used with Sears, and that it was impossible to integrate it with suppliers' existing computerized applications.
6.   Note that, if this is true, the blame for the slow rate of EDI adoption shifts from suppliers to retailers.

7

THE EFFECT OF MULTIMEDIA PRESENTATIONS ON IMPRESSION FORMATION

David B. Paradice

Information production and distribution is growing at a staggering rate. Few would argue that the average person of today is not literally bombarded by information, or more accurately, by attempts to gain the person's attention so that information may be received by the person (Huber, 1984). Anyone walking through an airport or a shopping mall, listening to a radio, or watching television is constantly a target for attention-grabbing efforts, which may be visual, audible, mobile, or all three.

Information technology is quickly reaching a point where very sophisticated presentation formats may be embedded in information systems. User interfaces are becoming increasingly graphics-oriented. Users are moving away from command driven systems to ones that rely on icon manipulation. Interfaces are becoming animated, with windows that open and menus that appear and disappear. Sound may be easily incorporated into systems, so that messages include a sound (or perhaps a recorded voice) to draw attention to situations requiring user intervention. Even full-motion video is becoming easily incorporated in systems with processors that are widely available today.

However, little has been done to determine whether these system capabilities can be manipulated to influence impressions formed by users. Certainly, advertisers and others believe that colors, animation, and images can be manipulated to some desired result (see Paivio, 1973; Snodgrass & Asiaghi, 1977; Lutz & Lutz, 1978; D'Agostino & Small, 1980). Studies also indicate that the attractiveness of an information source can influence attitude formation (Puckett et al., 1983; Haugtvedt et al., 1986). But, can the same be said for computer-based information? Would a computer-based multimedia presentation influence the initial impression formed by a consumer of information differently from the impression formed by someone that received the same information in a different format? This study provides an initial step toward answering these questions.

In the sections that follow, a study is described that examines the impact of a computer-based multimedia presentation on the formation of initial impressions. The study was conducted in an academic setting, where students were asked about their impression of a professor before and after being given information about the professor in one of two formats: printed text or computer-based multimedia.

In the next section, theoretical concepts from the growing field of impression management are placed in the context of the study. The subsequent section reviews characteristics of multimedia systems for readers who may be unfamiliar with these types of systems. The remaining sections describe the study's procedure and results.

IMPRESSION MANAGEMENT

Impression management has been studied in some form since the beginning of this century (Tedeschi, 1981; Giacalone & Rosenfeld, 1991). The seminal work, however, is traced to the sociology literature and the research by Goffman (1959). In setting the stage for his discussion of impression management, Goffman makes a point relevant to this study. He observed that "Information about the individual helps to define the situation, enabling others to know in advance what he will expect of them and what they expect of him" (1959, p. 1). Although Goffman focused on face-to-face interactions, in today's media-rich environment it seems reasonable to begin to explore other modes of communicating the information that helps to define the situation.

The situation examined herein involves professors and students. Although the role filled by someone influences the impression given, no study has been found that focuses on the professor/student relationship and construction of the "first impression." Since the professor is in some ways a "leader" in this situation, one might turn to impression management and leadership research for (at least) a beginning point of reference. Generally speaking, more empirical work on leader/subordinate interactions is needed (Leary, 1989). Liden and Mitchell (1989), however, is a notable study. They point out, however, that their work assumes that "leaders typically do not use the same style in dealing with all subordinates, but rather, differentiate among subordinates" (p. 343). Although professors treat students as individuals, the classroom setting creates an environment where, for practical purposes, the students all receive the same treatment. Indeed, to study the treatment effect in this work requires that no differentiation be made.

Another source for related work is Schneider's (1981) research. As Tedeschi observes, "Schneider examines attributional analyses that actors may make prior to self-presentations and their concerns about creating primary and secondary impressions in the eyes of others" (1981, p. xvi). Schneider notes that "There is almost no research literature on the use of appearance cues, possessions, and the like in impression management, although in everyday life they are commonly used." (1981, p. 27). Later, he states, "most of the relevant research on impression management has dealt exclusively with verbal presentations" (p. 28). This study seeks to address these issues by incorporating other cues and deviating from face-to-face interactions.

How impressions are formed and managed is a growing area of study. Leary and Kowalski (1990) reviewed literature on impression management and developed a two-component model of the process. The first component focuses on a person's motivation to manage the impression created. Impression motivation is conceptualized as a function of three factors. First is the goal relevance of the impression one creates. Second is the value of desired outcomes. Third is the discrepancy between the desired image and the current image.

Of particular importance for this study are the first two factors: goal relevance and the value of desired outcomes. Leary and Kowalski posit that people are more motivated to impression-manage when the impressions being made are relevant to the fulfillment of goals such as social and material outcomes, self-esteem maintenance, and identity development. They add that motivation will be stronger when one's behaviors are public. Additionally, when a person is dependent on others for valued outcomes, the impressions he or she makes on them are more important. Also, people who expect future interactions with another person are more likely to try to control how the other perceives them (Kowalski & Leary, 1990).

Most of these characteristics hold in academic environments. All of us probably remember classes or professors which had some type of "reputation." We may have entered some classes with very strong preconceived notions of what to expect, based on impressions formed indirectly from interactions with other students or simply based on the rumors that are associated with some classes. However, many faculty wish to create a classroom atmosphere that is conducive to effective learning (although ideas vary widely on exactly what characteristics such an environment exhibits!). Consciously and subconsciously the actions of professors in a classroom work to construct impressions of both the professor and the learning environment. In many cases, teaching evaluations are considered in the allocation of merit pay raises, making the professor to some degree dependent on the students for part of the reward structure. Professors may teach a student in more than one class, so the potential for future interactions exists. When professors fail to create an environment conducive to learning, the classroom experience becomes tedious, and in some cases even miserable, for everyone involved. Teaching evaluations are lower and both professor and student enter into future interactions with a feeling of apprehension. The impressions taken from such situations can have lasting effects.

The second component of Kowalski and Leary's model focuses on the actual construction of the impression created. They note five factors that comprise this component. First is the self-concept one has. Second is the desired identity image one wants. Third is the constraints inherent in the social role held by the individual and fourth is the values held by the persons forming the impression. Fifth is the current or potential impression one believes others have.

Of particular importance for this study are the first, second, and third factors. Professors may have a self-concept of integrity, but they may also be drawn into utilization of pretense through their social position in the academic setting. Leary and Kowalski note that although most people have internalized an ethic against lying, some conditions exist under which pretense is likely to occur. They cite a study by Buss and Briggs (1984) which indicates that pretense is more likely for individuals employed in highly visible positions, such as teachers.

One might ask, "What type of identity is desirable for someone that wishes to create the impression of an effective teacher?" A survey of students at one university characterized effective teachers as those which are caring, concerned, energetic, enthusiastic, accessible, approachable, and so forth (Gresham, 1993). Also, Kowalski and Leary note that "the effectiveness of people in positions of authority depends, to a degree, on their ability to maintain public images of being competent" (1990, p. 41). Obviously, professors who create such impressions (i.e., identities) will be more likely to be perceived as effective teachers. However, the social role of professor constrains how the professor may behave.

MULTIMEDIA

Multimedia processing combines multiple presentation modes such as text, graphics, photographic still images, animation, sound, and motion video into a single information processing environment. Multimedia technology has the potential to revolutionize information processing in a manner similar to the introduction of the microcomputer in the 1980s. Applications have already been developed in a wide variety of formats including visual databases, public access kiosks, policy and procedure manuals, education and training programs, and system prototyping.

A notable example of multimedia processing is the presentation developed recently by the Atlanta Olympic Committee (Teets, 1991). This system allowed members of the International Olympic Committee, at a meeting in Puerto Rico, to "tour" the Atlanta area. The system contained a combination of video pictures of existing Atlanta facilities and animated examples of proposed facilities. The Atlanta Olympic Committee believes this system played a major role in Atlanta being selected to host the games. The economic impact of hosting the Games will be significant. Similar significant competitive advantages are expected to accrue for enterprises that utilize this technology. For example, Florsheim Shoes have increased sales by 20 percent by using a multimedia information kiosk in its stores (see Table 7.1). These examples illustrate the perceived persuasive nature of multimedia systems (see also Ottinger, 1993).

As with most information system genres, multimedia systems occur on a continuum of complexity. At the "low end" of the continuum are systems that utilize only color and graphic images and allow for primarily linear navigation through the information in the system. For example, a computer-based presentation that has a well-defined beginning and end, utilizes text in color to emphasize major points, and perhaps includes a graph to convey a data-based issue would be an example of a "low-end" multimedia presentation.

At the "high end" of the spectrum are systems that contain animated images and full-motion video and allow users to dictate the navigation path through the system information via interactive responses. For example, a computer-based training system which allows the user to select the topic desired (perhaps via a menu) and then presents the subject matter using animated graphic images or full-motion video would be an example of a "high-end" multimedia presentation.

The design and implementation of multimedia systems is being greatly facilitated by the creation of extremely powerful development environments. "Programming," per se, is no longer a necessary skill, as new metaphors for systems development become commonplace. Low-end multimedia systems can be constructed using development software based on metaphors as simple as an outline. With these tools, the user simply types in an outline and each major point on the outline becomes a new screen in the presentation. Minor points in the outline become bullets on screens. These packages contain a variety of graphics tools that support drawing images to be placed on screens and they also contain interfaces to spreadsheet software so that data may be graphed in a variety of predefined formats. Many of these systems also support the display of scanned images and, in some cases, full motion video.

High-end systems frequently use slightly more complicated metaphors, but are primarily distinguished by their wider array of special features for managing transitions from screen to screen and their ability to support nonlinear traversal through the information in the system. One common metaphor used in the high-end systems is that of actors on a stage. Each item displayed on a screen is considered an actor; the screen is the stage. "Programming" consists of defining the actors (which may be a string of text, a graphic, or a video) and determining how they enter the stage, behave on the stage (e.g., by way of animation), and leave the stage. The logical units of action may be described as "scenes," and facilities typically exist to allow users to control which

Table 7.1
Sample Applications of Multimedia Processing

Task Area	Organization	Application
Interactive retailing	Florsheim Shoes	Customers can view and purchase shoes from store kiosk and have them shipped
Advertising	British Columbia Ministry of Tourism	Interactive system on attractions draws more tourists and visitors
Electronic mail/ video conferencing	Texas A&M University System	Multimedia teleconferencing being used for system-wide meetings
Public information	Tulare County Welfare System	General information for welfare applicants delivered via touch-screen system
Visual database	Fisher-Price Toys	Records product ideas submitted to company to reduce liability
Training	American Airlines	Pilots are trained without use of expensive simulators
Education	Texas Board of Education	Approved videodisc science program as an approved "textbook"
Education	Florida Department of Education	Approved laserdisc technology for use in schools
Persuasion	Atlanta Olympic Committee	Multimedia presentation heralded as key component of city's successful bid for 1996 Olympic Games
Presentation	Stryker vs. Zimmer	Artificial hip prostheses demonstrated to jury via multimedia

"scene" they wish to view next.

Multimedia processing is being forecast as having as significant an impact on people's lives and the ways in which they do everything as was the advent of electronic data processing (Arnett, 1990; Raskin, 1990; DeSimone, 1992). John Scully has stated flatly, "Multimedia will change the world in the 1990s as personal computing did in the 1980s." Bill Gates, CEO of Microsoft, states, "Multimedia will be bigger than everything we do today" (Gasper, 1990). The growing use of multimedia systems in industry, as illustrated in Table 7.1, will help drive further development. Additionally, today's youth are accustomed to receiving information in visual, animated fashion. They will also drive further development of these systems, through their efforts both as developers and consumers.

A STUDY OF PRESENTATION MODE EFFECTS

The study conducted sought to determine the impact of multimedia presentation of information on the formation of first impressions. The design of the study was a pretreatment measurement, treatment, posttreatment measurement design. Approximately 40 students from an introductory course in information systems were randomly divided into two groups. Both groups were surveyed to determine several factors. Of primary importance was their knowledge of this researcher in order to identify their initial impressions of the researcher as a faculty member. Other background information such as gender, expected major (students do not declare a major field until admitted to the "upper division" or junior class), and experience with multimedia-related technologies (e.g., photographic development, music composition, and so forth) was also collected. The researcher moved to a position across the room and well away from the students to reduce any reluctance on the part of the students to answer truthfully. On completion, the subject placed the questionnaire face-down in front of him or her. This instrument is provided in Appendix 7.A.

One group was then given a written excerpt from the researcher's Teaching Portfolio. The Teaching Portfolio is a description of a professor's teaching philosophy and documentation supporting the implementation of that philosophy (Seldin, 1993). The written excerpt was printed in black ink on white paper using a laser printer. Fresh copies were used as necessary so that subjects would not be distracted by stray marks or creases. The other group viewed a multimedia presentation of the same excerpt. The multimedia presentation included sound, animated text (i.e., text that moved), color photographic images, and a short (20 seconds long) video of a student making a comment about one of the researcher's classes. The text of the written excerpt was spoken in the multimedia version. The multimedia presentation was approximately 2.5 minutes long.   (Appendix 7.B contains a description of the multimedia presentation with the text of the written excerpt.) Both groups were instructed to read (or view) the information as many times as necessary until they felt they had absorbed the information content. When the subject indicated he or she was ready, the written material was removed or the subject was moved away from the multimedia presentation and the second questionnaire was administered.

The second survey was administered to determine the impression developed by the subject about the researcher, and to determine any change from the expectation indicated in the first questionnaire. Once again the researcher moved to a position across the room and well away from the students to reduce any reluctance on the part of the students to answer truthfully. On completion, the subjects were instructed to staple the second questionnaire to the first and place them in an envelope that contained other completed questionnaires. This survey is included in Appendix 7.C. On conclusion of this step, subjects were thanked for their participation and reminded of their promise to remain silent about the study until a date well after the conclusion of the study.

DATA ANALYSIS AND DISCUSSION

Table 7.2 shows the demographic data and skill characteristics for the two groups. Values can range from one to nine on these scales, with one representing no experience or less skill, as appropriate. As can be seen, the groups are similar in terms of the number of prior classes taken in the Business Analysis Department, their computer experience and comfort with computers, their reading ability, and their understanding of English.

The bottom section of Table 7.2 shows the characteristics of the groups for skills applicable in the development of multimedia systems. Again, values can range from one to nine, with lower values representative of lesser skill. Both groups have similar skill levels in these areas, giving themselves (on average) somewhat low evaluations of their capabilities in these areas.

Table 7.3 indicates how the two groups perceive faculty in a number of areas. This data gives a preliminary glimpse into the impressions students have about faculty at this university. Again, the scale goes from one to nine. In the first issue, the average student input of approximately 6.5 indicates that faculty are perceived to be somewhere between the anchors "Moderately Caring" (anchor point 5) and "Somewhat Caring" (anchor point 7). Subjects perceive the faculty make classes interesting at a point on the scale somewhere between "Moderately Interesting" (anchor point 5) and "Somewhat Interesting" (anchor point 7). The subjects believe faculty are "Somewhat Interested" (anchor point 7) in the subjects they teach, indicating on average values over seven for this question. And, the subjects find the course work somewhere between the anchor points of "Moderately Applied" (anchor point 5) and "Somewhat Real World" (anchor point 7).

The only issue on which a statistically significant difference can be found concerns the accessibility of faculty. The group receiving the multimedia-based presentation rated faculty more accessible than the group receiving the paper-based presentation. Both groups indicated they had been able to access professors outside of class somewhere between "Moderately Easily" (anchor point 5) and "With Ease" (anchor point 7). There is no obvious reason for this difference.

The lower section of Table 7.3 presents the subjects' ratings of the researcher, given only the knowledge that the researcher was affiliated with the Business Analysis and Research Department. This table indicates how the two groups perceive the primary researcher in a number of areas. This data gives a preliminary glimpse into the impressions students have about the individual, based on the reputation of the department or the subject area. Since only one student had taken a course offered by this department, virtually all of the

Table 7.2
Demographic and Skill Characteristics of Subjects

Demographic Variable	Paper-based Presentation Average	Multimedia-based Presentation Average	t-Test (p value)
Males/Females	15/6	14/8	
Age	20.62	21.24	
Number of Business Analysis Classes	1.15	1.00	
Computer Experience	4.33	4.09	0.353
Computer Comfort	5.57	5.55	0.481
Reading Ability	7.29	7.32	0.477
English Understanding Skills	7.62	8.18	0.129
Photography	3.29	3.36	0.437
Graphic Arts	2.62	3.23	0.158
Technical Editing	1.90	2.36	0.159
Sound Production	2.10	2.41	0.322
Video Production	1.86	2.09	0.279
Desk-top Publishing	1.86	2.14	0.188

subjects are basing their evaluation on conjecture. Again, the scale goes from one to nine.

In the first issue, the average student input of approximately 6.5 indicates that the researcher is perceived to be somewhere between the anchors

Table 7.3
Pre-Treatment Perceptions of Subjects

Issue	Paper-Based Presentation Average	Multimedia-Based Presentation Average	t-Test (p-value)
Professors are caring	6.52	6.41	0.388
Professors make interesting classes	5.86	7.41	0.233
Professors are interested in the subject	7.10	6.62	0.242
Professors are accessible	5.33	6.05	0.010 *
Faculty teach theoretical subjects	5.86	4.24	0.293
Faculty take student evaluations seriously	5.00	7.23	0.054
I fill out students evaluations seriously	7.00	6.26	0.273
Dr. Paradice is caring	6.71	6.25	0.199
Dr. Paradice makes classes interesting	6.19	7.52	0.422
Dr. Paradice is interested in the subject	7.86	6.38	0.183
Dr. Paradice teaches theoretical concepts	6.76	6.86	0.113

*   significant at p = .01

"Moderately Caring" (anchor point 5) and "Somewhat Caring" (anchor point 7). Subjects perceive the researcher makes classes interesting at a point on the scale somewhere between "Moderately Interesting" (anchor point 5) and "Somewhat Interesting" (anchor point 7). The subjects also believe the researcher is "Somewhat Interested" (anchor point 7) in the subjects he teaches, indicating on average values over seven for this question. The researcher is rated as accessible "Moderately Easily" to "With Ease." And, the subjects expect the course work to be somewhere between the anchor points of "Moderately Applied" (anchor point 5) and "Somewhat Real World" (anchor point 7). These responses reflect no significant deviation between the expectations for this researcher and the general faculty. There is no significant difference between the responses for the two treatment groups.

The top section of Table 7.4 presents the differences in the impressions between the faculty in general and the primary researcher for subjects receiving the paper-based information. The primary researcher is perceived to be more interested in the subjects he teaches and to teach more applied concepts in class. These differences could be attributable simply to having executed the study. First, the subjects were aware that Dr. Paradice was involved in the study. Also, executing the study in the lab would likely lead to a perception of an "applied" orientation. Otherwise, the primary researcher was considered very similar to faculty in general.

The lower section of Table 7.4 presents the differences in the impressions between the faculty in general and the primary researcher for subjects receiving the multimedia-based information. For this group, the primary researcher is perceived to be different only on the issue of teaching more applied concepts.

Table 7.5 contains the post treatment measurements of the impressions of the primary researcher for both treatment groups. Both groups showed shifts in the measurements relative to the pre-treatment questionnaire. However, the only significant difference between the treatments is for the issue of how theoretical or applied a class taught by the researcher would be. The group receiving the multimedia-based presentation perceived classes taught by the primary researcher would be more applied than subjects receiving the paper-based presentation.

The top section of Table 7.6 provides the first indication that receiving the information presented to the subjects affected their impressions. A statistically significant difference exists in the pre treatment versus post treatment ratings on four of the five issues for the group receiving the paper-based information. The data indicates the subjects in this group perceived the primary researcher to be more caring, make classes more interesting, be more interested in the subjects taught, and be more accessible, after reading the teaching philosophy. Of particular interest is the issue of accessibility, because no mention of accessibility is made in the teaching philosophy. The change on this issue must be due to some type of "halo effect" relative to the other issues.

The lower section of Table 7.6 presents the pre-treatment/post-treatment ratings for the group receiving the multimedia-based information. It shows some similar and some different results. Again, the post treatment ratings reflect a perception that the primary researcher is more caring, makes classes more interesting, and is more accessible. Unlike the paper-based treatment, the multimedia-based presentation also shows a significant difference in the perception of how applied the primary researcher's classes are, with a statistically significant shift toward the applied end of the scale.

Table 7.4
Pre-Treatment Differences in Impressions —
General Faculty Versus Primary Researcher

	Issues	General Faculty	Primary Researcher	t-Test (p-value)
Paper-Based Treatment	Faculty is caring	6.52	6.71	0.321
	Faculty makes classes interesting	5.86	6.19	0.230
	Faculty is interested in the subject	7.10	7.86	0.019 *
	Faculty is accessible	5.33	5.86	0.181
	Faculty teaches theoretical concepts	5.86	6.76	0.002**
Multimedia Treatment	Faculty is caring	6.41	6.26	0.346
	Faculty makes classes interesting	6.18	6.25	0.435
	Faculty is interested in the subject	7.14	7.52	0.403
	Faculty is accessible	6.62	6.38	0.278
	Faculty teaches theoretical concepts	6.05	6.86	0.016

*   significant at $p < .05$
**   significant at $p < .01$

However, the multimedia-based presentation also shows a decrease in perceived interest of the primary researcher toward interest in the subject. Since the information presented covers topics outside of the topic of teaching (e.g., reading industry publications and working in the Center for the Management of Information Systems), perhaps the subjects felt this implied a lack of interest in teaching functions, or that the researcher was simply more interested in these other activities. Since the same information (content) was presented in both treatments, the multimedia-based mode of presentation appears to have been the critical factor.

In summary, having the subjects exposed to the teaching philosophy of the primary researcher, whom they did not know, affected their impressions of him. Significant differences exist in the pre treatment versus post treatment measurements on almost all issues. The majority of the directions of the shifts were also consistent, with only one measurement moving in a different direction across the two treatment types. The mode of presentation appears to have no appreciable affect.

Table 7.5
Post-Treatment Impressions of the Primary Researcher

Issues	Paper-Based Presentation	Multimedia-Based Presentation	t-Test (p-value)
Dr. Paradice is caring	8.05	7.82	0.198
Dr. Paradice makes classes interesting	7.19	7.55	0.155
Dr. Paradice is interested in the subject	8.43	6.08	0.149
Dr. Paradice is accessible	6.71	7.05	0.213
Dr. Paradice teaches theoretical concepts	6.33	7.82	0.014 *

*   significant at $p < .05$

Table 7.6
Pre-Treatment/Post-Treatment Differences
in Impressions of Primary Researcher

	Issues	Pre-Treatment Average	Post-Treatment Average	t-Test (p-value)
Paper-Based Treatment	Dr. Paradice is caring	6.71	8.05	0.0000 **
	Dr. Paradice makes classes interesting	6.19	7.19	0.0002 **
	Dr. Paradice is interested in the subject	7.86	8.43	0.0073 **
	Dr. Paradice is accessible	5.86	6.71	0.0014 **
	Dr. Paradice teaches theoretical concepts	6.67	6.33	0.2387
Multimedia Treatment	Dr. Paradice is caring	6.26	7.82	0.0000 **
	Dr. Paradice makes classes interesting	6.25	7.55	0.0002 **
	Dr. Paradice is interested in the subject	7.52	6.08	0.0009 **
	Dr. Paradice is accessible	6.38	7.05	0.0038 **
	Dr. Paradice teaches theoretical concepts	6.86	7.82	0.0143 *

*   significant at $p < .05$
**   significant at $p < .01$

LIMITATIONS OF THE STUDY

Studies such as this can always be improved. This study employed simple statistical tests in an exploratory fashion. Larger sample sizes and more formal hypothesis tests should be employed, now that some basis for suggesting a hypothesis has been formed.

Although the study utilized state-of-the-art desk-top equipment, the technology is evolving so rapidly in this area that the experimental treatment is already likely to be dated by the time of this publication. Today's students are emersed in high-quality, technology-based images throughout much of the day. It is possible that some of the students that participated in the study viewed the multimedia presentation as somewhat crude, since it was constructed at a standard that was a little below "television quality." Today's hardware allows the study to be replicated with television-quality production as the standard.

Additionally, the study was conducted in a laboratory setting. This setting may have distracted those that received the paper-based treatment; they may have felt somehow disappointed that they were not selected to view the multimedia presentation. Although all participants were given the opportunity to view the multimedia presentation after the study, this option would not control for emotions that occurred during the study.

Finally, the primary researcher was also the subject of the treatments. Although steps were taken to minimize the interaction between the subjects and the researcher, some contamination of the results may have occurred due to this dual role played by the researcher. A better approach would have employed a neutral figure to conduct the study, or would have camouflaged the identity of the researcher in some manner.

CONCLUSIONS AND FUTURE WORK

This preliminary study gives some indication that multimedia presentations have no advantage over paper-based presentations in affecting the impressions of subjects with no prior knowledge of a person. The impressions formed by the subjects appear to be governed primarily by their role expectations of the researcher, that is, that he is a professor. When presented with information in two very different formats, the subjects appear to have processed the information in very similar manners, with one exception. Whether this exception is due to the subject matter or the mode of presentation requires further study.

The study has several characteristics worthy of further exploration. First, the results seem to indicate that role expectations were the primary impetus behind the formation of the subjects in the study. One may reasonably ask whether the influence of such role expectations extend to impressions of other persons, such as police, doctors, politicians, and so on. If so, one may question the usefulness of some advertisements from an impression-making orientation.

However, the efficacy of advertisements for purposes of persuasion would be a different area of study.

Second, the multimedia presentation was approximately 2.5 minutes in duration. The paper-based information was contained in one-half page of single-spaced text. Would the results of this study hold for longer or shorter presentations of information? A study of this type would help determine whether a payoff point occurs in terms of how to invest resources to construct impressions. Corporations desiring to manipulate impressions might be wise to invest in a much less expensive paper-based approach rather than a very expensive multimedia campaign.

Third, the study was conducted in a laboratory environment by someone who was the target of the impression formation. A better approach would have the study conducted by a third party, or have the target of the study be a fictitious person. This change would help to avoid possible contamination of the results due to the presence of the researcher during the study. Although steps were taken to avoid such contamination, it may have occurred.

Finally, as multimedia-based presentations become more commonplace, will the results of a study like this change? On the one hand, the mode of presentation appears to have no effect. However, familiarity may breed a more critical examination by subjects. Or paper-based sources of information may become somewhat dated. Multimedia presentations are growing in number and frequency. Their impact will require continued examination.

APPENDIX 7.A
Pre-Treatment Survey

Please answer the following questions. Note that scales may differ from question to question, so be sure to read the possible responses carefully.

Please indicate your gender: Male _____ Female _____

Your age: _____ Your (intended) major: _____

Please indicate how many BANA courses you
have taken (including courses being taken now): _____

My experience with computers is

1	2	3	4	5	6	7	8	9
Very Little		Some		Moderate		Good		Very Strong

When using computers, I feel

1	2	3	4	5	6	7	8	9
Very Uncomfortable		Some Discomfort		Moderate Comfort		Good		Very Comfortable

My reading ability is

1	2	3	4	5	6	7	8	9
Very Weak		A little Weak		Moderate		Good		Very Strong

My understanding of English is

1	2	3	4	5	6	7	8	9
Very Weak		A little Weak		Moderate		Good		Very Strong

My experience in photography is

1	2	3	4	5	6	7	8	9
None		Some		Hobby		A lot	Professional	

My experience in the graphic arts is

1	2	3	4	5	6	7	8	9
None		Some		Hobby		A lot		Professional

My experience in page layout or technical editing is

1	2	3	4	5	6	7	8	9
None		Some		Hobby		A lot		Professional

My experience in sound or music production is

1	2	3	4	5	6	7	8	9
None		Some		Hobby		A lot		Professional

My experience in video production is

1	2	3	4	5	6	7	8	9
None		Some		Hobby		A lot		Professional

My experience in desk top publishing is

1	2	3	4	5	6	7	8	9
None		Some		Hobby		A lot		Professional

Generally speaking, my professors have been _____ about students.

1	2	3	4	5	6	7	8	9
Very Uncaring		Somewhat Uncaring		Moderately Caring		Somewhat Caring		Very Caring

Generally speaking, my professors have made classes

1	2	3	4	5	6	7	8	9
Very Boring		Somewhat Dull		Moderately Interesting		Somewhat Interesting		Very Interesting

Generally speaking, my professors have been _____ by the subjects they teach.

1	2	3	4	5	6	7	8	9
Very Bored		Somewhat Bored		Moderately Interested		Somewhat Interested		Very Interested

Generally speaking, I have been able to access my professors outside of class

1	2	3	4	5	6	7	8	9
Hardly		With Some		Moderately		With		Very
Ever		Difficulty		Easily		Ease		Easily

Generally speaking, my professors have made subjects

1	2	3	4	5	6	7	8	9
Very		Somewhat		Moderately		Somewhat		Very
Theoretical		Theoretical		Applied		Real-world		Real-world

I think student evaluations are _____ by faculty

1	2	3	4	5	6	7	8	9
Largely		Glanced		Considered		Considered		Taken
Ignored		At		Some		Often		Seriously

I fill out student evaluations

1	2	3	4	5	6	7	8	9
With No		With Some		With		Thoughtfully		Very
Concern		Effort		Moderate Effort				Thoughtfully

Since Dr. Paradice is a BANA professor, I expect he is _____ about students.

1	2	3	4	5	6	7	8	9
Very		Somewhat		Moderately		Somewhat		Very
Uncaring		Uncaring		Caring		Caring		Caring

Since Dr. Paradice is a BANA professor, I expect he makes classes

1	2	3	4	5	6	7	8	9
Very		Somewhat		Moderately		Somewhat		Very
Boring		Dull		Interesting		Interesting		Interesting

Since Dr. Paradice is a BANA professor, I expect he is ____ by the subjects he teaches.

1	2	3	4	5	6	7	8	9
Very		Somewhat		Moderately		Somewhat		Very
Bored		Bored		Interested		Interested		Interested

Since Dr. Paradice is a BANA professor, I expect he is accessible

1	2	3	4	5	6	7	8	9
Hardly Ever		With Some Difficulty		Moderately Easily		With Ease		Very Easily

Since Dr. Paradice is a BANA professor, I expect he makes subjects

1	2	3	4	5	6	7	8	9
Very Theoretical		Somewhat Theoretical		Moderately Applied		Somewhat Real-world		Very Real-world

APPENDIX 7.B
Multimedia Presentation Script

In the script that follows, the left column contains all of the text provided in the written excerpt provided to subjects. The right column describes what was occurring in the multimedia presentation as the information in the left column was being presented.

Text/Script	Description
Teaching Philosophy of Dr. David Paradice, Associate Professor Department of Business Analysis & Research College of Business & Graduate School of Business Texas A&M University	This text displayed on screen in maroon for 15 seconds with background music. Background is grey with muted, pastel abstract patterns.
	Blue sky background with white clouds in lower right corner displayed. Also, heading of "Teaching Philosophy" in dark blue displayed in upper left corner. Music plays in background.
My philosophy of teaching varies somewhat according to the level of the class.	This sentence displayed on screen in blue across top of screen.
Each level of student typically brings different skill sets to the class. Thus, my teaching goals are tailored to these differences. However, at all levels I strive to bring students to a point where they are more than adequately prepared to complete the types of tasks I believe they will face in their careers.	Two pictures of Dr. Paradice lecturing fade in on screen. Pictures fade out, then single picture of Dr. Paradice appears from center out in middle of screen.

Text/Script	Description
I want them to be able to provide better solutions than their employer expects them to provide.	This sentence displayed on screen in blue below picture.
I want them to be confident of their ability to face new problems. This confidence creates leaders. In all cases, I treat students as adults and hold them responsible for their decisions.	Picture and text on screen fade out as spoken part ends.
The information systems field confronts teachers with two significant decision situations.	This sentence displayed on screen in blue at top of screen.
First, teachers must decide whether they will teach general concepts or specific tools.	This idea displayed on screen in red italics and as a question: "Should one teach concepts or tools?"
Second, they must decide how they will stay "up-to-date" with the technology of the field.	This idea displayed on screen in red italics and as a question: "How does one stay current in the field?"
I believe in teaching concepts, not tools.	Prior statement and two questions fade from screen. This sentence displayed on screen in blue.
Certainly, specific tools have a role in the classroom and I use them extensively. However, the tools are used to illustrate concepts. I believe the technology changes too quickly to take any other approach. Students must be able to pick up any manual for any specific tool, spend a few days with it, then be productive. This goal can only be achieved through a thorough grounding of the fundamental concepts of the field.	Picture of Dr. Paradice in front of class appears in a mosaic pattern. A picture of students appears in a bard door opening pattern. The picture of Dr. Paradice fades out, then a second picture of students appears in a barn door opening pattern. The two pictures of students fade out as spoken parts end.

Text/Script	Description
To stay current with industry, I once relied solely on attending the presentations made by corporations that recruit our students. Now, I supplement my attendance at these presentations by maintaining an active involvement in the Center for the Management of Information Systems.	"Data Processing Management Association" fades in on screen in navy blue (Chicago font). "Center for the Management of Information Systems" fades in on screen in red. DPMA and CMIS logos fade from screen.
I also subscribe to trade periodicals.	Scanned image of cover of *ComputerWorld* (a weekly trade periodical fades in on screen. Scanned image of cover of *MacWorld* (a monthly trade periodical) fades in on screen. Both logos fade out as music fades out.
A student once said about my class, "Dr. Paradice's database class really prepared me for what I have found in my job. His use of examples from his work experience has been invaluable to me."	Video of female student making comments displayed on screen. Video, blue sky, clouds, and "Teaching Philosophy" title fade from screen. Copyright notice for music appears for approximately 2 seconds then fades out. Background for opening screen displays with a button to restart the presentation appearing in the lower right corner.

APPENDIX 7.C
Post-Treatment Survey

Please answer the following questions.   Note that scales may differ from question to question, so be sure to read the possible responses carefully.

I think Dr. Paradice is _____ about students.

1	2	3	4	5	6	7	8	9
Very Uncaring		Somewhat Uncaring		Moderately Caring		Somewhat Caring		Very Caring

I think Dr. Paradice makes classes

1	2	3	4	5	6	7	8	9
Very Boring		Somewhat Dull		Moderately Interesting		Somewhat Interesting		Very Interesting

I think Dr. Paradice is ____ by the subjects he teaches.

1	2	3	4	5	6	7	8	9
Very Bored		Somewhat Bored		Moderately Interested		Somewhat Interested		Very Interested

I think Dr. Paradice is accessible

1	2	3	4	5	6	7	8	9
Hardly Ever		With Some Difficulty		Moderately Easily		With Ease		Very Easily

I think Dr. Paradice makes subjects

1	2	3	4	5	6	7	8	9
Very Theoretical		Somewhat Theoretical		Moderately Applied		Somewhat Real-world		Very Real-world

Indicate whether the following statements are true or false, based on the information you have just been presented.

T   F   Dr. Paradice tries to build confidence of students.

T   F   Dr. Paradice tells jokes in class to make classes enjoyable.

T   F   Dr. Paradice trains students to complete tasks they will face in their careers.

T   F   Dr. Paradice emphasizes specific tools over general concepts.

T   F   Dr. Paradice no longer attends meetings by corporations that recruit students.

T   F   Dr. Paradice subscribes to trade periodicals.

Circle the appropriate response:

Have you ever had a class from Dr. Paradice?   Yes   No

Have you ever heard about Dr. Paradice from friends?   Yes   No

8

IMPRESSION MANAGEMENT AND COMPUTER SURVEYS IN ORGANIZATIONS

Paul Rosenfeld
Stephanie Booth-Kewley

Researchers within the organizational sciences have been devoting increased attention to a theoretical framework that focuses on the concerns of individuals about making impressions on others. *Impression management theory* refers to the many ways by which individuals attempt to control the impressions others have of them: their behavior; motivations; morality; and personal attributes such as dependability, intelligence, and future potential (Giacalone & Rosenfeld, 1989, 1991; Rosenfeld, Giacalone, & Riordan, 1994). The impression management perspective assumes that a basic motive, both inside and outside of organizations, is to be viewed by others in a favorable manner and avoid being seen negatively. *Organizational impression management theory* (Giacalone & Rosenfeld, 1989, 1991; Rosenfeld, Giacalone, & Riordan, 1994) interprets much of organizational behavior as analogous to advertising campaigns on behalf of commercial products. Individuals and organizations act in a manner akin to publicity agents conducting public relations campaigns on their own behalf, highlighting strengths and virtues while minimizing deficiencies.

Impression management has increasingly become a recognized part of organizational behavior research. This perspective has been applied to areas such as employment interviews, performance evaluation, assessment centers, business ethics, communication, feedback, leadership, and diversity issues (Giacalone & Rosenfeld, 1989, 1991).

One recent organizational application of impression management theory has been to the area of computer surveys. A number of studies have employed an impression management framework to look at the implications of utilizing computers to administer organizational surveys (e.g., Booth-Kewley, Edwards, & Rosenfeld, 1992; Lautenschlager & Flaherty, 1990; Martin & Nagao, 1989;

Rosenfeld et al., 1991). These studies have addressed an issue that has both important theoretical and practical implications: To what degree are responses on computer surveys similar to or different than those obtained on standard paper surveys?

As computers have become more prevalent in U.S. society, computer administration of organizational surveys has gained popularity (Booth-Kewley, Rosenfeld, & Edwards, 1993; Dunnington, 1993). Although computer administration of surveys offers advantages compared to paper administration (e.g., the elimination of data transcription errors), it is only relatively recently that researchers have investigated the psychometric and statistical comparability of responses from computer- versus paper-administered surveys in organizational settings (e.g., Booth-Kewley, Edwards, & Rosenfeld, 1992; Lautenschlager & Flaherty, 1990)

Over the past years, some published studies (see Booth-Kewley et al., 1993, for a review) have reported that computer survey responses are more candid, less biased, and less influenced by social desirability or impression management motives than responses given on paper surveys. These studies have, however, been difficult to replicate. Comparisons between paper-and-pencil and computer surveys have frequently yielded virtually identical responses and internal validities, although computer respondents consistently find the survey more enjoyable than their paper-and-pencil counterparts (Rosenfeld, Doherty, & Carroll, 1987; Rosenfeld et al., 1989, 1991).

In the present chapter, we take a focused look at studies that address the issue of impression management in the form of socially desirable responding on organizational computer surveys. We first review past research that has painted a picture of inconsistency: Some studies have found that computer surveys are associated with reduced levels of socially desirable responding, whereas others have found an increase in socially desirable responding. Next, the results of our own Navy computer survey research program are described. Finally, we offer an analysis of past inconsistencies by proposing a "Big Brother Syndrome" integration of recent findings. This Big Brother Syndrome analysis attempts to clarify the impact of heightened monitoring of computer responding on surveys.

COMPUTER VERSUS PAPER SURVEYS

As computers have become more prevalent in organizational settings, they have become a popular means of administering organizational surveys. According to Booth-Kewley et al. (1993), this increased popularity is because administering a computer rather than paper survey has a number of advantages. Among these are: (1) errors resulting from entering data manually are eliminated by automated data entry; (2) missing responses are eliminated; (3) there are no out-of-range responses; and (4) complex item branching, transparent to the respondent, can be used. Of these, the fact that computer surveys allow data entry to take place as the survey is being completed is probably the most advantageous for organizational applications. Automatic data entry saves time and money and leads to more accurate data, because one of the stages at which errors are often introduced into a database is skipped.

Computer administration of surveys has some drawbacks as well (Booth-Kewley et al., 1993). There is the expense involved in purchasing the necessary computer hardware and software. Respondents who are "computer-anxious" may feel less comfortable answering questionnaires on computers. Furthermore, computers are much less portable than paper, and are subject to equipment failure and software problems that do not occur with paper.

A critical issue that remains unresolved in the use of computer surveys in organizations concerns the quality of data they obtain as compared to paper responses. Is data gathered using a computer of similar or of higher quality than data gathered using paper and pencil? In particular, what impact do computer surveys have on the tendency of survey respondents to engage in impression management in the form of socially desirable responding? We review research that has compared responses on computer and paper surveys and has considered the computer's purported impact of socially desirable responding.

COMPARING COMPUTER AND PAPER SURVEY RESPONSES: THE CENSUS PROJECT

Although aptitude tests, personality scales, and clinical-diagnostic instruments have been administered on computers since the early 1970s (Booth-Kewley et al., 1993), the use of computers to administer organizational scales and surveys is a later development. An extensive effort to develop a system where respondents could complete organizational surveys on computers was conducted by researchers at the Navy Personnel Research and Development Center (NPRDC) in San Diego during the mid- and late 1980s. As the Navy's lead organization for manpower and personnel research, NPRDC is often required to conduct surveys for Navy policy-makers. The logistic and technical requirements of large-scale paper surveys typically requires a year or more from start to finish. Therefore, the findings are often outdated by the time they are obtained (Tyburski, 1992).

Consequently, in 1983, the Navy's Office of Civilian Personnel Management directed NPRDC to conduct a feasibility study of a computer-based survey system that would automate and speed the process of survey administration. This resulted in the development of several prototypes of the Computerized Executive Networking Survey System (CENSUS) during the mid- and late 1980s. In its original form (CENSUS I), individuals completed surveys on a computer terminal linked to an industry-standard PC/XT or PC/AT host computer. This configuration allowed up to eight users to complete the survey simultaneously, either on-site or at remote locations using commercial phone connections.

As microcomputers became more sophisticated, the original CENSUS prototype was modified. CENSUS II used the multiuser XENIX operating system; this allowed up to 16 users to complete a survey simultaneously, either at direct or remote locations.

Although the multiuser capability of the CENSUS prototypes proved to be an advantage for surveys of large organizations, the system's requirement that respondents be linked to the host computer during administration limited its flexibility and usefulness. This resulted in the development of the Microcomputer-Based Assessment Surveys and Questionnaires (MASQ) system, which mimicked the features of the CENSUS system but on single floppy diskettes capable of running on any industry-standard or compatible personal computer. Using MASQ, a computer survey could be developed, run, stored, and analyzed without requiring a networked system or a complex operating system. MASQ allowed organizational surveys to be mailed out to respondents on diskettes; respondents completed them on their own personal computers and returned them to NPRDC for analysis. An additional version, suitable for portable machines (P-MASQ), allowed surveys to be administered on computers in field settings. This system enabled organizational surveys to be administered at respondents' work sites while avoiding the disruption of work caused by the requirement to report to a central location. (For more detailed descriptions of the CENSUS systems see Doherty & Thomas, 1986; Rosenfeld, Doherty, & Carroll, 1987; Rosenfeld, Doherty, Vicino, Kantor, & Greaves, 1989.)

When the CENSUS project first began, there were no widely available software products that could meet all the requirements necessary to conduct Navy surveys. More recently, however, commercial survey software such as Ci3 from Sawtooth Software, has become readily available (Dunnington, 1993). Subsequently, the most recent versions of CENSUS have adapted commercial survey software to Navy needs.

The development of the CENSUS prototypes at NPRDC set the stage for a number of research studies and field tests for the comparison of computer and paper administration of organizational surveys and standardized instruments. Doherty and Thomas (1986) administered a 60-item attitude survey regarding proposed changes to the civil service retirement system to over 300 civilian Navy employees. Comparisons between Census I and the paper survey revealed similar responses on both modes of administration, however, computer administration had fewer data entry errors than paper administration. Three percent of the total responses on the paper and pencil survey were in error (e.g., incorrect branching, multiple responses), whereas none of these errors occurred when CENSUS I was used.

When CENSUS II was developed, it became of interest to determine if responses differed on the two computer systems (CENSUS I versus CENSUS II) or if responses differed on computer versus paper administration modes.

Rosenfeld, Doherty, Carroll, Kantor, and Thomas (1986) administered an organizational survey that contained measures of job satisfaction to employees at a naval aircraft repair facility. Respondents completed the survey using either CENSUS I, CENSUS II, or paper and pencil. Results indicated that the attitudinal and job satisfaction scores were nearly identical on both CENSUS systems and the paper survey.

This pattern of findings was replicated and extended by Rosenfeld et al. (1989). The CENSUS project team had been requested by the Commanding Officer of a Navy facility that maintains and repairs fighter planes to design a survey assessing decision making and communication. Two-hundred ninety-six supervisors (e.g., shop foreman, department and division directors) were randomly assigned to one of four groups: CENSUS II, MASQ, P-MASQ, and paper. Once again, there were no differences between the computer and paper groups or between the three different computer groups. Although the computer and paper groups had equivalent decision-making and communication responses, all three computer groups found the survey more enjoyable than those who completed the survey on paper.

SOCIAL DESIRABILITY, IMPRESSION MANAGEMENT, AND COMPUTER SURVEYS

Although the CENSUS-based studies consistently found that computer and paper surveys yielded equivalent results, there were a number of claims by others researchers that computer surveys reduced the tendency of respondents to give socially desirable responses. For example, Kiesler and Sproull (1986) examined responses to surveys given via electronic-mail (E-Mail) or on paper to college students and university employees. The survey contained five items from the Marlowe-Crowne social desirability scale (Crowne & Marlowe, 1960), as well as items assessing health attitudes and computer use. Respondents completed the survey anonymously. No differences were found on attitudes towards health or computer use, but less socially desirable responding (as reflected on the Marlowe-Crowne items) was found in the computer group. This was interpreted as meaning that E-Mail respondents were more candid and less inhibited than those completing the paper survey. Sproull (1986) compared responses to a questionnaire administered via the same two administration modes. The questionnaire assessed E-Mail attitudes and behaviors, personal history, and how respondents would choose to perform a set of hypothetical tasks. Although no differences were obtained for the average responses, computer respondents were more likely to choose extreme responses on the set of questions asking how respondents would complete a set of hypothetical tasks. The author interpreted this finding as evidence of a greater willingness to respond candidly on computers. In an anecdotal report, Feinstein (1986) observed that people responding to marketing surveys on computers used harsher language in describing their supervisors than did individuals who completed an equivalent paper questionnaire.

More recently, Martin and Nagao (1989) had business undergraduates complete a simulated job-interview survey using a computer, paper, or face-to-face interview. The paper condition elicited more socially desirable responding on the Marlowe-Crowne scale than the computer condition. Respondents also showed less overreporting of scholastic aptitude (SAT) scores (but not grade point averages) in the computer than in the paper condition. The authors concluded that the computer mode of administration may reduce social desirability bias relative to the paper mode. In this study, respondents may have been more candid on the computer because they were under the impression that their computer responses could readily be checked and verified against other computer data bases.

These findings led NPRDC researchers to directly test the issue of whether respondents are more candid on computer surveys than on paper. In particular, we and our NPRDC colleagues sought to determine if specific conditions (e.g., anonymity) or subgroups of people (e.g., high self-monitors) would show greater candor (i.e., less social desirability) on the computer than on paper.

Vicino (1989) performed a study using college undergraduates in which responses to a social desirability inventory (the Marlowe-Crowne scale) given in computer and paper conditions were compared. He found no significant differences between the two conditions. Kantor (1991) administered the Job Descriptive Index (JDI), a widely used job satisfaction measure, to a sample of Navy civilian employees in either computer or paper conditions. He found that administration mode had no effect on mean responses on any of the five JDI scales or on scale reliabilities. Because the JDI assessed satisfaction with work, pay, supervision, promotion, and coworkers—dimensions that could be affected by respondent impression management motives to please significant audiences by indicating higher job satisfaction—it was assumed that equivalence in mean scores on the JDI paper and computer conditions indicated that responses were equally candid in both administration conditions. In addition, there was no difference in the respondents' perceptions of whether either method of survey administration elicited more truthful responses.

Rosenfeld et al. (1991) proposed an *individual differences* impression management approach in an attempt to clarify the social desirability—computer survey issue. It was reasoned that although respondents in general may not be more candid on the computer, there may be a subgroup of individuals particularly sensitive to social cues for impression management who might be more likely to modify their responses on the computer. It was hypothesized that individuals who are low self-monitors (i.e., exhibit behaviors that are generally consistent across situations; see Snyder, 1974) would tend to respond similarly across paper and computer modes of administration. Individuals who are high self-monitors (i.e., modify their behaviors depending on the situation) might be expected to answer more or less candidly on the computer (depending on the type of information requested and the manner in which it was requested) than on paper. Some support for this hypothesis had previously been obtained through a post hoc analysis of a computer versus paper study of job satisfaction among civilian employees at a naval shipyard described above (Rosenfeld et al., 1986). Although that study found no overall differences between computer and paper respondents in levels of job satisfaction, it did find computer-paper differences based on responses to an item that assessed how important people thought it was that they do as others thought they should. Individuals who endorsed this item had higher job satisfaction scores on paper than on the computer. Individuals who did not endorse this item responded similarly on job satisfaction in computer and paper conditions.

Rosenfeld et al. (1991) provided a more systematic test of this *individual differences* approach in a study using employed business students. Students completed a survey that contained the JDI and the self-monitoring scale either on a computer or on paper. As in previous studies, there were no differences in job satisfaction between computer and paper surveys. When respondents were divided into high and low self-monitors and their paper and computer survey responses contrasted, a self-monitoring by administration interaction for a global job satisfaction measure was obtained. The job satisfaction scores of high self-monitors were lower on computer than on paper. However, for low self-monitors, the opposite occurred: They had higher job satisfaction scores on computer than paper surveys. If, as Rosenfeld et al. (1991) hypothesized, it is socially desirable to indicate higher levels of job satisfaction, then the results suggest that the responses of high self-monitors are less socially desirable on computer than paper, while the responses of low self-monitors are more socially desirable on computer than paper. These findings for self-monitors are contrary, however, to the results of Vicino (1989) who found that high and low self-monitors *did not* respond differently on computer and paper instruments which included the Marlowe-Crowne scale. Thus, the idea that high and low self-monitors would show different levels of socially desirable responding on computer versus paper instruments has not received uneqivocal support.

DO COMPUTER SURVEYS RESULT IN
MORE SOCIALLY DESIRABLE RESPONSES?

Although the NPRDC studies typically found that computer surveys produced responses equivalent to paper surveys, they failed to support the claims that computer surveys reduce social desirability bias. However, the findings of studies that claimed computers reduce socially desirable responses or produce equivalent responses to paper were challenged in a study by Lautenschlager & Flaherty (1990). They compared responses of undergraduates on the impression management (IM[1]) and self-deception/self-deceptive enhancement (SD/SDE) scales of the Balanced Inventory of Desirable Responding (BIDR) (see Paulhus, 1991, for a review) completed in either computer or paper conditions. Contrary to previous findings, Lautenschlager & Flaherty (1990) found that respondents in the computer condition gave more socially desirable responses than their counterparts in the paper-and-pencil condition. Also, respondents who were identified had significantly higher scores on both the IM and SD/SDE scales than students in the anonymous condition. These results led the authors to conclude that "the administration of ... attitude questionnaires in organizational research may be adversely affected when converted from paper-and-pencil format. Increases due to impression management on such diagnostic measures may produce inaccurate and potentially misleading results" (Lautenschlager & Flaherty, 1990, p. 314).

Given that the findings of Lautenschlager and Flaherty (1990) contradicted the general literature and the results of our own work, Booth-Kewley et al. (1992) attempted to replicate Lautenschlager and Flaherty's method in a noncollege environment. Male Navy recruits completed surveys in either a computer or paper-and-pencil condition, and their responses were either identified or anonymous. In addition, respondents in the computer condition were split into two groups: half completed the questionnaire in a lock-step fashion that did not allow them to "backtrack"; the other half could backtrack within the questionnaire, meaning that they could review and change previous responses. These two different computer conditions were included because Lautenschlager and Flaherty had suggested that having computer respondents complete the questionnaire in a lock-step fashion may have caused them to engage in more impression management due to a need to maintain consistency.

The results of the Booth-Kewley et al. (1992) study supported Lautenschlager and Flaherty's (1990) finding that identified respondents had higher IM and SDE scores than anonymous respondents. Contrary to their findings, however, whether responses were made on the computer or on paper had no effect on either IM or SDE scores. As in the previous NPRDC-based studies, there were no significant differences between responses on the computer and paper surveys. In addition, whether respondents could backtrack or not on the computer had no effect on scores. Booth-Kewley et al. (1992) concluded that computer versus paper administration does not appear to affect mean scale scores, reliabilities, or socially desirable responding in any consistent way. They argued that, where financial and logistical considerations allow, organizations are justified in using computer-based surveys instead of paper-and-pencil administration.

RESOLVING PAST INCONSISTENCIES:
THE BIG BROTHER SYNDROME

Lautenschlager and Flaherty's (1990) findings that undergraduates who respondend to a computer survey had *higher* scores on an impression management/social desirability measure than did their counterparts who used a paper survey conflicts with Martin and Nagao's (1989) finding that individuals who responded on a computer gave *less* socially desirable answers and were less likely to over report their SAT scores than those answering in paper-and-pencil format. Although Booth-Kewley et al.'s (1992) study supports the continued use of computer surveys in military and civilian organizations, it did not address the issue of why these and other previous comparisons of computer and paper surveys have obtained conflicting results.

Two variables that may account for the different results obtained in past studies are the nature of the *social situation* created in the computer condition and the perceived *verifiability* of the survey information that is requested. Kiesler and Sproull (e.g., Kiesler & Sproull, 1986; Sproull & Kiesler, 1991) have previously suggested that computer surveys yield more candid responses than paper surveys because computers create an *impersonal social situation* where individuals are less concerned about how they appear to others. They contend that "when cues about social context are absent or weak, people ignore their social situation and cease to worry about how others evaluate them. Hence, they devote less time and effort to posturing and social niceties, and they may be more honest" (Sproull & Kiesler, 1991, p. 120). Similarly, Lautenschlager and Flaherty (1990, p. 310) note, "Researchers have hypothesized that computer administration of noncognitive instruments containing sensitive and personal items may reduce socially desirable responding, as it might offer greater anonymity and might be perceived as impersonal and nonjudgmental." This hypothesis is consistent with organizational impression management research (Giacalone & Rosenfeld, 1989, 1991) that has found socially desirable responding to be reduced in impersonal, anonymous situations.

Although the greater anonymity and depersonalized social situation created by computers can explain Martin and Nagao's (1989) results of increased candor on computer surveys, this analysis is hard-pressed to explain why respondents would dissimulate more on computers than on paper, as occurred in the Lautenschlager and Flaherty (1990) study. It is presently suggested that the social situation created by computers has changed in recent years with the message to the computer user of today being one of increased perceived surveillance and monitoring. Recently, newspaper and magazine articles (e.g., Betts, 1992; Bigelow, 1992; Coy, 1992; Green, 1991) have documented a growing and pervasive fear of computers monitoring and controlling people's lives. This fear has been labeled the "Big Brother Syndrome" (Martin & Nagao, 1989). Individuals are becoming more aware that computer communications can be monitored and information from diverse sources (e.g., parking tickets, tax information, credit history) can be linked with other information about them by police, government, and corporate authorities. Indeed, government agencies and private organizations now routinely monitor employee communication on both local and global E-Mail systems[2]. Computer-based communications have been introduced as evidence in legal proceedings, the most famous recent example being the racially insensitive remarks on an electronic messaging system made by officers involved in the Rodney King beating incident (And you thought your computer chat was private, 1993). In organizational settings, it has been estimated that more than 20 million people are electronically monitored at work. Much of this Big Brother surveillance is "silent monitoring," where employees are unaware of where and when their computers are being monitored. This practice is growing increasingly popular among banks, airlines, telephone companies, and other service industries that are heavily computerized (Bylinski, 1991). Big Brother monitoring has been associated with increased reports of anxiety, fatigue, exhaustion, and work stress (Eisman, 1991; Iadipaolo, 1992).

Thus, although computers previously may have created an impersonal, anonymous social situation, the Big Brother Syndrome of the 1990s is an unpleasant, stressful state conducive to *less* socially desirable responding. If Big Brother is watching, you may be more likely to tell the truth, especially if the truth can be checked against actual records. As Rosenfeld et al. (1991, p. 26) noted, "the possibility exists that individuals responding on computers perceive that they are being monitored and like those assessed on the bogus pipeline[3] are hesitant to overly inflate their responses."

The extent to which Big Brother acts to make responses more candid may depend on the degree to which the survey items ask for information the respondent perceives to be *verifiable*. In the Martin and Nagao (1989) study that found less social desirability (more candor) on the computer, some of the requested information (e.g., SAT scores) was verifiable; that is, it could be checked against an objective or factual standard. As the authors note, "That is, because the responses were on the computer rather than paper, they seemed more readily subject to instant checking and verification through other computer data bases. Thus, to avoid potential embarrassment, applicants may have been more likely to give truthful responses. If so, then the computer interview is operating in a manner reminiscent of the bogus pipeline technique" (Martin & Nagao, 1989, p. 78).

Although Big Brother may induce candor for verifiable responses, it may have the opposite effect if the responses are nonverifiable, such as those asked on personality inventories ("I always try to practice what I preach"). In the absence of a "reality check," previous impression management research (Schlenker, 1980) has found that individuals will act in self-enhancing ways to please significant audiences. However, when information exists that could repudiate an overly positive claim, individuals will present themselves in an accurate fashion, one that is more in line with what they really believe (Schlenker, 1975). As Schlenker (1980, p. 188) notes, "The more difficult it is for the audience to check the veracity of a self-presentation the more likely people are to self-aggrandize."

In the Lautenschlager and Flaherty (1990) study, the impression management/social desirability scales contained many items that were *not* verifiable (i.e., there was no correct or factual answer). Therefore, to the extent that the Big Brother Syndrome—rather than feelings of anonymity or depersonalization—was operating, an impression management analysis would predict greater socially desirable responding on computers than paper.

In sum, for individuals placed in an impersonal social situation (as Kiesler and colleagues have viewed the computer survey experience), the verifiability of requested information may have little impact on the social desirability of responses, but it might dramatically affect responses in a Big Brother scenario. When Big Brother is watching, responses to verifiable information should be more candid, and responses to nonverifiable information should be more socially desirable (i.e., less candid). Individuals should try to impress Big Brother when there is no reality check that would invalidate their responses but should make extra efforts at candor when the information might be verified. Although this pattern of responding has been reported in the impression management literature (e.g., Schlenker, 1975), it has never been found with regard to computer surveys in the same study.

In a recently completed experiment, Rosenfeld, Booth-Kewley, Edwards, and Thomas (1994) attempted to directly address these inconsistencies found in previous computer versus paper survey studies. They looked at the impact of the social situation and information verifiability on impression management and social desirability responding using paper and two computer conditions, linked and nonlinked. The computer-linked condition was included to simulate the Big Brother Syndrome. Rosenfeld et al. (1994) predicted that responses in the computer-linked condition would be more socially desirable than those in the computer-nonlinked and paper groups on items that cannot be verified (e.g., personality scales). It was expected that this effect would be enhanced when respondents were identified rather than anonymous. These hypotheses were tested using male Navy recruits who completed the BIDR, the MCSD scale, and some factual items. The results indicated that scores on the IM subscale of the BIDR and on the MCSD were higher in the identified than in the anonymous conditions. More importantly, in identified conditions, IM scores were significantly higher in the Big Brother condition than in the other two groups. No difference for the factual items was found. It was concluded that perceiving that one's responses are linked to a larger database may activate the Big Brother Syndrome, which may lead to greater impression management on computer surveys.

These results identified two conditions under which computer surveys produce responses equivalent to paper surveys. These are when responses are anonymous and when the computer is not thought to be linked to a larger data base. Under these two conditions—which are the common ways that computer surveys are administered—Booth-Kewley et al.'s (1992) conclusion that computer surveys yield essentially equivalent results to paper surveys remains valid. However, a limitation and caution in the use of computer surveys is now warranted. Under identified conditions and with the computer's linkage to larger databases made salient, the Rosenfeld et al. (1994) findings indicate that responses to computer surveys may be more influenced by socially desirable motives than are responses given in paper conditions.

The finding of no difference between "typical" computer and paper administration conditions is good news for organizational survey researchers and practitioners who may desire to administer computer surveys. The results also help clarify Lautenschlager and Flaherty's (1990) conclusion that computer assessment may lead to more socially desirable responding. The effect is apparently not a generalized characteristic of all computer surveys but may occur primarily when the Big Brother Syndrome is activated (i.e., under identified and computer-linked conditions). The conclusion to be drawn from these studies is that computer surveys are at best equal to paper surveys in controlling socially desirable responding and, under some conditions, (identified, computer-linked), may be worse.

The social implications of computer use may have changed in the past decade as computers became an integral part of daily life. In the "early days" (1960s-1980s), computers may have, indeed, created the impersonal, anonymous social setting that was associated with less social desirability responding. In the 1990s, however, the increased linkage of computers through local area networks, the worldwide Internet system, and the emerging information superhighway have increased the perception that what is typed into a computer today may be read, monitored, and reviewed by coworkers, supervisors, and competitors tomorrow. Under this sort of scrutiny it is not surprising that the computer may be emerging as a vehicle for increased levels of impression management, a trend that will need to be closely monitored by organizational survey researchers and practitioners.

SUMMARY AND CONCLUSIONS

The present chapter has reviewed research relating to impression management, socially desirability responding and organizational computer surveys. The results of past research suggest that computer and paper modes of administration yield similar results, although individual studies have reported both more and less socially desirable responding on computers as compared to paper surveys. We have offered a Big Brother Syndrome analysis as a means of integrating these diverse findings. Given the increased popularity of utilizing computers to administer organizational surveys, the resolution of the theoretical issues relating to impression management and responses to computer surveys will have important practical implications.

NOTES

The opinions expressed herein are those of the authors. They are not official and do not represent the views of the Navy Department.

1. "IM" is used in this chapter to indicate the impression management subscale of the BIDR. "Impression management" is used to indicate the more general use of this term as a theoretical construct, which includes socially desirable responding as one of its components. IM refers to the tendency to deliberately over report desirable behaviors and under report undesirable ones. SD/SDE refers to the tendency to give overly positive reports. SDE differs from IM in that respondents actually believe their positive SDE self-reports. On earlier versions of the BIDR, the SDE subscale was called SD.

2. One correlate of the increased pervasiveness of the Big Brother Syndrome may be greater concern for privacy. Public opinion polls have indicated that concern for privacy increased during the 1980s and that many in the United States feel that loss of privacy will be increasingly problematic in the future (Katz & Tassone, 1990).

3. The bogus pipeline refers to a set of procedures whereby respondents are convinced through an elaborate set of ruses that they are connected to a lie-detector-type device capable of assessing their "true" (i.e., private) attitudes and feelings (Jones & Sigall, 1971; Rosenfeld, 1990).

9

THE APPROPRIATE USE OF COMPUTER-BASED INFORMATION TECHNOLOGIES IN ORGANIZATIONS: AN IMPRESSION MANAGEMENT FRAMEWORK

K. Vernard Harrington
Jon W. Beard

The world is rapidly moving toward what Toffler (1980) referred to as the "intelligent environment" (p. 184) and Naisbitt (1982) described as the "information society" (p. 1). Computer-based information technologies (CBITs) have become ubiquitous. Without CBITs, banking and travel reservation systems would cease to function as we know them, and the automated factories now considered commonplace could not exist.

In the organizational world, the introduction and use of CBITs represents a meaningful form of organizational change (Barki & Huff, 1985; Keen, 1981; Markus & Robey, 1988). Any such change creates a potential disruption in the smooth functioning of an organization. Some forces within organizations promote change while other forces resist change. For example, what are the conditions that lead to the inappropriate use of CBIT, such as situations in which the technology is used but probably should not be? Or, what causes systems to not be used when they should be? To resolve these questions it is important to examine how the use of CBITs is affected by the dynamics of change within organizations and the impressions created by those changes.

In recognition of the dynamic and dramatic changes occurring, several studies have identified and examined the "key issues" for organizations in dealing with managing information systems (cf. Ball & Harris, 1982; Brancheau & Wetherbe, 1987; Dickson, Leitheiser, & Wetherbe, 1984; Neiderman, Brancheau, & Wetherbe, 1991; Watson, 1989; Watson & Brancheau, 1991). Browning (1990) stated in a discussion of the impact of information technology and automation on organizations in the 1990s that:

> In meeting the challenges of automation, each [organization] must rely on three sets of skills: engineering the technology (getting the machines to work), managing the technology (getting the machines to work with people), and managing the organization (getting our people and machines to work more efficiently than their people and machines). (1990, p. 9 of special section)

As noted by Culnan and Swanson (1986), one of the foundations for the study of information systems is the organization sciences. One perspective from the organization sciences that may offer some meaningful insight into this process of change and managing the technology is impression management (IM). Although this approach has been implied at various points in the MIS literature (cf. Mason & Mitroff, 1973; also see the "key issues" pieces noted above), the IM viewpoint has not been widely investigated in relation to information CBIT. In general, impression management, often also referred to as self-presentation, is the process where individuals seek to direct, manipulate, and control the impressions others form and have of them (Gardner & Martinko, 1988; Gardner & Peluchette, 1991; Goffman, 1959; Leary & Kowalski, 1990; Schlenker & Weigold, 1992). The focus has traditionally, although not exclusively, been on an individual managing the impressions others have of them. Broader interpretations do exist (cf. Giacalone & Rosenfeld, 1989, 1991; Rosenfeld, Giacalone, & Riordan, 1994). For our purposes, we will work with a broader interpretation of the IM process where it is concerned with the impression being formed of the technology and its capabilities. More specifically, can IM be directed at issues related to the appropriate use of CBIT in organizations? The next section in the chapter provides a more detailed explanation of impression management. This is followed by a definition and examination of computer-based information technology. Building from the CBIT definition, we investigate the factors that influence CBIT use and seek to link them with the impression management perspective. To conclude the chapter we suggest avenues for further exploration and research.

IMPRESSION MANAGEMENT

The organizational sciences have been devoting increased attention to impression management as a theoretical framework (cf. Gardner & Martinko, 1988; Giacalone & Rosenfeld, 1989, 1991; Leary & Kowalski, 1990). Derived from the seminal work of Goffman (1959), IM is an explanation of the behaviors people direct toward others to create and maintain desired perceptions of themselves (Schneider, 1981). The fundamental assumption of the IM approach is that a basic motive of individuals is to be viewed by others in a favorable manner (Goffman, 1959). Thus, individuals, and organizations, present themselves in ways that are compatible with the effects they seek to create and reinforce (e.g., highlight their strengths and virtues) and distance themselves from events and circumstances which are unfavorable to those images.

Goffman (1959), in *The Presentation of Self in Everyday Life*, promoted the belief that social interaction is much like the staging of a play. The "actors" (i.e., the people) are engaged in "performances" in their everyday lives. The "audience" consists of those who come into contact with the actors. The environment as a whole creates the setting and the context for the performance. Stimuli, that is, impressions, are derived from the characteristics and behavior of the audience and the actor in combination with environmental cues. Together, these characteristics and environmental cues provide a mutual understanding of the situation which serves as the framework for their interactions. Goffman (1959) suggests the definitions, or understanding, of the actor and audience will typically coincide in many respects, even while many aspects of the situation may be perceived differently. Behavior, therefore, is guided by a "definition of the situation" that is derived through the interaction of the actor and audience.

This is similar to the concept of interactional psychology, which explicitly recognizes that situations vary in cues, rewards, and opportunities and that people vary in cognitions, abilities, and motivation (Terborg, 1981, p. 569). Four propostions provide the foundation for the interactional psychology perspective:

1. Behavior is a function of interaction and/or feedback between the individual and the situation.
2. The individual is an active participant in the interaction, being both changed by and changing situations.
3. Individual motivation factors and ability are integral components of behavior.
4. The psychological meaning of situations for the individual and the behavior potential of situations for the individual are essential factors of behavior.

Gardner and Martinko (1988) developed a broader conceptual view of impression management to provide "a more thorough understanding of organizational behavior within its relevant context" (p. 322). Two issues from this view are especially important in this inquiry; that is, support for a set of actions can be influenced by the mechanisms of IM (Pfeiffer, 1981), and that the social construction of reality needs a framework for understanding behavior. Leary and Kowalski (1990) refined the concepts of IM further by developing a two-component model. This model suggests that two separate constituents of the IM process occur: impression motivation and impression construction. Impression motivation is the level of attention people direct at how they are "coming across to others" (Leary & Kowalski, 1990, p. 36). This dimension is conceptualized as consisting of three factors, including the goal-relevance of the impressions created, the value of the outcomes desired, and the variance between the current and desired images. Impression construction is the process of ascertaining the impression one wants to make and determining how to go about making the desired impression. This component consists of five factors, including the self-concept of the person and/or organization, the desired and undesired identity images, role constraints, the target's values, and the current social image (Leary & Kowalski, 1990).

In the pages that follow the general tenets of the IM framework will be used to suggest explanations for the dynamics of change due to CBIT. Obviously, information technology cannot be self-aware and adjust its own behavior as a method of self-presentation. However, people do respond to the presence of technology and the changes caused by technology. And, decisions on the technology—how it is to be designed, introduced, distributed, and used—are made by individuals who have a great deal invested, at both personal and professional levels, in the success of the technology. Therefore, the approach we will use is one of interpreting IM as a factor affecting decisions on the use (or lack thereof) of computer-based information technology.

COMPUTER-BASED INFORMATION TECHNOLOGY

Research into management information systems (MIS) can be argued to have begun with the conceptual work of Mason and Mitroff (1973). They suggested two tentative principles as a part of the research program informatiion systems. First, managers need information that is geared to their own psychology, not that of the system designers. Second, managers need a method of generating evidence that is geared to their problems, not those of the systems designers. The principle of CBIT, perhaps a broader conception of MIS, has developed to address the issues described by Mason and Mitroff (1973). The term *computer-based information technology* can be effectively broken down into three components: information, information technology, and computer-based systems. In order to provide a complete definition of CBIT, it is best to first provide working definitions of each of these components.

Information

The *American Heritage Dictionary* defines information as "Knowledge derived from study, experience, or instruction" (1985, p. 660). Although this definition is correct, for our purposes it is incomplete. The definition concentrates on where information comes from, but ignores how information is used. A somewhat broader perspective on information, including a variety of working definitions, has been supplied by researchers in the management information systems area (cf. Bakopoulos, 1985, for a summary).

Daft and Macintosh (1984) suggested that information is data that changes or confirms one's understanding of the external environment; that is, information describes the state of the world surrounding the organization. The better the information a decision maker has, the more aware of the external environment that individual will be, and, therefore, the better decisions that individual can potentially make.

Daft and Lengel (1986) suggest that two factors—uncertainty and equivocality—help determine the information contingencies in the external environment that should be of interest to decision makers in organizations. In this context, uncertainty is the difference between the amount of information needed to perform a task or make a decision and the amount of information already possessed (Galbraith, 1977). In contrast, equivocality deals with the question of ambiguity; the existence of multiple and conflicting interpretations about a situation (Daft, Lengel, & Trevino, 1987). Although a situation of high certainty is by nature unequivocal, an uncertain situation may or may not be equivocal.

The information processing requirements of a decision maker differ greatly according to whether the most pressing concern is uncertainty reduction or equivocality reduction. When presented with a situation of high uncertainty, managers tend to increase their acquisition of data. When faced with a highly equivocal situation, however, decision makers must first develop a common grammar to interpret the event. Therefore, when implementing an information processing system in an organizational unit, environmental uncertainty and equivocality must be evaluated. This must be done because different systems are more efficient and effective in dealing with these two information contingencies.

Information Technology

Perrow (1967) defined technology as a set of systems for getting the organization's work done. Bakopoulos (1985) suggested that information technology is

> the set of non-human resources dedicated to the storage, processing and communication of information, and the way in which these resources are organized into a system capable of performing a set of tasks. (p. 20)

From this perspective, technology can be seen as taking two forms: process technology and organizational technology. Process technology involves the tools, techniques, and actions used to transform organizational inputs into outputs. It defines the method in which organizational resources are allocated. Organizational technology concentrates on the systems that the organization uses to deal with its external environment (Perrow, 1967). The external environment can cause individuals within an organization to either wish to process more information or develop interpretation systems by which information already obtained can be more effectively used. When implementing an information processing system, the organization must decide whether emphasis should be placed on process technology, organizational technology, or both.

The concept of categorizing technology forms has been further developed by other researchers. Thompson (1967) divided technological systems into three types—sequential, intensive, and mediating—based on their level of interdependence among organizational units. Sequential systems involve single inputs and single outputs. Intensive technologies use multiple inputs to achieve single outputs. Mediating technologies involve multiple inputs and multiple outputs. Mason (1984) added a fourth type to this classification—extensive technology, which uses a single input to create multiple outputs. This classification suggests that an organization can treat information as another component of production in an extensive technology, with the raw material (i.e., the single input) being environmental data and the output being information used by decision makers.

Computer-Based Systems

A computer-based system is a collection of computer hardware and software brought together to facilitate the processing of information for an organization. They are used for a variety of functions within organizations, including component design and manufacturing, customer recordkeeping, presentation development, decision making, training, budgeting, planning, and controlling. Although a given system will serve a specific purpose in an organization, these systems have one overriding purpose in common—they are all designed to process information for the organizational unit.

Leifer (1988) noted that the term computer-based system is a generic one. Several categories of systems fall under this umbrella, including centralized systems, distributed systems, decentralized systems, and stand-alone systems (refer to any MIS textbook for definitions of these terms). Although the specific definitions of each type of system are different, they all have two fundamental concepts in common. First, they are all based on some form of computer technology, whether it is mainframe, minicomputer, or microcomputer (personal computer or PC) technology. Second, these systems change and/or enhance the way organizational tasks are performed after their installation. This change in organizational procedures implies a probable need for the training of users and possibly modifying fixed installations; that is, bringing a computer-based system into an organizational unit usually calls for a good deal more than simply placing a "black box" in a room, plugging it in, and expecting users to be instantly productive with it.

CBITs

Drawing from the above elemental definitions, a CBIT is any computer-based information processing system using an extensive technology designed to allow decision makers within organizational units to process data from their external environment into information to reduce uncertainty and/or equivocality. A wide variety of systems potentially fall under this definition. The distinction lies in how the system is actually being used. For example, if a computer-based system is being used primarily for functions such as word processing, it will not be considered a CBIT. If, however, this same system is used with a software application such as an electronic spreadsheet or database, this system is a CBIT.

End-User Computing

The result of the growth and expansion of activities toward CBIT has often and increasingly led to end-user computing (EUC). EUC is the practice of allowing individuals to develop, maintain, and use their own CBITs (Sein, Bostrom, & Olfman, 1987). EUC has become important because of the rapidly decreasing cost of computing power and increasing capabilities of off-the-shelf software. Rockart and Flannery (1983) concluded that EUC was growing at a rate of 50 to 90 percent per year. Benjamin (1982) predicted that by the mid-1990s, EUC will absorb as much as 75 percent of the corporate computing resource. User-perceived reasons for this growth included an increased awareness of EUC potentials, improvements in technical capabilities that make EUC increasingly more feasible and less costly, business conditions that have intensified the need in organizations for more effective analysis, increased planning and control capabilities (that an efficient EUC program can provide), and increasing needs for information that cannot be met through the traditional information systems organization.

EUC is one of the most important phenomena to occur in the information systems area in the last decade (Cheney, Mann, & Amoroso, 1986). To a major extent, this is due to the changes in the information flow within organizations caused by the introduction of EUC. Before EUC is introduced into an organization, environmental data collected by the organization flows through the organization's traditional data processing (DP) mechanism and is reduced to standardized reports before being passed on to end-users. Chances are good that this information is not in a form end-users could understand or make the best use of, but they use it unless they want to take the time and expense of requesting specialized reports. Thus, end-users are faced with the situation of possibly having inadequate information with which to make their decisions.

After the introduction of EUC, end-users can receive information in the form they need from their own EUC facilities, as well as the traditional data processing mechanism (although the importance of the data processing mechanism is lessened greatly). If the information is not exactly what end-users need, it is relatively simple for them to make adjustments and receive it in another form.

In a conceptual paper examining organizational factors affecting the success of EUC, Cheney, Mann, and Amoroso (1986) suggested that identifying these factors is extremely important to organizations. This is because confusion, inefficiency, and a perceived or real lack of productivity by CBIT users may force management into constraining what could well be the major force in the management of the information resources within organizations. Alavi and Weiss (1985) also pointed to several organizational risks of improper EUC implementation including ineffective use of organizational resources, solving the wrong problem, and inefficient expenditure of non-DP personnel time. These points suggest that although EUC has the potential to play a major role in an organization's CBIT plan, without proper implementation it can actually be detrimental to the organization.

The concept of end-user computing and the potential pitfalls identified above suggest the boundaries of this inquiry. What is it that creates a situation that encourages individuals to use CBIT when it is inappropriate? Alternatively, what causes people to aviod technology when it should be used? In the next section we construct a framework that will orient the discussion throughout the remainder of the chapter.

A CHANGE FRAMEWORK

Change within organizations can be viewed from a variety of different perspectives. Two change perspectives dominate and are presented here as the "rational" perspective and the "emotional" perspective.

Rational Perspective

The rational perspective toward change is derived from the concept of economic optimization. Economic optimization pertains to the efficient allocation of scarce resources. Assuming that efficiency is a goal of an organization, economic optimization seeks to differentiate between a number of alternative courses of action because "the alternative that produces a result most consistent with the [organization's] goal is the optimal action" (Pappas, Brigham, & Hirschey, 1983, p. 21). If the benefits of a change, no matter how they may be calculated, outweigh the costs of implementation, then the change is appropriate for the organization and will be implemented. However, if the costs of change outweigh the benefits, then the change is inappropriate and will not be implemented. Several forces can contribute to the choice of implementing an appropriate change, including external forces such as competitors, customers, and suppliers, and internal forces such as stockholders, employees, and the changing state of the production process.

In the case of CBITs, the major determinants of change appropriateness involve two categories of variables: characteristics of the task and characteristics of the CBIT as required by the task. Task characteristics and task design have been studied for more than two centuries. Research in task design and task characteristics has had a variety of goals, including increased productivity and job satisfaction (Griffin, 1982). Three characteristics of the task are important: feedback requirements, work pace, and task integration requirements.

Feedback. Feedback requirements relate to the degree that the task requires a knowledge of the results of previous work activities. When feedback requirements are low, job incumbents do not need to know a great deal about outcomes in order to continue performing the task. The higher the feedback requirements of a task are, the more appropriate a CBIT is in performing that task.

Work pace. Work pace refers to the speed with which task-related decisions must be made. When presented with a task requiring a rapid work pace, individual cognitive limitations become evident. The more rapidly tasks must be performed, the more appropriate a CBIT is for use in that task.

Task integration. Task integration requirements are closely related to the dimensions of component complexity and coordinative complexity (Wood, 1986). Situations of high task integration are similar to Thompson's (1967) idea of reciprocal interdependence, where the different tasks of a job are tightly linked. The more the individual components of a given job need to be highly integrated, the more appropriate CBIT use will be for that job.

In addition, as the information processing and retrieval requirements of a task increase, the individual cognitive limitations of a decision maker become problematic, also indicating a possible appropriate use of CBIT.

In summary, therefore, from the rational perspective, CBIT use is appropriate to the extent that the unique characteristics of CBITs are required by individuals to perform their tasks effectively.

Emotional Perspective

The emotional perspective to organizational change lies in obvious contrast to the rational perspective. From this perspective, change is viewed from the standpoint of the individual and is focused on individual differences. Individual differences are the variations in the ways individuals think, how they interpret their environment, and the ways in which they respond to that environment (Moorhead & Griffin, 1995). Individuals vary in terms of cognitions, affect, motivation, and skills (Nelson, 1990). Zmud (1979) suggested that of the numerous factors believed to influence CBIT success, the area of individual differences has been the most widely studied. A major assumption linking

CBIT success with use is the idea that from the organization's perspective, the more a CBIT is used in support of decision making, the more successful the CBIT (Swanson, 1974, 1982; Zmud, 1979). Therefore, the individuals affected by the change must be taken into account in order to determine whether the change will be accepted and the CBIT will be used. By failing to take individual differences into account in CBIT implementation decisions, organizations run the risk of not achieving their (assumed) goal of increasing organizational efficiency.

The Framework

These two perspectives of organizational change create the two dimensions of CBIT use that are the basis for this framework. The rational perspective is an objective dimension of CBIT appropriateness. It is our premise that for any given task, the costs and benefits of CBIT use can be measured in order to determine whether the CBIT should be used. Yet, there is still opportunity for affecting this dimension through managing impressions. The emotional perspective, on the other hand, creates a perceptual dimension of CBIT use. With this perspective, the premise is that by examining the factors related to individual differences and perceptions, the likelihood of CBIT use by an individual in performance of the task can be determined.

Figure 9.1 is the result of combining these two dimensions and is a graphical depiction of the framework. Cells 2 and 3 depict situations where the rational perspective is consistent with the emotional perspective. For example, in cell 2 it is appropriate from the organizational perspective for the CBIT to be used, and it is being used effectively by individuals within the organization. In cell 3, CBIT use is inappropriate, and they are not being used.

Cells 1 and 4 are the cells of primary interest in this inquiry. Using one of the research principles originally delineated by Mason and Mitroff (1973), managers are seeking a method to generate evidence needed for their decision making. Unfortunately, the approach is improper in these two circumstances. In cell 1, the organization finds itself in the situation of having a CBIT that should be used (i.e., is appropriate) but, for one reason or another, is not being used. For organizational units with individuals who find themselves in this cell, resources are being wasted because these individuals are not using systems when they should be. In other words, negative affect/emotions toward (i.e., resistance to) the technology are overriding rationality.

In cell 4, the organization finds itself in a situation where the CBIT should not be used, but individuals are using them. In this situation, organizational resources are being used inappropriately because emotion for the technology is overriding rationality.

IMPRESSION MANAGEMENT AND THE
RATIONAL/EMOTIONAL FRAMEWORK

As noted in the preceeding sections and portrayed in Figure 9.1, the rational perspective is the situational side, whereas the emotional perspective comprises the person side of the interaction. The discussion now turns to a more detailed examination of the components of the rational and emotional perspectives on change.

Figure 9.1
A Change Framework

Likelihood of CBIT Use
Person/Perceptual Factors

Emotional Perspective

	Low	High
High Appropriateness of CBIT Use	Emotions Override Rationality **Underuse** 1	Rational & Emotional Perpsectives Consistent **Appropriately Used** 2
Situational/Objective Factors Rational Perspective Low	3 Rational & Emotional Perspectives Consistent **Appropriately Unused**	4 Emotions Override Rationality **Overuse**

A number of factors have been identified in the literature as influencing the likelihood of CBIT use by individuals. These include organizational context (Trice & Treacy, 1988; Nelson, 1990); attitudes toward the CBIT (Dambrot, Watkins-Malek, Silling, Marshall, & Garver, 1985; Rafaeli & Sutton, 1986; Robey, 1979); individual differences (Nelson, 1990; Trice & Treacy, 1988) and individual locus of control or causation (Arndt, Feltes, & Hanak, 1983; Coovert & Goldstein, 1980; Russell, 1982; Russell & McAuley, 1986; Russell, McAuley, & Tarico, 1987); perceived quality, usefulness, training, and ease of use of the CBIT (Davis, Bagozzi, & Warshaw, 1989; O'Reilly, 1982; Robertson, 1989); and the social environment of the work unit as it relates to CBIT use (Kling, 1980; Nelson, 1990; Ostberg & Chapman, 1988; Robertson, 1989; Safayeni, MacGregor, Lee & Bavelas, 1987). All of the factors discussed in the following sections play an important role in determining CBIT use because users react to and interact with a given CBIT in different ways based on these differences and contexts. As these factors are explored, brief suggestions will be made for linking them with IM.

Organizational Change Considerations

The foundation for the framework in Figure 9.1 is the concept of organizational change. An organizational change is the adoption of a new idea or behavior by an organization (Pierce & Delbecq, 1977). As noted, the introduction of CBITs into the organizational unit implies some form of change within that unit. (See Chapter 4 for a broad interpretation of changing organizations and information technology.) Factors within and external to the organization may force it to introduce a change that involves CBITs and resistance is a common occurrence in the change process. Factors external to the organization include competitors, customers and suppliers.

External factors. Competitors can force the organization to adopt CBITs by increasing their own information processing capacity, leaving the organization at a competitive disadvantage if it fails to react. By the same token, merely existing in a competitive environment may cause an organization (depending upon its specific strategies) to seek to obtain first-mover advantages wherever possible. Adopting CBITs to increase information processing capabilities can give major advantages to the first mover. For example, the SABRE flight reservation system created such a great competitive advantage for American Airlines (i.e., revenues from SABRE became greater than American's flight revenues over time, and, in recent years, have been a profit center while flight operations have been barely profitable or have lost money) that most major airlines scrambled to develop their own systems, while those that could not pursued lawsuits charging American with unfair competition.

Consider another example. An organization exists at a particular point in a value-added chain. Most manufacturing firms (the exception being those firms that are completely vertically integrated) are faced with the situation of having to purchase their raw materials from a supplier outside of their organizational hierarchy, and sell their finished goods to a party that is not the final consumer. Within this value-added chain, certain "links" have a greater amount of power than others. For example, the sole supplier of a scarce raw material has a large amount of power over the organization seeking to buy this material. On the other hand, when the organization makes a product that is sold to a limited customer group (e.g., defense contractors in dealing with the Pentagon) these customers have power over the organization. These are situations of resource dependence (Ulrich & Barney, 1984).

In either of these situations, the organization can be forced to introduce a CBIT change to accommodate the group that holds power over the organization. In the supplier situation, the organization may be required to install a specialized order-entry system designed to streamline the supplier's operation. (See Chapter 6 of this volume for a more extensive exploration of this issue from an impression management perspective.) In the customer power situation, the customer may require the organization to provide specialized cost tracking, which may mean a new or modified CBIT. An example of this exists in the government, which regularly engages in the practice requiring standardization among organizations wishing to bid on government contracts. (Chapter 5 examines service-level agreements from an impression management perspective.) This standardization is beginning to include areas that relate to CBITs.

Internal focus. Within the organization, the major factors which can help promote CBIT-related change are the people. In the organization, the individuals who have the greatest exposure to the external environment are the top-level strategic managers. These individuals are ideally the individuals who are best able to tell whether the organization is effectively and efficiently processing information. If it is not, then it is incumbent on these managers to determine ways in which to increase this capacity.

Lederer and Mendelow (1988) noted that top managers may be needed to be convinced of the potential of CBIT use. If this is the case, then the organization must have a CBIT "champion." This champion very often is a mid-level manager who sees the potential advantage of a CBIT change. The champion pushes the ideas for a change through the organization. (Chapter 3 provides an investigation of the symbolic value of information technology in the organization.)

Resistance to change. Markus and Robey (1988) have stated that the literature on information technology and organizational change do not currently support reliable generalizations about the relationship between information technology and organizational change. There are, however, several things we do know. First, changes in information technology can cause changes in the structure of the organization and of jobs within the organization. Spans of control are restructured because the introduction of one PC-based system can eliminate one or more clerks within an organizational unit. For those clerks who do remain with the organization, the way they perform their jobs can change dramatically. In addition, in order to do essentially the same job as before, workers may need to be retrained. Also, because the CBIT can allow a worker to do the same job in a shorter amount of time, more duties may be assigned.

Second, CBIT induced changes can create changes in organizational decision-making practices. Simon (1977) argued that decision making would be recentralized, line structures would shrink in size, staff structures would increase in number, the number of hierarchical levels would decrease, and structures would become more complex and require more lateral coordination. Although it is true that CBIT change can mean recentralized decision making, this does not have to be the case. If the system is installed in a decentralized manner, decision making will tend to become decentralized as well. Whatever the resulting changes caused by the introduction of a CBIT, one thing is certain: not everyone in the organization will be happy with the change. In other words, some will most likely resist the change. This resistance is one of the major factors organizational change agents must take into consideration and resolve.

Resistance to change has two major sources: organizational (Katz & Khan, 1978) and individual (Nadler, 1983). Each of these sources manifests itself in several ways. Organizational sources include inertia, threatened expertise and power, and resource allocation. Individual sources include habit, security, fear of the unknown, lack of awareness, and group norms. It is important for the change agent to identify the specific causes of the resistance to the CBIT change and take steps to reduce them to the point that will allow the change to take place. If the resistance to the change is too strong, then the CBIT implementation will be doomed to failure.

One significant and particularly damaging form of resistance is counter-implementation (Keen, 1981). Counter-implementation crosses the fine line from honest resistance to a misguided process of selfish sabotage of a necessary innovation. Counter-implementation often occurs because CBITs tend to redistribute data and can sometimes be used to break up information monopolies of organizational units. These information monopolies are many times a source of power for individuals within the unit and for the unit within the organization. Therefore, the unit will often resist any change that it perceives to be an attempt to limit its power. Counter-implementation is most likely to occur when outsiders control the implementation of the CBIT (Argyris, 1971). In this situation, a CBIT champion, an internal figure, becomes very important to successful CBIT implementation. However, this is only the case when the champion has credibility within the units to be affected by the CBIT.

The need for change and the common resistance to change, for both external and internal constituencies, can be examined using Leary and Kowalski's (1990) two-component model. As suggested, one component of impression management is impression motivation, that is, the degree to which people (and organizations) are motivated to regulate how they are seen by others. The "others" in the situations described above are varied, and may range from competitors to suppliers to customers. The factors of goal-relevance, desired outcomes, and distance between current and desired images drive the process. For example, how important is it that the organization, or the individual, make the change to CBIT? How much change is necessary to transform the process to CBIT? The second component of the model is impression construction, and consists of the factors necessary to actually make the tranisition, that is, the current concept, constraints, the target's values, and the current image. Whose image is damaged? Can the change process proceed without the negative consequences?

Although it may be intuitively obvious that impression management is an ingredient, little systematic work from this perspective has been done to date to provide guidance on how to proceed with the change process.

Organizational Context

In their seminal piece on information systems research, Mason and Mitroff (1973) proposed that an information system:

> consists of at least one person of a certain psychological type who faces a
> problem within some organizational context for which he needs evidence to
> arrive at a solution (i.e, select some course of action) and that the evidence
> is made available to him through some mode of presentation (p. 475).

The organizational context that these authors refer to consists of two components: structure and people. Building on this work, Ein-Dor and Segev (1978) developed a conceptual framework that examines the factors of organizational context as they relate to CBIT use. This scheme is based on the degree of controllability of these factors and the consequent ability of the organization to change them if necessary. These factors are classified as uncontrollable, partially controllable, and controllable.

Uncontrollable factors. Factors in the uncontrollable group include organizational size, structure, time frame, and the extra-organizational, or task, environment. These variables are considered to be uncontrollable because "the time required to change their values is well beyond the time frame of [CBIT] implementation, and ... because there is very little the [organizational unit] can do to induce changes in these variables even in the long run" (Ein-Dor & Segev, 1978, p. 1066).

Perhaps the most interesting uncontrollable organizational context factor relating to CBIT use is the task environment. Dess and Beard (1984) suggested that there are three dimensions by which an organization's task environment can be measured: munificence (capacity), complexity (homogeneity-heterogeneity, concentration-dispersion), and dynamism (stability-instability, turbulence). These dimensions refer to "the nature and the distribution of resources in environments, with different values on each dimension implying differences in appropriate structures and activities" (Aldrich, 1979, p. 63).

Environmental munificence involves the extent to which the environment can support sustained growth. A high level of munificence can allow an organization to generate slack resources. This slack can allow the organization to buffer itself in times of scarcity, provide resources for organizational innovation, and provide a means for maintaining organizational coalitions.

Environmental dynamism involves the rate of change in the environment. There are two forms of environmental change: predictable and unpredictable. Dess and Beard (1984) suggested that dynamism should be restricted to change which is hard to predict. This hard-to-predict change increases uncertainty for organizational decision makers. As uncertainty increases, information processing requirements for decision makers also increase.

Environmental complexity refers to the heterogenity and range of activities an organization is involved in. The greater the range and the more heterogeneous the activities, the more complex the task environment for the organization. A more complex environment means greater uncertainty and thus higher information processing needs.

These three dimensions of the task environment help to determine the information processing capacity needs of an organizational unit. If the needs are high and capacity is low, the organizational unit will find itself unable to cope with environmental demands. If, on the other hand, too many slack resources are created (i.e., there is a great deal of unused information processing capacity), then the organizational unit is misallocating its resources.

Partially controllable factors. Partially controllable organizational context variables include organizational resources, organizational maturity, and the psychological climate of the organization (Cheney et al., 1986; Ein-Dor & Segev, 1978). Resource availability problems tend to occur for CBITs because the information function is considered to be a staff function and, therefore, tend to not get the attention or respect of line functions, such as production and marketing. There is a tendency for organizations to ignore their information needs until they become acute. Thus, members of the organizational unit championing the CBIT function may find themselves in a situation of "feast or famine" in the area of resource allocation.

Ein-Dor and Segev (1978) define mature organizations to be those that have formalized and quantified systems and produce data appropriate to their decision and control processes. An effective information system requires not only that these processes be well understood, but that their output also be presented in a form suitable for analysis by end-users. Another important part of organizational maturity is the degree to which the sociopolitical structure of the organization is rational and compatible with CBIT use. This topic will be explored in the section on implementation process variables.

Fully controllable factors. Fully controllable contextual factors include organizational EUC policies, the rank of the EUC executive, and end-user training. The existence of well-documented EUC policies tends to create a form of continuity that is important to organizational units because if new CBITs are being introduced without any coordination, then end-users may have a tendency to avoid supporting any one system, fearing the likelihood that it will be replaced shortly.

The rank and location in the organization of the executive responsible for information in general and EUC in particular is also important to end-users. The closer to the chief executive officer (CEO) the chief information officer (CIO) is within the organizational hierarchy, the stronger the signal to end-users and other organizational members as to how dedicated to EUC the organization really is.

CBIT use is related to information processing capacity needs in organizational units through the perceptions of individuals within these units. Every organization develops its own psychological climate with respect to CBIT use. If individuals feel that they need to increase their information processing capacity in order to perform their jobs more effectively, they will be more likely to turn to CBITs in order to fill the void. These excessive expectations as to the usefulness of the system can be both self-induced and fostered by experts. On the other hand, it is possible to play down the capabilities of CBITs in order to avoid creating exaggerated expectations. Returning to the work of Daft and Lengel (1986), the concepts of uncertainty and equivocality are relevant. Do the individuals who must work with CBIT understand CBIT capabilities and limitations? Is this an honest process of resolving uncertainty by the individual or an attempt at equivocality reduction? What impression of the situation are leading to attempts to overcome uncontrollable and partially controllable factors? An impression management perspective should yield some insight to these questions.

The Social System

Robertson (1989) suggested that the social system of an organization has a significant affect on how and where a CBIT will be used. This social effect can occur in two ways: (1) by affecting the manner in which an individual perceives the work environment in relation to the CBIT and (2) by creating social pressures and demands from the group on the individual using the CBIT.

It has been widely acknowledged that the social system of an organization can change an individual's perception of unchanging physical objects. Turkle (1980) argued that computers are highly abstract physical objects that can be interpreted in many ways. Due to individual differences, to be discussed in a later section, individuals within organizational units will obviously have different views of a CBIT and its capabilities. These perceptions are refined through experience with the system, and over time tend to converge within the group. As Goffman (1959) suggested in his siminal work on IM, the actors and audience arrive at a common understanding of the situation. These prevailing attitudes can then become a part of the norms of the organizational unit. These norms, if important to the members of the unit, will be enforced (Staw, 1981), thus contributing to the use or the avoidance of the CBIT. By influencing individual perceptions, the social system of the organizational unit can have three general impacts on the CBIT use, affecting the level and quality of working life (QWL), the degree of centralization, and the height of the organizational hierarchy (Robertson, 1989).

Research on the relationship between QWL and CBIT use focuses on the impact on job content. Some researchers have found that CBITs tend to decrease QWL of clerical jobs by increasing job stress, lowering job content, and deskilling jobs (Iacono & Kling, 1987; Turner, 1984). Other research, however, has shown CBITs to improve QWL by enlarging jobs, and increasing influence (Crawford, 1982; Foster & Flynn, 1984). This pattern of conflicting results can also be found in the degree of centralization caused by the introduction of a CBIT. Some research has postulated that CBITs would allow management to "micro-manage" subordinate's activities, thus centralizing authority (Noble, 1978), while other research has found no such relationship (Pfeffer & Leblebibi, 1977).

Once again, the results are mixed as to CBITs affect on the organizational hierarchy. Some research has found CBITs tend to flatten the hierarchy (i.e., reduce the number of organizational levels) (Whisler, 1970); other outcomes suggest that CBITs actually increase the number of management levels (Pfeffer & Leblebibi, 1977). Robertson (1989) has no problem with these mixed results in social impacts. As he notes; "individuals in different social groups [i.e., different organizational units] will have different influences on [other individuals within their units] and will thus use [CBITs] differently" (p. 57). (Chapter 2 presents a model of a self-presentational perspective through computer-mediated communication.)

The second social determinant of CBIT usage comes from individual role pressures and demands. These pressures can arise when others in the organization working on interdependent tasks request the use of a particular CBIT. In addition, an individual may use a CBIT out of fear, envy, or curiosity if rivals are using it.

How can the relationship between the social system of the organizational unit and CBIT use be operationalized? Robertson (1989) suggests using the concept of structural equivalence. Structural equivalence is a measure of similarity in interaction patterns (Boorman & White, 1976). It attempts to capture a social system characteristic that is different from that captured by formal titles in the organization chart. For example, two individuals are said to be structurally equivalent if they work with the same others, go to the same others for help, or report to the same person. These individuals are said to occupy the same structural position (at least to the extent that their roles are structurally equivalent).

Robertson (1989) tested and found support for the following two hypotheses related to structural equivalence and CBIT use: (1) individuals in different structural positions will interpret and use CBITs in different ways and (2) individuals in different structural positions will have different social pressures and demands, and thus will use CBITs in different ways. IM should be able to add insight to the effects of the social system on CBIT use.

CBIT Characteristics

The characteristics of the CBIT are of concern to this inquiry because they have an effect on the efficiency of the end-user's interaction with the system (Trice & Treacy, 1988). If the physical characteristics of the CBIT present obstacles to users, then the system will tend to be avoided. This is the case not only for computer anxious-individuals, who will attempt to avoid the CBIT for a variety of reasons, but even potential users who display a proclivity toward CBIT usage will avoid it if they perceive it to be inefficient.

A number of CBIT characteristics have been studied in the past, including response time (Fuerst & Cheney, 1982), presentation format (Fuerst & Cheney, 1982; Srinivasan, 1985), stability and security (Srinivasan, 1985), and the user interface (Fuerst & Cheney, 1982). The basic thrust of this research has been to determine how best to create positive perceptions of the usefulness and/or ease of use of the CBIT (Davis, 1989; Robertson, 1989). These increased perceptions can then contribute to increased CBIT use by individuals within organizational units. Interestingly, however, these studies do not address the concept of impression management, at least not directly. Here again, is an opportunity to extend our understanding of the process of managing impressions in relation to CBIT.

CBIT Training

As noted in the previous section, in order for a CBIT to have any realistic chance of contributing to individual and organizational efficiency, end-users must be trained in the use of the system. In a case study examining the issue of end-user training, Nelson and Cheney (1987) discovered a sad state of affairs relating to this important area. Of the 20 organizations studied, about 80 percent reported training budgets of less than 2 percent of the total CBIT budget. In addition, a majority of the participants in the study reported two or fewer full-time trainer staff. However, there has been substantial growth in the number of information centers in organizations (Garcia, 1985), suggesting that the need for systems training has not been completely ignored by organizations. Information centers are specialized facilities that act as resources to end-users in their work with CBITs, providing training for new users as well as recommendations for what types of hardware and software to select for a particular application.

The objective of a training program is to provide the trainee with the knowledge and the desire to use the CBIT appropriately on the job (Sein et al., 1987). In EUC environments where the user has a choice of whether or not to use the CBIT in their tasks, it is especially important for the trainee to have a high motivation to use the CBIT. How can this objective be achieved? Proper development of training programs can go a long way toward creating motivation to utilize a CBIT. Sein et al. (1987) note there has been very little research conducted in the area of EUC training. Their research suggests that an effective training program should concentrate on the physical aspects of the training environment, conceptual models of trainees, motivational planning and management, and the social environment of use. Each of these aspects of the training situation is an opportunity to capitalize on concepts from IM. (See Chapter 8 for a discussion of the effects of computer-based surveys in organizations.)

Physical aspects of the training environment deal with creating a stimulating learning environment. The training environment can be formal or self-instructional. A formal training environment provides a degree of structure for the training experience and tends to be conducted in a hands-on classroom situation with an instructor present. Self-instructional environments are unstructured and self-paced, using an on-line tutorial to train users, without direct interaction with an instructor. Results from a study conducted by Harrington, McElroy, and Morrow (1990) suggest that the type of training environment that should be used depends on the individual being trained. If the individual is computer anxious, anxiety can be lessened if they receive their choice of training environments. Formal training environments were found to be especially useful for computer-anxious individuals.

Conceptual models allow trainees to transfer prior knowledge of other situations to the EUC training environment. The Macintosh computer provides an excellent example of the use of conceptual models. The Macintosh uses a "desk top" metaphor intended to simulate the user's actual desk top on the computer screen. Thus, the user is presented with a conceptual model (the desk top), which they intuitively understand and can draw from when they use the Macintosh to perform their tasks.

If the ultimate goal is to get the trainee to use the system, motivation is highly important. Sein et al. (1987) give suggestions on how to instill a high level of motivation to learn in trainees. The factors to consider during training include alleviating computer anxiety, the design of learning tasks, and the development of learning materials.

As discussed earlier, the social environment can play a major role in determining system use. Every organizational unit has individuals who are known to be "experts" or "lead users" on a particular system who can serve as "informal consultants" (Lee, 1986). This informal grapevine, if managed properly by the organization, can be a positive contributor to the training of new users.

Attitudes Toward CBITs

Attitudes toward CBITs are perhaps the most important set of individual difference variables to consider when evaluating the likelihood of CBIT use. Reviews suggest that attitudes are the most studied individual difference relating to CBIT use (Nelson, 1990). When individuals possess negative attitudes toward these technologies, chances are good that any attempted CBIT implementation will be unsuccessful (i.e., the system will not be used or users will be dissatisfied with it) (Day, 1985).

A variety of researchers have investigated the effect of attitudes on CBIT use. Lucas (1975) developed a model of the use and performance of a CBIT in which attitudes and perceptions toward the system directly affected CBIT use. Robey (1979) used a sample of industrial salespeople to relate objective and subjective measures of system use to attitudes, finding that user attitudes are significant correlates of objective measures of system use, but are less powerful predictors of subjective assessment of perceived CBIT worth. In spite of these promising results, Goodhue (1988) argued that there is a lack of a convincing theoretical model that links user attitudes and use.

Negative attitudes toward CBITs can manifest themselves as a phenomenon known as computer anxiety that can cause individuals to avoid CBIT use (Harrington et al., 1990). Anxiety is defined by the *American Heritage Dictionary* as: "Intense fear or dread lacking an unambiguous cause or a specific threat" (1985, p. 117). Turner wrote that "Anxiety is an explanatory term which allows prediction from a variety of situations to a complex and variable set of reactions" (1984, p. 52). May (1950) distinguished between anxiety and fear by saying: "fear is a reaction to a specific threat while anxiety is unspecific, 'vague', 'objectless'" (p. 191).

Attitudes toward CBITs and computer anxiety influence each other through factors internal to the individual. It stands to reason that a positive attitude toward computers should be related to a low level of computer anxiety, whereas a negative attitude would correlate with a high level of computer anxiety (Harrington, et al., 1990; Howard, 1983; Morrow, Prell & McElroy, 1986; Raub, 1981).

Exactly how a positive attitude towards computers is formed is a question that is not easily answered. Because of its two-way relationship with computer anxiety, it is difficult to postulate which comes first, computer anxiety or a negative attitude toward computers. Results reported by Harrington et al. (1990) suggest that the proper training environment can go a long way toward eliminating computer anxiety. If this is the case, and computer anxiety is in fact not a permanent condition (i.e., not a form of trait anxiety), then this individual difference can be managed.

It can be speculated that the role of computer anxiety in determining CBIT use by individuals within organizational units should diminish in the future since so many individuals are now being exposed to CBITs at a younger and younger age. As these individuals enter the workplace, they will be less likely to display anxiety toward CBITs because they are familiar with them. The current workforce, however, did not grow up with these technologies and thus computer anxiety is still an important consideration today. Still, even if there is past experience with technology, a change in technology may continue to be traumatic to and resisted by even the most experienced individuals. (See Chapter 7 for an examination of impression formation and multimedia presentations.)

Locus of Control

Locus of control is a concept developed by Rotter (1966) to measure perceived control of reinforcement. This measure was developed after it was realized that individuals reacted differently to success or failure when the outcome of the task they were to perform was said to be due to either skill (i.e., factors internal to the individual) or chance (i.e., factors external to the individual) (Lefcourt, 1981).

Past research has found that perceived control of reinforcement is positively associated with access to opportunity. Individuals who are given opportunities to attain valued positive outcomes are more likely to hold internal control expectancies than individuals who do not have access to these opportunities. Individuals who are deprived of such things as positions with status, group memberships, and the like, are often found to hold fatalistic, external control beliefs. Thus, some individuals have learned to believe that valued reinforcement occurs only by chance, and that they have no control over their fate, while others believe that they control their own fate (Lefcourt, 1982).

The locus of control concept can play a role in CBIT use because individuals with an internal locus of control, who require a say in how their lives are run, will be less apt to view the CBIT as a threat to their position and will be more apt to utilize it to their advantage. On the other hand, individuals with an external locus of control, with their natural tendency to believe they are not in control of their lives, will tend to view the CBIT as just another way for the organization to control them (Arndt et al., 1983; Coovert & Goldstein, 1980; Russell, 1982; Russell & McAuley, 1986; Russell, et al., 1987).

Past Experiences with CBITs

Although it is true that it would be extremely difficult, if not impossible, for individuals to completely avoid CBITs in today's organizations, there are nonetheless different levels of exposure to CBITs. Individuals with high levels of exposure can be characterized by activities such as owning or voluntarily using personal computers in the home or workplace, consistently using automatic teller machines (ATMs) to do their banking, or enjoying video games. Individuals with low levels of exposure, on the other hand, would not be voluntarily involved in the above activities and would have a distinct disinterest in becoming involved with information technology even when they were given the opportunity to do so. Individuals with low levels of exposure to CBITs would, all other things being equal, tend to possess a lower likelihood of CBIT acceptance than individuals with high exposure levels.

Koester and Luthans (1979) found that individuals who have had very little direct exposure to CBITs were influenced to a greater extent by the computer and its output than by more traditional information forms, such as mimeographed data. Individuals with CBIT experience reacted differently. These individuals were more pessimistic about computer generated data when compared to the more traditional forms.

This concept of past experience with CBITs affecting potential use also has implications in the area of attitudes toward CBITs of future workers. Many of these individuals are being exposed to CBITs at an early age in the schools. Thus, by the time they reach adulthood and go to work in organizations, CBITs are second nature to them. This idea is supported by the work of Howard (1983) and Howard and Smith (1986) who found that younger managers had more positive attitudes toward CBITs than older managers.

Once again, Leary and Kowalski's (1990) two-component model provides a possible structure on which to build. In this case, past expereince has led to the construction of user perceptions of CBIT. These perceptions must be understood, destinations due to the change process must be determined, the discrepancy between the current situation and the desired one must be assessed, and concrete action can be planned and implemented to move toward the desired outcome.

DISCUSSION

Keen (1980) described MIS research as study dealing with "the effective design, delivery, and use of [CBITs] in organizations" (p. 16). Since the advent of large-scale information systems for data processing, information distribution, and organizational communication, research has been directed at discerning the factors important to the success of these large and complex systems (cf. Beatty, 1986; Dykman, 1986; Lucas, 1975; Mawhinney, 1986; Robey, 1979; Schewe,

1976; Sokol, 1986). Many of these studies have used an organizational science approach. None, however, has specifically focused on or incorporated the impression management perspective.

Using IM, we suggest that one avenue of research that might be of interest is an examination of the inappropriate use and lack of use of CBIT. We combined the rational perspective on change (i.e., the organization's perspective) and the emotional perspective (i.e., the personal, perceptual perspective) to create the model presented in Figure 9.1. In this model are four general categories, or cells, of CBIT use/nonuse. Cells 2 and 3 are appropriate in CBIT use in that the rational and emotional perspectives lead to the same conclusion on system use or nonuse. For example, in cell 2 both the rational and emotional perspectives would suggest that the CBIT would be used in an appropriate fashion; in cell 3 both perspectives indicate appropriate nonuse of the CBIT. However, cells 1 and 4 indicate an inconsistency between the two perspectives. In cell 1 we find an underuse of the CBIT due to the effects of the emotional perspective suppressing the effects of the rational perspective. In other words, from an organizational perspective, the system is capable of being used more extensively for relevant work-related needs and activities. In cell 4 we have a situation of overuse of the CBIT, where the system is used inappropriately; that is, too much.

To briefly highlight several opportunities for further research, there are aspects of both the rational and emotional perspectives that are open to investigation from an IM perspective. The trend in CBIT has been toward end-user computing (Benjamin, 1982; Rockart & Flannery, 1983); that is, placing most of the control and responsibility for computing at the hands of the user of the information produced (Sein et al, 1987). This provides for less specific organizational control over computing uses, increasing the need for a conscious management of impressions of technology capabilities and limitations. It also raises the effects of individual differences of the users. Several specific areas of interest were advanced.

Uncertainty and equivocality create different dynamics in the process of seeking information (Daft & Lengel, 1986). Depending on employee understanding of a situation and information needs, different approaches to using CBIT may occur. The dynamics of organizational change are also open to investigation from an IM perspective. What are the internal factors to change? The external factors? How can resistance to change be overcome? Even the context of the organization, including controllable, partially controllable, and uncontrollable factors need additional evaluation. Other interesting factors are more focused on the individual, including the social system, individual differences, locus of control, attitudes toward and past experiences with CBIT, training for new technology, and characteristics of the CBIT itself. Impression management offers an unexplored avenue of research for all of these issues.

It must be noted again that the perspective we have taken is broader than the original conception of impression management. As typically portrayed, IM is self-presentation, that is, an individual's attempts to assess and manage the impressions they make and that others have of them. Our approach is broader in that we are talking about managing the effects of the impressions people have of computer-based information technology and the impressions caused by the technology. Although some broader conceptions have appeared in the literature, in general, none have focused on information technology as we have done in this chapter and in this book.

CONCLUSION

Throughout this chapter, and in many of the preceeding chapters of this volume, we have examined in a cursory, tentative, and suggestive fashion the possibility of impression management providing a useful approach to gaining additional understanding of the use of computer-based information technologies. Our goal has been to raise questions and suggest avenues for investigation. We believe that impression management is a fertile perspective, one that has not been explicitly investigated to date, for the examination and understanding of many of the dynamics of people's interactions with, and even through, computer-based information technology. It is our aspiration that the material presented in this and the preceeding chapters can provide a foundation for the start of a fruitful avenue of theory development and applied research.

BIBLIOGRAPHY

Ahn, J. H. (1987). End-user computing: A task referent approach. Unpublished doctoral dissertation, New York University, Graduate School of Business Administration.

Alavi, M., & Weiss, I. R. (1985). Managing the risks of end-user computing. *Journal of Management Information Systems, 11*, 5-20.

Alcalay, R., & Pasick, R. J. (1983). Psycho-social factors and the technologies of work. *Social Science and Medicine, 17*(16), 1075-1084.

Aldrich, H. E. (1979). *Organizations and environments.* Englewood Cliffs, NJ: Prentice-Hall.

Alexander, C. N., & Knight, G. W. (1971). Situated identities and social psychological experimentation. *Sociometry, 34*, 65-82.

Alexander, E. R., Penley, L. E., & Jernigan, I. E. (1991). The effect of individual differences on media choice. *Management of Communication Quarterly, 5*, 155-173.

Allen, D. (1988). New telecommunications services. *Telecommunications Policy, 12*(3), 257-271.

American Heritage Dictionary, 2nd College Edition. (1985). Boston, MA: Houghton Mifflin.

And you thought your computer chat was private. (1993, February 7). *New York Times*, p. A 10.

Andersen Consulting. (1992). Strategic Vendor Partnership Survey Results, National Retail Federation.

Anderson, R. E., Hassen, T., Johnson, D. C., & Klassen, D. L. (1979). Instructional computing: Acceptance and rejection by secondary school teachers. *Sociology of Work and Occupations, 6*, 227-250.

Anthes, G. H. (1990, December 17).   EDI user numbers growing stronger. *Computerworld, 24*(51), 48.

Applegate, L. M., Cash, J. I., & Mills, D. Q. (1988).   Information technology and tomorrow's manager. *Harvard Business Review, November-December,* 104-112.

Argyris, C. (1971).   Management information systems: The challenge to rationality and emotionality. *Management Science, 17,* 275-292.

Argyris, C., & Schon, D. A. (1978).   *Organizational learning.* Reading, MA: Addison-Wesley Publishing.

Arndt, S., Feltes, J., & Hanak, J. (1983).   Secretarial attitudes towards word processors as a function of familiarity and locus of control. *Behaviour and Information Technology, 2,* 17-22.

Arnett, N. (1990).   The PC evolution continues: Multimedia. *The Computer Shopper, June,* 126+.

Artle, R., & Averous, C. (1973).   The telephone system as a public good: Static and dynamic aspects.   *The Bell Journal of Economics and Management Science, 4*(1), 89-100.

Babad, E. Y., Bernieri, F., & Rosenthal, R. (1989).   Non-verbal communication and leakage in the behavior of biased and unbiased teachers. *Journal of Personality and Social Psychology, 56,* 89-94.

Bakopoulos, J. Y. (1985).   Toward a more precise concept of information technology.   In L. Gallegos, R. Welke, & J. Wetherbe (Eds.), *Proceedings of the Sixth International Conference on Information Systems,* pp. 17-24.

Ball, L., & Harris, R. (1982).   SMIS members: A membership analysis. *MIS Quarterly, 6*(1), 19-38.

Banker, R. D., and Kaufmann, R. (1988).   Strategic contributions of information technology: an empirical study of ATM networks.   In J. I. DeGross & M. H. Olson (Eds.), *Proceedings of the Ninth International Conference on Information Systems,* pp. 141-150.

Banker, R. D., Kaufmann, R. J., and Morey, R. C. (1989).   "Measuring input productivity gains from information technology." Working Paper Number 196, Center for Research on Information Systems, Stern School of Business, New York University.

Barki, H., & Huff, S. L. (1985).   Change, attitude to change, and decision support system success. *Information & Management, 9,* 261-268.

Baumeister, R. F., & Tice, D. M. (1984).   Role of self-presentation and choice in cognitive dissonance under forced compliance: Necessary or sufficient cahses? *Journal of Personality and Social Pscyhology, 46,* 5-13.

Baumeister, R. F., Tice, D. M., & Hutton, D. G. (1989). Self-presentational motivations and personality differences in self-esteem.   *Journal of Personality, 57,* 547-579.

Beatty, C. A., & Gordon, J.R.M. (1988). Barriers to the implementation of CAD/CAM systems. *Sloan Management Review, Summer*, 25-33.

Beatty, W. A. (1986). Determining factors of microcomputer-based management information user satisfaction. Unpublished doctoral dissertation, Florida State University.

Becker, F. D. (1982). *The Successful Office*, Reading MA: Addison Wesley.

Becker, M. H. (1970). Factors Affecting Diffusion of Innovations among Health Professionals. *American Journal of Public Health, 60*, 294-305.

Belitsos, B. (1988). EDI becomes a necessity. *Computer Decisions, October*, 38-40.

Bender, D. H. (1986). Financial impact of information processing. *Journal of Management Information Systems, 3*, 2.

Benjamin, R. I. (1982). Information technology in the 1990s: A long range planning scenario. *MIS Quarterly, 6*, 11-31.

Benjamin, R. I., de Long, D. W, & Scott Morton, M. S. (1990). Electronic data interchange: How much competitive advantage? *Long Range Planning, 23*(1), 29-40.

Berger, C. R., and Calabrese, R. J. (1975). Some explorations in initial interaction and beyond: Toward a developmental theory of interpersonal communication. *Human Communication Research, 1*(2), 99-112.

Berger, P., & Luckmann, T. (1967). *The social construction of reality: A treatise in the sociology of knowledge*. New York: Anchor Books.

Betts, M. (1992, March 9). Personal data more public than you think. *Computerworld, 26*, 1-4.

Betts, M. (1994, January 31). Manage My Inventory or Else! *Computerworld, 28*(5), 93-96.

Bies, R. J., & Shapiro, D.L. (1988). Voice and justification: Their influence on procedural fairness judgements. *Academy of Management Journal, 31*, 676-685.

Bigelow, B. V. (1992, June 20). Computer wiretap new Big Brother? *San Diego Union*, pp. A1, A7.

Bikson, T. K., & Gutek, B. A. (1983). *Advanced office systems: An empirical look at utilization and satisfaction* (N-1970/NSF). Santa Monica, CA: RAND Corp.

Bikson, T. K., Gutek, B. A., & Mankin, D. (1987). *Implementation of information technology in office settings: Influences and outcomes*. (Final Report to the National Science Foundation, Productivity Improvement Section R-3077-NSF/IRIS). Santa Monica, CA: Rand Corporation.

Blumer, H. (1969). *Symbolic interactionism: Perspectives and methods*. Englewood Cliffs, NJ: Prentice-Hall.

Bond, M. H. (1991). Cultural influences on modes of impression management: Implication for the culturally diverse organization. In R. A. Giacalone &

P. Rosenfeld (Eds.), *Applied impression management* (pp. 195-215). Newbury Park, CA: Sage Publications.

Booker, E. (1990, February 12). IS trailblazing puts retailer on top. *Computerworld, 24*(7), 69, 73.

Booker, E., & Fitzgerald, M. (1990, July 9). Retailers try EDI hard sell. *Computerworld, 24*(28), 1, 8.

Boorman, S., & White, H. (1976). Social structure from multiple networks II: Role structures. *American Journal of Sociology, 81*, 1384-1446.

Booth-Kewley, S., Edwards, J. E., & Rosenfeld, P. (1992). Impression management, social desirability, and computer administration of attitude questionnaires: Does the computer make a difference? *Journal of Applied Psychology, 77*, 562-566

Booth-Kewley, S., Rosenfeld, P., & Edwards, J. E. (1993). Computer-administered surveys in organizational settings: Alternatives, advantages, and applications. In P. Rosenfeld, J. E. Edwards, & M. D. Thomas (Eds.), *Improving organizational surveys: New directions, methods, and applications* (pp. 73-101). Newbury Park, CA: Sage.

Bouchard, L. (1992). Business partnerships and the adoption of collective innovations: The case of EDI. Unpublished Doctoral Dissertation, University of California at Los Angeles, CA.

Bowen, W. (1986). The puny payoff from office computers. *Fortune*, May 26, 20-24.

Brancheau, J., & Wetherbe, J. C. (1987). Key issues in information systems—1986. *MIS Quarterly, 11*(1), 23-45.

Brown, M. (1994). Do you believe in magic? A theory of information technology cultures. Working paper. York University, Toronto, Ontario.

Browning, J. (1990, June 16). A survey of information technology: A question of communication. *The Economist* (special section—20 pages).

Brynjolfsson, E., & Hitt, L. (1993). Is information systems spending productive? New evidence and new results. In J. I. DeGross, R. P. Bostrom, & D. Robey (Eds.), *Proceedings of the Fourteenth International Conference on Information Systems*, p. 384.

Burt, R. S., (1982). *Toward a Structural Theory of Action*, New York: Academic.

Burt, R. S. (1987). Social contagion & innovation: Cohesion versus structural equivalence. *American Journal of Sociology, 92*(6), 1287-1335.

Buss, A., & Briggs, S. (1984). Drama and the self in social interaction. *Journal of Personality and Social Psychology, 47*, 1310-1324.

Bylinsky, G. (1991, November 4). How companies spy on employees. *Fortune, 124*, 131-140.

Caminiti, S. (1990, September 24). The new champs of retailing. *Fortune*, 85-100.

Cheney, P. H., Mann, R. L., & Amoroso, D. L. (1986). Organizational factors affecting the success of end-user computing. *Journal of Management Information Systems, 3*, 65-80.

Christie, R., & Geis, F. L. (1970). *Studies in Machiavellianism*. New York: Academic Press.

Cialdini, R. B. (1989). Indirect tactics of image management: Beyond basking. In R. A. Giacalone & P. Rosenfeld (Eds.), *Impression management in the organization* (pp. 45-56). Hillsdale, NJ: Erlbaum.

Clement, A. (1988). Office automation and the technical control of information workers. In V. Mosco & J. Wasko (Eds.) *The political economy of information* (pp. 217-246). Madison, WI: The University of Wisconsin Press.

Cohen, R. L. (1986). *Justice: View from the social sciences*. New York: Plenum.

Computerworld, (1990, December 12). Sears pushing EDI with suppliers. *24*, 51, 95.

Connolly, T., Jessup, L., & Valacich, J. (1990). Effects of anonymity and evaluative tone on idea generation in computer-mediated groups. *Management Science, 36*, 689-703.

Coovert, M. D., & Goldstein, M. (1980). Locus of control as a predictor of user's attitude toward computers. *Psychological Reports, 47*, 1167-1173.

Copeland, D. G., & McKenney, J. L. (1988). Airline reservation systems: lessons from history. *MIS Quarterly, 12*, 3, 353-370.

Coy, P. (1992, August 17). Big brother, pinned to your chest. *Business Week*, 38.

Crane, F. G. (1989). A practical guide to professional services marketing. *Journal of Professional Services Marketing, 5*, 3-15.

Crawford, A. B., Jr. (1982). Corporate electronic mail: A communication-intensive application of information technology. *MIS Quarterly, 6*, 1-13.

Cron, W., & Sobol, M. (1983). "The relationship between computerization and performance: a strategy for maximizing economic benefits of computerization." *Information and Management, 6*, 171-181.

Crowne, D. P., & Marlowe, D. (1960). A new scale of social desirability independent of psychopathology. *Journal of Consulting Psychology, 24*, 349-354.

Crowne, D. P., & Marlowe, D. (1964). *The approval motive*. New York: Wiley.

Culnan, M. J., & Markus, M. L. (1987). Information technologies. In F. M. Jablin, L. L. Putnam, K. H. Roberts, & L. W. Porter (Eds.), *Handbook of organizational communication: An interdisciplinary perspective* (pp. 420-443). Newbury Park, CA: Sage Publications.

Culnan, M. J., & Swanson, E. B. (1986). Research in management information systems, 1980-1984: Points of work and reference. *MIS Quarterly, 10,* 289-301.

Daft, R. L., & Lengel, R. H. (1984). Information richness: A new approach to managerial behavior and organization design. In B. M. Staw & L. L. Cummings (Eds.), *Research in organizational behavior* (Vol. 6, pp. 191-233). Greenwich, CT: JAI Press.

Daft, R. L., & Lengel, R. H. (1986). Organizational information requirements, media richness and structural design. *Management Science, 32,* 554-571.

Daft, R. L., Lengel, R. H., & Trevino, L. K. (1987). Message equivocality, media selection, and manager performance: Implications for information systems. *MIS Quarterly, 11,* 355-368.

Daft, R. L., Lengel, R. H., & Trevino, L. K. (1987). The relationship among message equivocality, media selection, and manager performance: Implications for information support systems. *MIS Quarterly, 11,* 355-368.

Daft, R. L., & Macintosh, N. B. (1981). A tentative exploration into the amount and equivocality of information processing in organizational work units. *Administrative Science Quarterly, 26*(2), 207-224.

Daft, R. L., & Steers, R. M. (1986). *Organizations: A micro/macro approach.* Glenview, IL: Scott, Foresman & Co.

D'Agostino, P., & Small, K. (1980). Cross-modality transfer between pictures and their names. *Canadian Journal of Psychology, 34*(2), 113-118.

Daly, J. A. (1985). Writing apprehension. In M. Rose (Ed.), *When a writer can't write* (pp. 43-82). New York, NY: Guilford.

Dambrot, F. H., Watkins-Malek, M. A., Silling, S. M., Marshall, R. S., & Garver, J. A. (1985). Correlates of sex differences in attitudes toward and involvement with computers. *Journal of Vocational Behavior, 27,* 71-86.

Dandridge, T. C. (1983). Symbol's function and use. In L. R. Pondy, P. J. Frost, G. Morgan, & T. D. Dandridge (Eds.), *Organizational symbolism.* Greenwich, CT: JAI Press.

Dandridge, T. C., Mitroff, I., & Joyce, W. F. (1980). Organizational symbolism: A topic to expand organizational analysis. *Academy of Management Review, 5,* 77-82.

Danziger, J. N., & Dutton, W. H. (1977, December). Computers as an innovation in American local government. *Communications of the ACM, 20,* 945-956.

Danziger, J., Dutton, W., Kling, R., & Kraemer, K. (1982). *Computers and politics.* NY: Columbia University Press.

Davis, F. D. (1989). Perceived usefulness, perceived ease of use, and user acceptance of information technology. *MIS Quarterly, 13,* 319-340.

Davis, F. D., Bagozzi, R. P., & Warshaw, P. R. (1989). User acceptance of computer technology: A comparison of two theoretical models.

Management Science, 35, 982-1003.

Davis, G. B. (1983). Evolution of information systems as an academic discipline. Paper presented at the Information Systems Education Conference, Chicago.

Davis, T. R. V. (1984). The influence of the physical environment in offices. *Academy of Management Review, 9*, 271-283.

Davis, T. R. V. (1991). Information technology and white-collar productivity. *Academy of Management Executive, 5*(1), 55-67.

Day, C. R. (1985, January 21). Anxiety "busters" tackle computers. *Industry Week*, 65-67.

DeSanctis, G., & Gallupe, R. B. (1987). A foundation for the study of group decision support systems. *Management Science, 33*, 589-606.

DeSimone, D. (1992). *Multimedia—minds merging*. Institute for Information Studies.

Dess, G., & Beard, D. W. (1984). Dimensions of organizational task environments. *Administrative Science Quarterly, 29*, 52-73.

Dickson, G. W. (1981). Management Information Systems: Evolution and status. *Advances in Computers, 20*, 1-37.

Dickson, G. W., Leitheiser, R. L., & Wetherbe, J. C. (1984). Key information systems issues for the 1980's. *MIS Quarterly, 8*(3), 129-159.

Doherty, L., & Thomas, M. D. (1986). Effects of an automated survey system upon responses. In O. Brown, Jr., & H. W. Hendrick (Eds.), *Human factors in organizational design management--II* (pp. 157-161). New York: Elsevier Science Publishers.

Dos Santos, B. L., Peffers, K., & Mauer, D. C. (1993). The impact of information technology investment announcements on the market value of the firm. *Information Systems Research, 4*(1), 1-23.

Dreyfuss, J. (1988, September 26). Catching the computer wave. *Fortune*, pp. 78-79, 82.

Drucker, P. F. (1991). The new productivity challenge. *Harvard Business Review, November-December*, 69-79.

Dunlop, C., & Kling, R. (1991). *Computerization and controversy: Value conflicts and social choices*. San Diego: Academic Press.

Dunnington, R. A. (1993). New methods and technologies in the organizational survey process. In P. Rosenfeld, J. E. Edwards, & M. D. Thomas (Eds.), *Improving organizational surveys: New directions, methods, and applications* (pp. 102-121). Newbury Park, CA: Sage.

Dykman, C. A. (1986). Electronic mail systems: An analysis of the use/satisfaction relationship. Unpublished doctoral dissertation, University of Houston.

Eden, D. (1988) Pygmalion, goal setting, and expectancy: Compatible ways to raise productivity. *Academy of Management Review, 13*, 639-652.

Eden, D. (1990). *Pygmalion in management: Productivity as a self-fulfilling prophecy.* Lexington, MA: Lexington.

Eden, D. (1991). Applying impression management to create productive self-fulfilling prophecies at work. In R. A. Giacalone & P. Rosenfeld (Eds.), *Applied impression management* (pp. 13-40). Newbury Park, CA: Sage Publications.

EDI, spread the word! (October 1992—September 1993). *EDI Yellow Pages: Business Partner Directory, Edition VIII, Volume II.*

EDP Analyzer. (1987). The rise of "cooperative" systems. *25*(6).

EDP Analyzer. (1989). The strategic value of EDI. *27*(8).

Edwards, R. (1979). *Contested terrain: The transformation of the workplace in the twentieth century.* New York: Basic Books.

Ein-Dor, P., & Segev, E. (1978). Organizational context and the success of management information systems. *Management Science, 24*, 1064-1077.

Eisman, R. (1991, June). Big Brother lives. *Incentive, 165*, pp. 21-27, 103.

Emerson, R. M. (1962). Power-dependence relations. *American Sociological Review, 27*, 31-41.

Feinstein, S. (1986, October 9). Computers replacing interviewers for personnel and marketing tasks. *The Wall Street Journal*, p. 35.

Feldman, M., & March, J. G. (1981). Information as signal and symbol. *Administrative Science Quarterly, 26*, 171-186.

Felson, R. B. (1981). An interactionist approach to aggression. In J. T. Tedeschi (Ed.), *Impression Management Theory and Social Psychological Research* (pp. 181-200). New York: Academic Press.

Fenigstein, A., Scheier, M., & Buss, A. H. (1975). Public and private self-consciousness: Assessment and theory. *Journal of Consulting and Clinical Psychology, 43*, 522-527.

Festinger, L., Pepitone, A., & Newcomb, T. (1952). Some consequences of deindividuation in a group. *Journal of Abnormal and Social Psychology, 47*, 382-389.

Finholt, T., & Sproull, L. S. (1990). Electronic groups at work. *Organization Science, 1*, 41-64.

Fireman, B., & Gamson, W. A. (1979). Utilitarian logic in the resource mobilization perspective. In N. Z. Mayer & J. D. McCarthy (Eds.), *The Dynamics of Social Movements: Resource Mobilization, Social Control, and Tactics* (pp. 8-44). Cambridge, MA: Winthrop Publishers, Inc.

Fitzgerald, M. (1990, July 16). Sears puts foot down, insists on EDI ability. *Computerworld, 24*, 29, 132.

Fitzgerald, M. (1990, October 8). "When?" is now at Sears. *Computerworld, 24*, 41, 67, 71.

Fletcher, C. (1979). Candidates' beliefs and self-presentation strategies in selection interviews. *Personnel Review, 10*, 14-17.

Fletcher, C. (1990). The relationship between candidate personality, self-presentation strategies, and interviewer assessments in selection interviews: An empirical study. *Human Relations, 43*, 739-749.

Foster, L. W., & Flynn, D. M. (1984). Management information technology: Its effects on organizational form and function. *MIS Quarterly, 8*(4), 229-235.

Fox, B. (1991). Kmart tackles distribution with "Clas." *Chain Store Age Executive, 67*(1), 60-68.

Frenzel, C. W. (1992). *Management of information technology* (pp. 316-337). Boston, MA: Boyd and Fraser.

Fuerst, W. L., & Cheney, P. H. (1982). Factors affecting the perceived utilization of computer-based decision support systems in the oil industry. *Decision Sciences, 13*, 554-569.

Fulk, J., Schmitz, J., & Steinfield, C. W. (1990). A social influence model of technology use. In J. Fulk & C. Steinfield (Eds.), *Organizations and communication technology* (pp. 117-140). Newbury Park, CA: Sage.

Fulk, J., Steinfield, C. W., Schmitz, J., & Power, J.G. (1987). A social information processing model of media use in organizations. *Communication Research, 14*, 529-552.

Galbraith, J. (1977). *Organizational design.* Reading, MA: Addison-Wesley.

Galbraith, J. R. (1982). Designing the innovating organization. *Organizational Dynamics, Winter*, 5-25.

Galeskiewickz, J., & Burt, R. S. (1991). Interorganization contagion in corporate philanthropy. *Administrative Science Quarterly, 36*(1), 88-105.

Garcia, B. 1985. The second CRWT information center survey. *CRWT News for Better Training, 3*, 2.

Gardner, W. L. 1992. Lessons in organizational dramaturgy: The art of impression management. *Organizational Dynamics, 21*(1), 33-46.

Gardner, W. L., & Martinko, M. J. (1988). Impression management in organizations. *Journal of Management, 14*, 321-338.

Gardner, W. L., & Martinko, M. J. (1988). Impression management: An observational study linking audience characteristics with verbal self-presentations. *Academy of Management Journal, 31*, 42-65.

Gardner, W. L., & Peluchette. J. V. (1991). Computer-mediated communications in organizational settings: A self-presentational perspective. In E. Szewczak, C. Snodgrass, & M. Khosrowpour (Eds.), *Management impacts of information technology: Perspectives on organizational growth and change* (pp. 165-206). Harrisburg, PA: Idea Publishing Group.

Gasper, E. (1990). *HyperAnimation News*, 3.

Giacalone, R. A., & Pollard, H. G. (1989). Comparative effectiveness of impression management tactics on the recommendation of grievant punishment: An exploratory investigation. *Forensic Reports*, *2*, 147-160.

Giacalone, R. A., & Rosenfeld, P. (Eds.) (1989). *Impression management in the organization*. Hillsdale, NJ: Lawrence Erlbaum.

Giacalone, R. A., & Rosenfeld, P. (Eds.) (1991). *Applied impression management: How image making affects managerial decisions*. Newbury Park, CA: Sage.

Gilmore, D. C., & Ferris, G. R. (1989). The effects of applicant impression management tactics on interviewer judgements. *Journal of Management*, *15*, 557-564.

Goodhue, D. (1988). I/S attitudes: Toward theoretical and definitional clarity. *Data Base*, *19*(3-4), 6-15.

Goffman, E. (1959). *The presentation of self in everyday life*. Garden City, NY: Doubleday Anchor.

Grandjean, E. (1987). *Ergonomics in computerized offices*. London: Taylor & Francis.

Granovetter, M. (1978). Threshold models of collective behavior. *American Journal of Sociology*, *83*(6), 1420-1443.

Green, F. (1991, May 23). Big brother is on-line. *San Diego Union*, C1, C3.

Greenberg, J. (1990). Looking fair vs. being fair: Managing impressions of organizational justice. In B. M. Staw & L. L. Cummings (Eds.), *Research in organizational behavior* (Vol. 12, pp. 111-15). Greenwich, CT: JAI.

Greenberg, J., Bies, R. J., & Eskew, D. E. (1991). Establishing fairness in the eye of the beholder: Managing impression of organizational justice. In R. A. Giacalone & P. Rosenfeld (Eds.), *Applied impression management* (pp. 111-132). Newbury Park, CA: Sage Publications.

Gresham, L. (1993). Report from The College of Business Administration and Graduate School of Business Task Force on Teaching Excellence, L. Gresham (chairman).

Griffin, R. W. (1982). *Task design: An integrative approach*. Glenview, IL: Scott, Foresman.

Gurbaxani, V. (1990). Diffusion in computing networks: The case of BITNET. *Communications of the ACM*, *33*(12), 65-75.

Gutek, B. A. (1989). Implications of information technology for professional/managerial and clerical work. Unpublished manuscript.

Hardin, R. (1982). *Collective action*. Baltimore: The John Hopkins University Press.

Harrington, K. V., McElroy, J. C., & Morrow, P. C. (1990). Computer anxiety and computer-based training: A laboratory experiment. *Journal of Educational Computing Research*, *6*, 343-358.

Harris, S. E., & Katz, J. L. (1988). Profitability and information technology capital intensity in the insurance industry. *Proceedings of the Twenty-First Annual Hawaii International Conference on System Sciences*, pp. 124-130.

Hatch, M. J. (1990). The symbolics of office design. In P. Gagliardi (Ed.), *Symbols and Artifacts: Views of the Corporate Landscape* (pp. 129-146). New York: Aldine de Gruyter.

Haugtvedt, C., Petty, R., & Cacioppo, J. (1986). Need for cognition and use of peripheral cues. Presented at the Annual Meeting of the Midwest Psychological Association, Chicago.

Haynes, R. M. (1990). The ATM at age twenty: A productivity paradox. *National Productivity Review, 9*(3), 273-280.

Helmreich, R. (1987). Changing potential users to actual users: An evolutionary approach to office system acceptance. In M. Frese, E. Ulich, & W. Dzida (Eds.) *Psychological issues of human computer interaction in the work place* (pp. 81-95). New York: Elsevier.

Hickson, D. J., Hinnings, C. A, Schneck, R. E., & Pennings, J. M. (1971). A strategic contingencies theory of intraorganizational power. *Administrative Science Quarterly, 16*, 216-229.

Hiltz, S. R., & Johnson, K. (1990). User satisfaction with computer-mediated communication systems. *Management Science, 36*, 739-764.

Hiltz, S. R., & Turoff, M. (1981). The evolution of user behavior in a computerized conferencing system. *Communications of the ACM, 24*, 739-759.

Hiltz, S. R., & Turoff, M. (1985). Structuring computer-mediated communication systems to avoid information overload. *Communications of the ACM, 28*, 680-689.

Hiltz, S. R., Turoff, M., Johnson, K. (1989). Experiments in group decision making: Disinhibition, deindividuation, and group process in pen name and real name computer conferences. *Decision Support Systems, 5*, 217-232.

Hirschheim, R. (1986). The effect of a priori views on the social implications of computing: The case of office automation. *Computing Surveys, 18*(2), 165-195.

Hirschheim, R., & Newman, R. (1991). Symbolism and information systems development: Myth, metaphor and magic. *Information Systems Research, 2*(1), 29-62.

Hollander, E. P. (1958). Conformity, status, and idiosyncracy credit. *Psychological Review, 65*, 117-127.

Howard, G. S. (1983). Computer anxiety and other determinants of managers' attitudes toward the usefulness of microcomputers in management. Unpublished doctoral dissertation, Kent State University, Kent, Ohio.

Howard, G. S., & Smith, R. D. (1986). Computer anxiety in management: Myth or reality? *Communications of the ACM, 29*, 611-615.

Huber, G. (1984). The nature and design of post-industrial organizations. *Management Science, 30*(8), 928-951.

Huber, V. L., Latham, G. P., & Locke, E. A. (1989). The management of impressions through goal setting. In R. A. Giacalone & P. Rosenfeld (Eds.), *Impression management in the organization* (pp. 203-217). Hillsdale, NJ: Lawrence Erlbaum.

Iacono, S., & Kling, R. (1987). Changing office technologies and transformations of clerical jobs: A historical perspective. In R. E. Kraut (Ed.), *Technology and the transformation of white-collar work* (pp. 53-76). Hillsdale, NJ: Lawrence Erlbaum Associates.

Iadipaolo, D. M. (1992, June). Monster or monitor? *Insurance and technology*, *17*, 47-54.

Ives, B., & Mason, R. (1990). "Can information technology revitalize your customer service." *Academy of Management Executive*, *4*(4), 52-69.

Izzo, J. (1987). *The Embattled Fortress*, San Francisco: Jossey-Bass Publishing Co.

James, L. R., & Jones, A. P. (1974). Organizational climate: A review of theory and research. *Psychological Bulletin*, *81*, 1096-1112.

Jarvenpaa, S. L., & Ives, B. (1990). Information technology and corporate strategy: A view from the top. *Information Systems Research*, *1*(4), 351-376.

Jessup, L., Connolly, T., & Galegher, J. (1990). The effects of anonymity on GDSS group process with an idea-generating task. *MIS Quarterly*, *14*(3), 313-321.

Johnston, H. R., & Carrico, S. R. (1988). Developing capabilities to use information strategically. *MIS Quarterly*, *12*(1), 37-48.

Jones, E. E., & Pittman, T. S. (1982). Toward a general theory of strategic self-presentation. In J. Suls (Ed.), *Psychological perspectives on the self* (pp. 231-262). Hillsdale, NJ: Erlbaum.

Jones, E. E., & Sigall, H. (1971). The bogus pipeline: A new paradigm for measuring affect and attitude. *Psychological Bulletin*, *76*, 349-364.

Jones, E. E., & Wortman, C. (1973). *Ingratiation: An attributional approach*. Morristown, NJ: General Learning Press.

Kantor, J. (1991). The effects of computer administration and identification on the Job Descriptive Index (JDI). *Journal of Business and Psychology*, *5*, 309-323.

Katz, D. & Khan, R. L. (1978). *The social psychology of organizations* (2nd ed.). New York, NY: John Wiley.

Katz, J.A. (1987). Playing at innovation in the computer revolution. In M. Frese, E. Ulich, & W. Dzida (Eds.), *Psychological issues of human computer interaction in the work place* (pp. 97-112). North Holland: Amsterdam.

Katz, J. E., & Tassone, A. R. (1990). Public opinion trends: Privacy and information technology. *Public Opinion Quarterly*, *54*, 125-143.

Kaufmann, R. J., & Weill, P. (1989). An evaluative framework for research on the performance effects of information technology investment. In J. I. DeGross, J. C. Henderson, & B. R. Konsynski (Eds.), *Proceedings of the Tenth International Conference on Information Systems*, pp. 377-388.

Keefe, P. (1980, January 6). Can you afford to ignore EDI? *Computerworld*, 39-41.

Keen, P. G. (1980). MIS research: Reference disciplines and a cumulative tradition. In E. R. McLean (Ed.), *Proceedings of the First International Conference on Information Systems*, pp. 9-18.

Keen, P. G. (1981). Information systems and organizational change. *Communications of the ACM, 24*, 24-33.

Kerr, E. B., & Hiltz, S. R. (1982). *Computer-mediated communication systems*. New York: Academic Press.

Kiely, T. (1990, October). The two faces of EDI. *CIO, 4*(1), 80-91.

Kiesler, S. (1986). The hidden messages in computer networks. *Harvard Business Review, 64*(1): 46-60.

Kiesler, S., Siegel, J., & McGuire, T. W. (1984). Social psychological aspects of computer-mediated communication. *American Psychologist, 39*, 1123-1134.

Kiesler, S., & Sproull, L. (1986). Response effects in the electronic survey. *Public Opinion Quarterly, 50*, 402-413.

King, J. L. (1983). Centralized versus decentralized computing: Organizational considerations and management options. *Computing Surveys, 15*(4), 319-349.

King, W. C., Dent, M. M., & Miles, E. W. (1991). The persuasive effect of graphics in computer-mediated communication. *Computers in Human Behavior, 7*, 269-279.

Klein, S. M. & Ritti, R. R. (1980). *Understanding Organizational Behavior*. Boston: Kent.

Kletke, M., Trumbly, J. E., & Nelson, L. (1991). The integration of microcomputers into the organization: A human adaptation model and the organizational response. *Journal of Microcomputer Systems Management, 3*(1), 23-35.

Kling, R. (1980). Social analysis of computing: Theoretical orientations in recent empirical research. *Computing Surveys, 12*(1), 61-110.

Kling, R., & Iacono, S. (1984). The control of information systems developments after implementation. *Communications of the ACM, 27*(12), 1218-1226.

Kling, R., & Iacono, S. (1989). Desktop computerization and the organization of work. In T. Forester (Ed.), *Computers in the human context: Information technology, productivity, and people* (pp.). Cambridge, MA: The MIT Press.

Kling, R., & Scachi, W. (1982). The web of computing: Computer technology and social organization. *Advances in Computers, 21*, 1-90.

Koester, R., & Luthans, F. (1979). The impact of the computer on the choice activity of decision makers: A replication with actual users of computerized MIS. *Academy of Management Journal, 22*, 416-422.

Komsky, S. H. (1991). A profile of users of electronic mail in a university. *Management of Communication Quarterly, 4*, 310-340.

Konar, E., & Sundstrom, E. (1985). Status demarcation in the office. In J. Wineman (Ed.), *Behavioral issues in office design* (pp. 203-223). New York: Van Nostrand.

Konar, E., Sundstrom, E., Brady, C., Mandel, D. & Rice, R. (1982). Status markers in the office. *Environment and Behavior, 14*(3), 561-580.

Konovsky, M. A., & Jaster, F. (1989). "Blaming the victim" and other ways business men and women account for questionable behavior. *Journal of Business Ethics, 8*, 391-398.

Korda, M. (1977). *Success!* New York: Random House.

Kraemer, K. L., & Dutton, W. H. (1979). The interests served by technological reform. *Administration and Society, 11*(1), 80-106.

Larwood, L. (1991). Start with a rational group of people: Gender effects of impression management in organizations. In R. A. Giacalone & P. Rosenfeld (Eds.), *Applied impression management* (pp. 177-194). Newbury Park, CA: Sage Publications.

Lautenschlager, G. J., & Flaherty, V. L. (1990). Computer administration of questions: More desirable or more socially desirable? *Journal of Applied Psychology, 75*, 210-314.

Lawrence, P. R., & Lorsch, J. W. (1967). *Organizations and environment.* Boston: Harvard Business School, Division of Research.

Leary, M. (1989). Self-presentational processes in leadership emergence and effectiveness. In R. A. Giacalone & P. Rosenfeld (Eds.), *Impression Management in the Organization* (pp. 363-374). Hillsdale, NJ: Lawrence Erlbaum.

Leary, M. R., & Kowalski, R. M. (1990). Impression management: A literature review and two-component model. *Psychological Bulletin, 107*, 34-47.

Leavitt, H. J., & Whisler, T. L. (1958). Management in the 1980s. *Harvard Business Review, November-December*, 41-48.

Lederer, A. L., & Mendelow, A. L. (1988). Information resource planning: Overcoming difficulties in identifying top management's objectives. *MIS Quarterly, 11*, 389-399.

Lee, D.M.S. (1986). Usage patterns and sources of assistance for personal computer users. *MIS Quarterly, 10*, 313-325.

Lefcourt, H. M. (1981). *Research with the locus of control construct.* New York: Academic Press.

Lefcourt, H. M. (1982). *Locus of control: Current trends in theory and research*, 2nd edition. Hillsdale, NJ: Lawrence Erlbaum Associates.

Leifer, R. (1988). Matching computer-based information systems with organizational structures. *MIS Quarterly, 12*, 63-73.

Levitt, E. E. (1967). *The psychology of anxiety.* Indianapolis, IN: Bobbs-Merrill.

Liden, R., & Mitchell, T. (1989). Ingratiation in the development of leader—member exchanges. In R. A. Giacalone & P. Rosenfeld (Eds.), *Impression Management in the Organization* (pp. 343-362). Hillsdale: Lawrence Erlbaum Publishers.

Lipman, A., Cooper, I., Harris, R., & Tranter, R. (1978). Power: A neglected concept in office design. *Journal of Architectural Research, 6*(3), 28-37.

Loveman, G. W. (1988). "An assessment of the productivity impact on information technologies." MIT Management in the 1990s Working Paper #88-054, July.

Lucas, H. C., Jr. (1975). Performance and the use of an information system. *Management Science, 21*, 908-919.

Ludlam, D. A. (1989, September 11). IS services keep airline aloft despite AMR's new competition. *Computerworld Premier 100, supplement to Computerworld*, pp. 20-22.

Lutz, K., & Lutz, R. (1978). Imagery-Eliciting Strategies: Review and Implications of Research, In H. K. Hunt (Ed.), *Advertising Consumer Research* (pp. 611-620). Ann Arbor, MI: Association for Consumer Research.

Maccoby, M. (1991). Closing the motivation gap. *Research-Technology Management, 34*(1), 50-51.

Malone, T. W. (1980). What makes things fun to learn? A study of intrinsically motivating computer games. Cognitive and Instructional Sciences Series, Vol. CIS-7 (SSL-80-11). Palo Alto, CA: Xerox.

Mandell, M. (1991, August 12). Kmart's $1 billion bar-code bet. *Computerworld, 25*(32), 53, 55.

March, J. G. (1987). Old colleges, new technology. In S. B. Kiesler & L. S. Sproull (Eds.), *Computing and change on campus* (pp. 16-27). New York: Cambridge University Press.

March, J. G., & Sproull, L. S. (1990). Technology, management, and competitive advantage. In P. S. Goodman & L. S. Sproull & Associates (Eds.), *Technology and organizations* (pp. 144-173). San Francisco: Jossey-Bass.

Markus, M. L. (1981). Implementation politics: Top management support and user involvement. *Systems/Objectives/Solutions, 1*(4), 203-215.

Markus, M. L. (1987). Toward a "critical mass" theory of interactive media. *Communications Research, 14*(5), 491-511.

Markus, M. L. (1990). Toward a "critical mass" theory of interactive media. In J. Fulk & C. Steinfield (Eds.), *Organizations and communication technology* (pp. 194-218). Newbury Park, CA: Sage.

Markus, M. L., & Robey, D. (1988). Information technology and organizational change: Causal structure in theory and research. *Management Science, 34*, 583-598.

Martin, C. L., & Nagao, D. H. (1989). Some effects of computerized interviewing on job applicant responses. *Journal of Applied Psychology, 74*, 72-80.

Martin, J., Feldman, M. S., Hatch, M. J., & Sitkin, S. B. (1983). The uniqueness paradox in organizational studies. *Administrative Science Quarterly, 28*, 438-453.

Mason, R. O. (1984). Information systems strategy and corporate strategy. In F. W. McFarlan (Ed.), *Harvard 75th Anniversary MIS Research Colloquim* (pp. 261-304).

Mason, R. O., & Mitroff, I. (1973). A program for research on management information systems. *Management Science, 19*, 475-487.

Matheson, K. (1991). Social cues in computer-mediated negotiations: Gender makes a difference. *Computers in Human Behavior, 7*, 137-145.

Matheson, K., & Zanna, M. P. (1988). Persuasion as a function of self-awareness in computer-mediated communication. *Social Behavior, 4*, 99-111.

Mawhinney, C. H., III. (1986). Factors affecting the utilization of personal computers by managers and executives. Unpublished doctoral dissertation, University of Pittsburgh.

May, R. (1950). *The meaning of anxiety*. New York, NY: Ronald Press.

McCosh, A. (1984). Factors common to the successful implemention of twelve decision support systems and how they differ from three failures. *Systems, Objectives, Solutions, 4*, 17-28.

McCroskey, J. C. (1977). Oral communication apprehension: A summary of recent theory and research. *Human Communication Research, 4*, 78-96.

Mehrabian, A. (1971). *Silent messages*. Belmont, CA: Wadsworth.

Miles, M. B., & Huberman, A. M. (1984). *Qualitative Data Analysis: A Sourcebook of New Methods*. Newbury Park, CA: Sage Publications.

Moorhead, G., & Griffin, R. W. (1995). *Organizational behavior: Managing people and organizations* (4th ed.). Boston, MA: Houghton Mifflin.

Morgan, G., Frost, P. J., & Pondy, L. R. (1983). Organizational symbolism. In L. R. Pondy, P. J. Frost, G. Morgan, & T. D. Dandridge (Eds.), *Organizational symbolism* (pp. 3-35). Greenwich, CT: JAI Press.

Morrow, P. C., Prell, E. R., & McElroy, J. C. (1986). Attitudinal and behavioral correlates of computer anxiety. *Psychological Reports, 59*, 1199-1204.

Nadler, D. A. (1983). Concepts for the management of organizational change. In J. R. Hackman, E. E. Lawler, III, & L.W. Porter (Eds.), *Perspectives on behavior in organizations* (pp. 551-561). New York: McGraw Hill.

Naisbitt, J. (1982). *Megatrends: Ten new directions transforming our lives.* New York: Warner.

Nash, J. (1990, March 5). EDI sprinters find partners on slow track. *Computerworld, 24*(120), 1, 12.

Nash, J. (1990, March 5). When push comes to shove. *Computerworld, 24*(120), 12.

Neiderman, F., Brancheau, J. C., & Wetherbe, J. C. (1991). Information systems management issues for the 1990s. *MIS Quarterly, 15*(4), 475-500.

Nelson, D.L. (1990). Individual adjustment to information-driven technologies: A critical review. *MIS Quarterly, 14*, 78-98.

Nelson, R. R., & Cheney, P. H. (1987). Educating the CBIS user: A case analysis. *Data Base, 18*, 11-21.

Newcomb, T. M. (1953). An approach to the study of communicative acts. *Psychology Review, 60*, 393-404.

Newcomb, T. M. (1961). *The acquaintance process.* New York: Holt, Reinhart, & Winston.

Noble, D. (1978). Social change in machine design: The case of automatically controlled machine tools and a challenge for labor. *Politics and Society, 8*, 313-347.

Nunamaker, J. F., Jr., Applegate, L. M., & Konsynski, B. R. (1987). Facilitating group creativity: Experience with a group decision support system. *Journal of Management Information Systems, 3*(4), 5-19.

O'Leary, M. (1991, October 1). Store-crossed lovers. *CIO, 5*(1), 40-48.

Oliver, P. (1980). Rewards and punishments as selective incentives for collective action: Theoretical investigations. *American Journal of Sociology, 85*(6), 1356-1375.

Oliver, P., Marwell, G., & Teixeira, R. (1985). A theory of the critical mass. I. Interdependence, group heterogeneity, and the production of collective action. *American Journal of Sociology, 91*(3), 522-556.

Olson, M. (1965). *The logic of collective action: Public goods and the theory of groups.* Cambridge, MA: Harvard University Press.

Ord, J. G. (1989). Who's joking? The information system at play. *Interacting with Computers: The International Journal of Human Computer Interaction, 1*, 118-128.

O'Reilly, C. A., III. (1982). Variations in decision makers' use of information sources: The impact of quality and accessibility of information. *Academy of Management Journal, 25*, 756-771.

O'Reilly, C. A., & Caldwell, D. (1979). Informational influence as a determinant of perceived task characteristics and job satisfaction. *Journal of Applied Psychology, 64*, 157-165.

Ornstein, S. (1986). Organizational symbols: A study of their meaning and influences on perceived psychological climate. *Organizational Behavior and Human Decision Processes, 38*, 207-229.

Ornstein, S. (1989). Impression management through office design. In R. A. Giacalone & P. Rosenfeld (Eds.), *Impression management in the organization* (pp. 411-426). Hillsdale, NJ: Lawrence Erlbaum.

Osgood, C. E. (1962). *An alternative to war or surrender*. Urbana, IL: University of Illinois Press.

Osgood, C. E. (1966). *Perspective in foreign policy*. Palo Alto, CA: Pacific Books.

Ostberg, O., & Chapman, L. J. (1988). Social aspects of computer use. In M. Helander (Ed.), *Handbook of human-computer interaction* (pp. 1033-1049). New York: Elsevier Science Publishers.

Ottinger, L. (1993). Understanding the effectiveness of multimedia technology as a persuasive tool: An experimental investigation. Unpublished Ph.D. Dissertation, Texas A&M University College of Business & Graduate School of Business, Department of Business Analysis & Research, College Station, TX, 77843.

Paivio, A. (1973). Picture superiority in free recall: Imagery or dual coding? *Cognitive Psychology, 5*(2), 176-206.

Pappas, J. L., Brigham, E. F., & Hirschey, M. (1983). *Managerial economics* (4th ed.). Chicago, IL: Dryden Press.

Pastore, R. (1992, February). The high price of nice. *CIO*, pp. 56-63.

Paulhus, D. (1982). Individual differences, self-presentation, and cognitive dissonance: Their concurrent operation on forced compliance. *Journal of Personaltiy and Social Psychology, 43*, 838-852.

Paulhus, D. L. (1991). Measurement and control of response bias. In J. P. Robinson, P. R. Shaver, & L. S. Wrightsman (Eds.), *Measures of personality and social psychological attitudes* (pp. 17-59). San Diego: Academic Press.

Payne, S. L., & Giacalone, R. A. (1990). Social psychological approaches to the perception of ethical delimmas. *Human Relations, 43*, 649-655.

Perrow, C. (1967). A framework for comparative analysis of organizations. *American Sociological Review, 32*, 194-204.

Perrow, C. (1970). *Organizational analysis: A sociological view*. Belmont, CA: Wadsworth.

Pfeffer, J. (1981). Management as symbolic action: The creation and maintenance of organization paradigms. In L. L. Cummings & B. Staw (Eds.), *Research in Organizational Behavior)* (Vol. 3, pp. 1-52). Greenwich, CT: JAI Press.

Pfeffer, J., & Leblebibi, H. (1977). Information technology and organizational structure. *Pacific Sociological Review, 20,* 241-261.

Pierce, J. L., & Delbecq, A. L. (1977). Organization structure, individual attitudes and innovation. *Academy of Management Review, 2,* 27-37.

Porter, M. E., & Millar, V. E. (1985). How information gives you competitive advantage. *Harvard Business Review, July-August,* 149-160.

Powell, D. (1992). The productivity paradox. *Computing Canada, 18*(24), 1-8.

Pruitt, D. G., & Smith, D. L. (1981). Impression management in bargaining: images of firmness and trustworthiness. In J. T. Tedeschi (Ed.), *Impression Management Theory and Social Psychological Theory* (pp. 247-267). New York: Academic Press.

Puckett, J., Petty, R., Cacioppo, J., & Fisher, D. (1983). The relative impact of age and attractiveness stereotypes on persuasion. *Journal of Gerontology, 38,* 340-343.

Rafaeli, A., & Sutton, R. I. (1986). Word processing technology and perceptions of control among clerical workers. *Behavior and Information Technology, 5,* 31-37.

Raskin, R. (1990, July). Multimedia: The Next Frontier for Business? *PC Magazine,* pp. 151+.

Raub, A. C. (1981). Correlates of computer anxiety in college students. Unpublished doctoral dissertation, University of Pennsylvania, Philadelphia.

Rice, R. E. (1984). New media technology: Growth and integration. In R. E. Rice & Associates (Eds.), *The new media: Communication, research, and technology* (pp. 33-54). Beverly Hills, CA: Sage.

Rice, R. E. (1988). Issues and concepts in research on computer-mediated communication systems. In J. A. Anderson (Ed.), *Communication yearbook, 12* (pp. 436-476).

Rice, R. E., & Case, D. (1983). Electronic message systems in the university: A description of use and utility. *Journal of Communication, 33,* 131-152.

Richardson, D. D., & Cialdini, R. B. (1987). Basking and blasting: Tacts of indirect self-presentation. In J. T. Tedeschi (Ed.), *Impression management theory and social psychological research* (pp. 41-53). New York: Academic Press.

Riordan, C. A. (1989). Images of corporate success. In R. A. Giacalone & P. Rosenfeld (Eds.), *Impression management in the organization* (pp. 87-103). Hillsdale, NJ: Lawrence Erlbaum.

Roach, S. S. (1987). Technology and the service sector: America's hidden competitive challenge. In *Economic perspectives.* New York: Morgan Stanley & Co.

Roach, S. S. (1988). Technology and the service sector: the hidden competitive advantage. *Technological forecasting and social change, 34*(4), 387-403.

Roach, S. S. (1989). Pitfalls on the "New" assembly line: Can services learn from manufacturing? *Economic perspectives*, New York: Morgan Stanley & Co.

Robertson, D. C. (1989). Social determinants of information systems use. *Journal of Management Information Systems, 5*, 55-71.

Robey, D. (1979). User attitudes and MIS use. *Academy of Management Journal, 22*, 527-538.

Robey, D., & Azevedo, A. (in press). Cultural analysis of the organizational consequences of information technology. *Accounting, Management, and Information Technologies*.

Robey, D., & Rodriguez-Diaz, A. (1990). The organizational & cultural content of systems implementation: Case experiences from Latin America. *Information & Management, 17*, 229-239.

Rockart, J. F., & DeLong, D. W. (1988). *Executive support systems: The emergence of top management computer use*. New York: Dow Jones-Irwin.

Rockart, J. F., & Flannery, L. S. (1983). The management of end-user computing. *Communications of the ACM, 26*, 776-784.

Rogers, E. M. (1983). *Diffusion of Innovations*, New York: The Free Press.

Rogers, E. M. (1991). The "critical mass" in the diffusion of interactive technologies in organizations. In *The information systems research challenge: Survey research methods* (pp. 245-263). Boston, MA: Harvard Business School.

Rogers, E. M., & Bhowmik, D. K. (1970-1971). Homophily-heterophily: Relational concepts for communication research. *Public Opinion Quarterly, 34*(4), 523-538.

Rohlfs, J. (1974). A theory of interdependent demand for a communications service. *The Bell Journal of Economics and Management Science, 5*(1), 16-37.

Roll, R., President of the Uniform Code Council. (1993, June 4). Personal communication.

Rosenberg, M. J. (1965). When dissonance fails: On elimination of evaluation apprehension from attitude measurement. *Journal of Personality and Social Psychology, 1*, 28-42.

Rosenfeld, P. (1990). Self-esteem and impression management explanations for self-serving biases. *Journal of Social Psychology, 130*, 495-500.

Rosenfeld, P., Booth-Kewley, S., Edwards, J. E., & Thomas, M. D. (1994). Responses on computer surveys: Impression management, social desirability, and the Big Brother Syndrome. Unpublished manuscript. San Diego, CA: Navy Personnel Research and Development Center.

Rosenfeld, P., Doherty, L. M., & Carroll, L. (1987). Microcomputer-based organizational survey assessment: Applications to training. *Journal of Business and Psychology, 2*, 182-193.

Rosenfeld, P., Doherty, L., Carroll, L., Kantor, J., & Thomas, M. (1986, November). Does microcomputer-based testing encourage truthful responses? Paper presented at the 28th annual meeting of the Military Testing Association, Mystic, CT.

Rosenfeld, P., Doherty, L. M., Vicino, S. M., Kantor, J., & Greaves, J. (1989). Attitude assessment in organizations: Testing three microcomputer-based survey systems. *Journal of General Psychology*, *116*, 145-154.

Rosenfeld, P., & Giacalone, R. A. (1991). From extreme to mainstream: Applied impression management in organizations. In R. A. Giacalone & P. Rosenfeld (Eds.) *Applied impression management: How image-making affects managerial decisions* (pp. 3-12). Newbury Park, CA: Sage.

Rosenfeld, P., Giacalone, R. A., Knouse, S. B., Doherty, L., Vicino, S. M., Kantor, J., & Greaves, J. (1991). Impression management, candor, and microcomputer-based organizational surveys: An individual differences approach. *Computers in Human Behavior*, *7*, 23-32.

Rosenfeld, P., Giacalone, R. A., & Riordan, C. (1994). Impression management theory and diversity: Lessons for organizational behavior. *American Behavioral Scientist*, *37*(5), 601-604.

Rotter, J. B. (1966). Generalized expectancies for the internal versus external control of reinforcement. *Psychological Monographs*, *80*, 1-28.

Rousseau, D. M. (1979). Assessment of technology in organizations: Closed versus open systems approaches. *Academy of Management Review*, *4*(4), 531-542.

Russ, G. S., Daft, R. L., & Lengel, R. H. (1990). Media selection and managerial characteristics in organizational communications. *Management Communication Quarterly*, *4*, 151-175.

Russell, D. (1982). The causal dimension scale: A measure of how individuals perceive causes. *Journal of Personality and Social Psychology*, *42*, 1137-1145.

Russell, D., & McAuley, E. (1986). Causal attributions, causal dimensions, and affective reactions to success and failure. *Journal of Personality and Social Psychology*, *50*, 1174-1185.

Russell, D., McAuley, E., & Tarico, V. (1987). Measuring causal attributions for success and failure: A comparison of methodologies for assessing causal dimensions. *Journal of Personality and Social Psychology*, *52*, 1248-1257.

Safayeni, F., MacGregor, J., Lee, E., & Bavelas, A. (1987). Social and task-related impacts of office automation: An exploratory field study of a conceptual model of the office. *Human Systems Management*, *7*, 103-114.

Safayeni, F. R., Purdy, R. L., & Higgins, C. A. (1989). Social meaning of personal computers for managers and professionals: Methodology and results. *Behaviour and Information Technology*, *8*(2), 99-107.

Salancik, G. R., & Pfeffer, J. (1977, September). An examination of need-satisfaction models of job attitudes. *Administrative Science Quarterly*, *22*, 427-456.

Salancik, G. R., & Pfeffer, J. (1977). Who gets power—and how they hold onto it: A strategic-contingency model of power. *Organizational Dynamics*, *Winter*, 3-21.

Samuelson, P. A. (1954). The pure theory of public expenditures. *Review of Economics and Statistics*, *36*(1), 387-389.

Sanders, G. L., & Courtney, J. F. (1985). A field study of organizational factors influencing DSS success. *MIS Quarterly*, *9*, 77-93.

Saporito, B. (1989, December 18). Retailing's winners & losers. *Fortune*, pp. 69-80.

Saporito, B. (1991, May 6). Is Wal-Mart unstoppable? *Fortune*, pp. 50-59.

Savage, G. T., Blair, J. D., & Sorenson, R. L. (1988). Consider both relationships and substance when negotiating strategically. *Academy of Management Executive*, *3*(1), 37-47.

Schein, E. H. (1985). *Organizational culture and leadership*. San Francisco: Jossey-Bass.

Schewe, C. D. (1976). The management information system user: An exploratory behavioral analysis. *Academy of Management Journal*, *19*, 577-590.

Schlenker, B. R. (1975). Self-presentation: Managing the impression of consistency when reality interferes with self-enhancement. *Journal of Personality and Social Psychology*, *32*, 1030-1037.

Schlenker, B. R. (1980). *Impression management: The self-concept, social identity, and interpersonal relations*. Monterey, CA: Brooks/Cole.

Schlenker, B. R. (1985). Identity and self-identification. In B. R. Schlenker (Ed.), *The self and social life*. New York: McGraw-Hill.

Schlenker, B. R., & Weigold, M. (1992). Interpersonal processes involving impression regulation and management. *Annual Review of Psychology*, *43*, 133-168.

Schlenker, B. R., & Weigold, M. F. (1989). Self-identification and accountability. In R. A. Giacalone & P. Rosenfeld (Eds.), *Impression management in the organization* (pp. 21-43). Hillsdale, NJ: Lawrence Erlbaum.

Schneider D. J. (1981). Tactical self-presentations: Toward a broader conception. In J. T. Tedeschi (Ed.), *Impression management theory and social psychological research* (pp. 23-40). New York: Academic Press.

Scholz, C. (1990). The symbolic value of computerized information systems. In P. Gagliardi (Ed.), *Symbols and Artifacts*. New York: Aldine de Gruyter.

Schwoerer, C., & Rosen, B. (1989). Effects of employment-at-will policies and compensation policies on corporate image and job pursuit intentions. *Journal of Applied Psychology*, *74*, 653-656.

Sears Communication Company: publicity.

Sein, M. K., Bostrom, R. P., & Olfman, L. (1987). Training end-users to compute: Cognitive, motivational and social issues. *INFOR*, *25*, 236-255.

Seldin, P. (1993). *Successful Use of Teaching Portfolios*. Boston, MA: Anker Publishing Company.

Sheppard, B. H., & Lewicki, R. J. (1987). Toward general principles of managerial fairness. *Social Justice Research*, *1*, 161-176.

Short, J., Williams, E., & Christie, B. (1976). *The social psychology of telecommunications*. New York: Wiley.

Siegel, J., Dubrovsky, V., Kiesler, S., & McGuire, T. W. (1986). Group processes in computer-mediated communication. *Organizational Behavior and Human Decision Processes*, *37*, 157-187.

Simon, H. A. (1977). *The new science of management decision*. Englewood Cliffs, NJ: Prentice-Hall.

Singleton, J. P., McLean, E. R., & Altman, E. N. (1988). Measuring information systems performance: Experience with management by results systems at Security Pacific Bank. *MIS Quarterly*, *17*(3), 325-336.

Smolensky, M. W., Carmody, M. A., & Halcomb, C. G. (1990). The influence of task type, group structure, and extraversion on uninhibited speech in computer-mediated communication. *Computers in Human Behavior*, *6*, 261-272.

Snodgrass, J., & Asiaghi, A. (1977). The picture superiority of effect in recognition memory. *Bulletin of the Psychonometrics Society*, *10*(1), 1-4.

Snyder, M. (1974). Self-monitoring of expressive behavior. *Journal of Personality and Social Psychology*, *30*, 526-537.

Snyder, M. (1987). *Public appearances/private realities: The psychology of self-monitoring*. New York: W. H. Freeman.

Sokol, M. B. (1986). Innovation utilization: The implementation of personal computers in an organization. Unpublished doctoral dissertation, University of Maryland, College Park.

Sokol, P. K. (1989). *EDI: The competitive edge*. New York: Intertext Publications.

Sproull, L. S. (1986). Using electronic mail for data collection in organizational research. *Academy of Management Journal*, *29*, 159-169.

Sproull, L., & Kiesler, S. (1986). Reducing social context cues: Electronic mail in organizational communication. *Management Science*, *32*, 1492-1512.

Sproull, L., & Kiesler, S. (1991). Computers, networks and work. *Scientific American*, *265*, 116-123.

Srinivasan, A. (1985). Alternative measures of system effectiveness:

Associations and implications. *MIS Quarterly*, *9*, 243-254.

Standard & Poor's Corporation. (1990, April 19). *Industry surveys: Retailing—basic analysis*. *158*, 15, Section 1.

Standard & Poor's Corporation. (1991, May 2). *Industry surveys: Retailing—basic analysis*. *159*, 17, Section 1.

Standard & Poor's Corporation. (1992, January 9). *Industry surveys: Retailing—current analysis*. *160*, 2, Section 1.

Staw, M. E. (1981). *Group dynamics: The psychology of small group behavior*. New York: McGraw-Hill.

Steele, F. I. (1973). *Physical settings and organization development*. Reading, MA: Addison-Wesley.

Steinfield, C. W. (1986). Computer-mediated communication in an organizational setting: Explaining task-related and socioemotional uses. In M. McLanghlin (Ed.), *Communication yearbook 9* (pp. 777-804). Newbury Park, CA: Sage.

Steinfield, C. (1992). Computer-mediated communications in organizational settings. *Management Communication Quarterly*, *5*, 348-365.

Steinfield, C. W., & Fulk, J. (1987). On the role of theory in research on information technologies in organizations: An introduction to the special issue. *Communications Research*, *14*, 479-490.

Sundstrom, E. (1986). *Work places: The psychology of the physical environment in offices and factories*. Cambridge: Cambridge University Press.

Swanson, E. B. (1974). Management information systems: Appreciation and involvement. *Management Science*, *21*, 178-188.

Swanson, E. B. (1982). Measuring user attitudes in MIS research: A review. *Omega*, *10*, 175-165.

Szewczak, E. J., & Gardner, W. L. (1989). Social and organizational impact of local and telecommunications systems—open questions. *Information Resources Management Journal*, *2*(1), 14-25.

Tapscott, D., & Caston, A. (1993). *Paradigm shift: The promise of new information technology*. New York: McGraw-Hill.

Tedeschi, J. T. (Ed.) (1981). *Impression management theory and social psychological research*. New York: Academic Press.

Tedeschi, J. T., Lindskold, S., & Rosenfeld, P. (1985). *Introduction to social psychology*. St. Paul, MN: West.

Tedeschi, J. T., & Norman, N. (1985). Social power, self-presentation, and the self. In J. T. Tedeschi (Ed.), *Impression management theory and social psychological research* (pp. 293-322). New York: Academic Press.

Tedeschi, J. T., & Reiss, M. (1981). Identities, the phenomenal self, and laboratory research. In J. T. Tedeschi (Ed.), *Impression management theory and social psychological research* (pp. 3-22). New York: Academic Press.

Tedeschi, J. T., & Rosenfeld, P. (1981). Impression management theory and the forced compliance situation. In J. T. Tedeschi (Ed.), *Impression management theory and social psychological research* (pp. 147-180). New York: Academic Press.

Tedeschi, J. T., Schlenker, B. R., & Bonoma, T. V. (1971). Cognitive dissonance: Private ratiocination or public spectacle. *American Psychologist*, *26*, 685-695.

Teets, J. (1991). Atlanta wins 1996 Olympics with gold medal presentation. *Presentation Products Magazine*, pp. 18+.

Terborg, J. R. (1981). Interactional psychology and research on human behavior in organizations. *Academy of Management Review*, *6*, 569-576.

Tetlock, P. E., & Manstead, A.S.R. (1985). Impression management versus intrapsychic explanation in social psychology: A useful dichotomy? *Psychological Review*, *92*, 59-77.

The trouble with open offices. (1978, August 7), *Business Week*, pp. 84ff.

Thompson, J. (1967). *Organizations in action*. New York: McGraw-Hill.

Toffler, A. (1980). *The third wave*. New York: William Morrow.

Tornatzky, L. G., & Fleisher, M. (1990). *The processes of technological innovation*. Lexington, MA: Lexington Books.

Trevino, L. K., Lengel, R. H., & Daft, R. L. (1987). Media symbolism, media richness, and media choice in organizations. *Communication Research*, *14*, 553-574.

Trevino, L. K., Lengel, R. H., Gerloff, E. A., & Muir, N. K. (1990). The richness imperative and cognitive style. *Management Communication Quarterly*, *4*, 176-197.

Trice, A. W., & Treacy, M. E. (1988). Utilization as a dependent variable in MIS research. *Data Base*, *19*(3-4), 33-41.

Turkle, S. (1980). Computer as Rorschach. *Society*, *17*(2), 15-24.

Turner, S. M. (Ed.). (1984). *Behavioral theories and treatment of anxiety*. New York: Plenum Press.

Turoff, M., & Hiltz, S. R. (1982). Computer support for group versus individual decision. *IEEE Transactions on Communications*, *30*, 82-91.

Tyburski, D. A. (1992). Computer enhanced Navy survey system: Final report. Unpublished manuscript. San Diego: Navy Personnel Research and Development Center.

Tyburski, D. A., Petrey, J. L., Wilson, S., & Kewley, B. (1989). *OCPM-CENSUS bulletin board system user's manual* (NPRDC TN 90-6). San Diego: Navy Personnel Research and Development Center.

Tyler, T. R., & Bies, R. J. (1990). Beyond formal procedures: The interpersonal context of procedural justice. In J. Carroll (Ed.), *Applied social psychology and organizational settings* (pp. 77-98). Hillsdale, NJ: Lawrence Erlbaum.

Ulrich, D. & Barney, J. B. (1984).   Perspectives in organizations: Resource
    dependence, efficiency, and population. *Academy of Management Review*,
    9(3), 471-481.

Verity, J. W., & Lewis, G. (1987, November 30). Computers: The new look.
    Business Week, pp. 112-123.

Vicino, S. M. (1989).   Effects of computer versus traditional paper-and-pencil
    survey administration on response bias among self-monitors. Unpublished
    Master's Thesis, San Diego State University, San Diego, CA.

Vitale, M., Ives, B., & Beath, C. (1986).   Identifying strategic information
    systems: finding a process or building an organization. In L. Maggi, R.
    Zmud, & J. Wetherbe (Eds.), *Proceedings of the Seventh International
    Conference on Information Systems*, pp. 15-17.

Walker, J. L. (1971). Innovation in state politics. In H. Jacob & K. N. Vines
    (Eds.), *Politics in the American states: A comparative analysis*. Boston,
    MA: Little, Brown.

Wall, J. A., Jr. (1991).   Impression management in negotiation. In R. A.
    Giacalone & P. Rosenfeld (Eds.), *Applied impression management* (pp.
    133-156). Newbury Park, CA: Sage Publications.

Watson, R. T. (1989).   Key issues in information systems management: An
    Australian perspective—1988. *Australian Computer Journal*, *21*(3), 118-
    129.

Watson, R. T., & Brancheau, J. C. (1991).   Key issues in information systems
    management: An international perspective. *Information & Management*,
    20(3), 213-223.

Weary, G., & Arkin, R. M. (1981). Attributional self-presentation. In J. H.
    Harvey, W. J. Ickes, & R. F. Kidd (Eds.), *New directions in attribution
    research* (Vol. 3, pp. 223-246). New York: Erlbaum.

Weill, P. (1992).   The relationship between investment in information
    technology and firm performance: A study of the valve manufacturing
    sector. *Information Systems Research*, *3*(4), 307-333.

Weill, P., & Olson, M. (1989). Managing investment in IT. *MIS Quarterly*,
    13(1), 3-17.

Weisband, S. P., Schneider, S. K., & Connolly, T. (1992).   Participation
    equality and influence: Status effects in computer-mediated decision making
    groups. Paper presented at the 1992 Annual Meeting of the Academy of
    Management.

Weiss, H. M., & Shaw, J.B. (1979).   Social influences on judgments about
    tasks. *Organizational Behavior and Human Performance*, *24*, 126-140.

Wexler, M. N. (1986).   Impression management and the new competence:
    Conjectures for seekers. *Et Cetera, Fall*, 247-258.

Whisler, T. L. (1970). *The impact of computers on organizations*. New York:
    Prager.

White, S. E., & Mitchell, T. R. (1979). Job enrichment versus social cues: A comparison and competitive test. *Journal of Applied Psychology, 64,* 1-9.

Winter, S. (1993). The symbolic potential of computer technology: Differences among white-collar workers. In J. I. DeGross, R. P. Bostrom, & D. Robey (Eds.), *Proceedings of the Fourteenth International Conference on Information Systems,* pp. 331-344.

Winter, S. J. (1993). Computer technology: Evidence of symbolic potential among white-collar workers. In J. I. DeGross, R. P. Bostrom, & D. Robey (Eds.), *Proceedings of the Fourteenth International Conference on Information Systems,* pp. 331-344.

Wood, R. E. (1986). Task complexity: Definition of the construct. *Organizational Behavior and Human Decision Processes, 37,* 60-82.

Wortman, C., & Linsenmeier, J. (1977). Interpersonal attraction and techniques of ingratiation in organizations. In B. M. Staw & G. R. Salancik (Eds.), *New directions in organization behavior* (pp. 133-178). Chicago: St. Clair.

Wotton, E. (1976). Some considerations affecting the inclusion of windows in office facades. *Lighting Design and Application, 6*(2), 32-40.

Yin, R. K. (1989). *Case study research: Design and method* (Revised Edition). Newbury Park, CA: Sage Publications.

Zartman, I. W. (1977). Negotiation as a joint decision-making process. *Journal of Conflict Resolution, 21,* 619-638. Reprinted in I. W. Zartman (Ed.). (1978). *The negotiation process.* Beverly Hills, CA: Sage Publications, 1978.

Zimmerman, S. (1990, May 17). Sold on EDI. *Purchasing, 108*(9), 86-87.

Zimmerman, W. (Ed.), (1988). *American Banker 1988 Managing Technology Survey: The impact of the bottom line.* New York: International Thompson Publishing Corporation.

Zinn, L., Power, C., & Flynn, J. (1990, November 26). Retailing: Who will survive? *Business Week,* pp. 134-144.

Zmud, R. W. (1979). Individual differences and MIS success: A review of the empirical literature. *Management Science, 25,* 966-979.

Zuboff, S. (1982). New worlds of computer-mediated work. *Harvard Business Review, 60*(5), 142-152.

Zuboff, S. (1988). *In the age of the smart machine: The future of work and power.* New York: Basic Books.

AUTHOR INDEX

SUBJECT INDEX

ABOUT THE CONTRIBUTORS

JON W. BEARD is the editor of this book. His research interests focus on the management of technology, incorporating topics such as creativity, job design, organizational learning, and the organizational implications of information technology. He has published several journal articles, including recent publications in the *Organizational Development Journal*, *Journal of Business Ethics*, *American Behavioral Scientist*, and *Humanities Review*, and has contributed chapters to several books.

STEPHANIE BOOTH-KEWLEY is Personnel Research Psychologist at the Navy Personnel Research and Development Center (NPRDC) in San Diego. Her many research interests include personality assessment, health psychology, survey methodology, and gender issues. She has published in *Psychological Bulletin*, *American Psychologist*, and the *Journal of Applied Psychology*.

LYNE BOUCHARD is teaching and conducting her research at Laval University in Quebec City, Canada. Her research interests include interorganizational communications, geographical information systems, information technology and organizational change, and the role of the information systems department in organizations.

JANE M. CAREY is Associate Professor of Management Information Systems at Arizona State University (ASU) West. Her research is focused primarily in the areas of system development methodologies and human factors in information systems. She is the editor of a series of books resulting from an ongoing symposia series on Human Factors in Information Systems, which she founded in 1986. She has also published many journal articles and book chapters.

WILLIAM L. GARDNER III is Hearin-Hess Associate Professor of Management at the University of Mississippi. His current research interests include impression management, leadership, women in management, managerial work, learned helplessness, cognitive style, and computer-mediated communications. He has published in the *Academy of Management Journal*, *Academy of Management Review*, *Journal of Management*, *Journal of Management Studies*, and *Organizational Dynamics*.

K. VERNARD HARRINGTON is Assistant Professor in the Department of Organization and Management at Syracuse University. His research interests include intergroup behavior, the management of diversity, organizational conflict, communication and learning, and the use of computing technology in organizations.

GEORGE M. MARAKAS is Assistant Professor at the University of Maryland at College Park. His current research interests are impression management theory, symbolic aspects of information technology, DSS, and information requirements determination issues.

M. LYNNE MARKUS is Associate Professor in the Programs in Information Science, affiliated with the Peter F. Drucker Graduate Management Center at The Claremont Graduate School (CGS) and is a consultant to the RAND Corporation. Her research focuses on the role of information technology in organizational performance and change, the implementation of information systems, electronic communication media, and group support technologies. She is the author of *Systems in Organizations; Bugs and Features* and has contributed articles to *Organization Science*, *The Information Society*, *Information Technology and People*, *Management Science*, *Communication Research*, *Communications of the ACM*, *Management Information Systems Quarterly*, and *Interfaces*.

MARK J. MARTINKO is Professor in the Department of Management at the Florida State University. His research is focused on the observation of leader behaviors, impression management, learned helplessness, and performance management. He is the author or coauthor of three books and more than 40 research articles in journals including the *Academy of Management Journal*, *Academy of Management Review*, *Journal of Management*, and *Journal of Management Studies*.

AFSANEH NAHAVANDI is Associate Professor of Management at Arizona State University (ASU) West. Her research is focused primarily in the areas of organizational behavior and leadership. Her work on the role of leadership and culture has been published in national and international journals. She is a coauthor of a book on the organizational cultural aspects of mergers and acquisitions.

DAVID B. PARADICE is Associate Professor in the Department of Business Analysis and the Center for the Management of Information Systems at Texas A&M University. He has published numerous articles focusing on the use of computer-based systems in support of managerial problem formulation. He has also published several papers regarding the influence of computer-based systems on ethical decision-making processes. He has coauthored a book on database management systems and coedited a book of readings on ethical issues in the information systems field.

JOY VAN ECK PELUCHETTE is Assistant Professor in the Department of Management and Marketing at the University of Southern Indiana. Her research interests include issues relating to careers, mentoring, gender, work-family interface, impression management, and computer-mediated communications. She has published in the *Journal of Vocational Behavior*, *Management Communication Quarterly*, and the *Journal of Applied Business Research*.

DANIEL ROBEY is Professor in the College of Business at Georgia State University. His current research deals with the consequences of information systems in organizations and the processes of system development and implementation. He is the author of three books and numerous journal articles in *Management Science*, *Organization Science*, *Information Systems Research*, *MIS Quarterly*, *Communications of the ACM*, *Human Relations*, *Academy of Management Review*, *Academy of Management Journal*, and *Decision Sciences*.

PAUL ROSENFELD is Personnel Research Psychologist at the Navy Personnel Research and Development Center (NPRDC) in San Diego, California. He has coauthored *Introduction to Social Psychology* (1985) and has coedited (with Robert A. Giacalone) *Impression Management in the Organization* (1989) and *Applied Impression Management* (1991). Recently, he has coedited *Hispanics in the Workplace* (1992) and *Improving Organizational Surveys* (1993).

SUSAN J. WINTER is Assistant Professor in the School of Business at the University of Victoria, Canada. Her current research interests in the role of computers in organizations include their symbolic aspects, computer literacy, and their impact on the way in which work is organized.

9 780899 308487